CLASSICAL INDIAN PHILOSOPHY

CLASSICAL
Indian Philosophy

A Reader

DEEPAK SARMA

Columbia University Press / *New York*

Columbia University Press
Publishers Since 1893
New York Chichester, West Sussex

Library of Congress Cataloging-in-Publication Data
Sarma, Deepak, 1969–
Readings in classical Indian philosophy / Deepak Sarma.
p. cm.
Includes bibliographical references and index.
ISBN 978-0-231-13398-2 (cloth : alk. paper) — ISBN 978-0-231-13399-9 (p)
1. Indian philosophy. I. Title.
B5131.S27 2011
181'.4—dc22
2010016122

Columbia University Press books are printed on permanent and durable acid-free paper.
This book is printed on paper with recycled content.
Printed in the United States of America
c 10 9 8 7 6 5 4 3 2 1
p 10 9 8 7 6 5 4 3

In service of Lord Kṛṣṇa and the Mādhva Saṃpradāya

OṂ

jīveśvarabhidā caiva jaḍeśvarabhidā tathā | jīvabhedo mithaś caiva jaḍajīvabhidā tathā | mithaś ca jaḍabhedo 'yaṃ prapañco bhedapañcakaḥ | so 'yaṃ satyo.

The universe has five [intrinsic] differences: There is a difference between [each] *jīva* (enduring self), and Lord [Viṣṇu]. There is a difference between Lord [Viṣṇu] and *jaḍa* (nonsentient material entities). There is difference between the individual *jīvas*. There is a difference between *jīvas* and *jaḍas*. There is a difference between one *jaḍa* and another. The [difference between these five] is real.

—Madhvācārya, *Viṣṇutattva(vi)nirṇaya*

CONTENTS

ACKNOWLEDGMENTS

This project originates from work that I began on Indian philosophy as an undergraduate in 1990 at Reed College with Professor Edwin Gerow and in Udupi with Śrī Bananjee Govindācārya. I was fortunate to be able to continue my study under Professor Paul J. Griffiths at the Divinity School at the University of Chicago. Scholars of the Pūrṇaprajña Saṃśodhana Mandiram (PPSM) under the auspices of the Pūrṇaprajña Vidyāpiṭham of the Pejāvara *maṭha* have helped tremendously in my study of Indian philosophy. Professors K. T. Paṇḍurangi, D. Prahlādācārya, and Sīta Nambiar in India were guides to whom I am deeply indebted. For assistance on this book, I am grateful to Dan Arnold, Francis X. Clooney, John Cort, Mario D'Amato, Paul Dundas, Andy Fort, Eli Franco, Paul Griffiths, Gerald Larson, Larry McCrea, Ramaswamy Sharma, and Pravin Shah. I also acknowledge the financial assistance provided by the Reisacher Family Endowment and the College Stimulus Funds at Case Western Reserve University, with special thanks to Professor Peter Haas and Dean Cyrus Taylor. I also want to thank the students in my Indian philosophy class, taught in the spring of 2009 at Case Western Reserve University. They were very careful and critical readers of earlier drafts of this reader. Thanks to the second reader of the manuscript, whose constructive suggestions were very useful indeed. Wendy Lochner at Columbia University Press has been a patient and encouraging editor and a fantastic guide of the astral plane. I am indebted to all of those sages of the magic grove who encouraged me to wonder if this is all a dream we dreamed one afternoon long ago on days when the sky was yellow and the sun was blue.

Many thanks to the translators of the texts that I have used here. Their work makes this work possible.

My greatest thanks are to my past and future students. This reader is for them.

The editor and publisher gratefully acknowledge the permission granted to reproduce the copyright material in this book:

1. Excerpts from E. B. Cowell and A. E. Gough, trans., *The Sarva-darśana-saṃgraha of Mādhavāchārya* (Delhi: Motilal Banarsidass, 1996), pp. 2–11. Reproduced by permission of Motilal Banarsidass Publishers (P) Ltd.

2. Excerpts from M. Rangacarya, trans., *The Sarva-Siddhānta-Saṃgraha of Śaṅkarācārya* (New Delhi: Ajay Book Service, 1983), pp. 5–6. Reproduced by permission of Ajay Book Service.

3. Excerpts from J. J. Jones, trans., *The Mahāvastu* (London: Pali Text Society, 1978), pp. 322–327. Reproduced by permission of the Pali Text Society.

4. Excerpts from Stefan Anacker, trans., *Seven Works of Vasubandhu* (Delhi: Motilal Banarsidass, 1996), pp. 161–179. Reproduced by permission of Motilal Banarsidass Publishers (P) Ltd.

5. Excerpts from Frederick J. Streng, trans., *Emptiness* (New York: Abingdon Press, 1967), pp. 222–227. Reproduced by kind permission of Susie Streng.

6. Excerpts from Olle Quarnstrom, trans., *The Yogaśāstra of Hemacandra* (Cambridge, Mass.: Department of Sanskrit and Indian Studies, Harvard University), pp. 19–61. Reproduced by kind permission of Michael Witzel.

7. Excerpts from Nagin J. Shah, trans., *Samantabhadra's Āptamīmāṃsā Critique of Authority* (Ahmedabad: Jagruti Dilip Sheth), pp. 29–65. Reproduced by kind permission of Nagin J. Shah.

8. Excerpts from M. M. Satisa Chandra Vidyābhūṣana, trans., *The Nyāya Sūtras of Gotama* (Delhi: Motilal Banarsidass, 1990), pp. 1–79. Reproduced by permission of Motilal Banarsidass Publishers (P) Ltd.

9. Excerpts from Bimal Krishna Matilal, trans., "A Critique of Buddhist Idealism," in L. Cousins, A. Kunst, and K. R. Norman, eds., *Buddhist Studies in Honour of I. B. Horner* (Dordrecht: D. Reidel Publishing Company), pp. 163–168. Reproduced by permission of Springer Publishers.

10. Excerpts from Debasish Chakrabarty, trans., *Vaiśeṣika Sūtra of* Kāṇada (New Delhi: D. K. Printworld (P) Ltd., 2003). Reproduced by kind permission of Debasish Chakrabarty and D. K. Printworld (P) Ltd.

11. Excerpts from Gerald James Larson, *Classical Sāṃkhya* (Delhi: Motilal Banarsidass, 1979), pp. 255–277. Reproduced by permission of Motilal Banarsidass Publishers (P) Ltd.

12. Excerpts from Gerald James Larson, trans., "Yogasūtras," in Gerald James Larson and Ram Shankar Bhattacharya, eds., *Yoga: India's Philosophy*

of Meditation (Delhi: Motilal Banarsidass, 2008), pp. 161–183. Reproduced by permission of Motilal Banarsidass Publishers (P) Ltd.

13. Excerpts from Ganganatha Jha, trans., *Śabara-bhāṣya* (Baroda: Oriental Institute, 1973), pp. 4–8. Reproduced by permission of M. L. Wadekar and the Oriental Institute.

14. Excerpts from Swami Gambhirananda, trans., *Brahma-Sūtra-Bhāṣya* (Calcutta: Advaita Ashrama, 1972), pp. 1–6.

15. Excerpts from J. A. B. van Buitenen, trans., *Rāmānuja's Vedārtha-saṃgraha* (Poona: Deccan College Postgraduate and Research Institute, 1956), pp. 184–188, 233–238, and 296–299.

Every effort has been made to trace copyright holders and to obtain their permission for the use of copyright material. The author apologizes for any errors or omissions in the above list and would be grateful if notified of any corrections that should be incorporated in future reprints or editions of this book.

Errors that remain in this text are entirely my own responsibility. If any are found I beg your forgiveness and hope that they inspire you to further study Indian philosophy.

INTRODUCTION

Classical Indian Philosophy seeks to provide a concise and convenient way to learn about the basic language, positions, and issues of an extraordinarily well-developed and sophisticated intellectual tradition. If those who peruse this volume are inspired to become aware of, and question, their own presuppositions (be these ontological, epistemological, soteriological, or otherwise), and perhaps even to entertain the possible truth of those put forth by the schools included here, then the book will have served one of its purposes.

By definition, no reader is comprehensive, nor can it be. If it were, then it would contain the entire corpus of texts, rather than a select few. That stated, one must appreciate that the history of Indian philosophy spans more than 2,500 years. This introduction simply could not take into account the growth and development of the schools of Indian philosophy over such an enormous time span without alienating novice readers. Ideally, this work will give rise to more complex analyses that are able to explicitly recognize these nuances, while inspiring in its readers an interest in and awareness of Indian philosophy.

The texts and passages that I have chosen are integral to the history of Indian philosophy. To this end I have included selections from Cārvāka, Jain, Buddhist (Yogācāra and Mādhyamaka) texts, traditions deemed to be Nāstika (heterodox) as they do not base themselves on the Vedas, as well as representative texts of the six "classical" schools, Mīmāṃsā, Nyāya, Vaiśeṣika, Sāṃkhya, Yoga, Advaita, Viśiṣṭādvaita, and Mādhva (also known as Dvaita), deemed Āstika (Orthodox) as they, at least nominally, base themselves on the Vedas. Three of these (Advaita, Viśiṣṭādvaita, and Mādhva), the so-called schools of Vedanta, have been given their own separate section in this book (part III).

The entries for each school are self-contained and include brief introductions as well as suggestions for further reading. Like the book itself, these introductions are meant to point readers in the right direction, rather than to be comprehensive surveys. They are intended as starting points and expedients leading toward much larger projects and readings.

DOXOGRAPHIES AND INDIAN PHILOSOPHY

The history of Indian philosophy[1] includes a number of doxographies (compilations of, and commentaries on, earlier philosophical positions), most notably Haribhadra's *Ṣaḍdarśana-samuccaya* (*Compendium of the Six Systems*) and Mādhava-Vidyāraṇya's *Sarvadarśana-saṃgraha* (*Summary of All the Systems*).[2] The classical doxographies contain depictions of views attributed to the schools of Indian philosophy with little or no textual evidence. Each doxography was composed or written by a scholar who identified with a particular school. While Haribhadra was a Jain, Mādhava was a follower of the Advaita school of Vedānta. In fact Jains and adherents to the Advaita school of Vedānta compiled most of the classical doxographies. The doxographies written by Advaita scholars, moreover, were hierarchically arranged, culminating with Vedānta, and specifically with Advaita Vedānta. In this way, the structure of the doxography itself was an argument proclaiming the inevitable truth of Advaita Vedānta, leaving what they believed to be the best for last.

I am a member of the Mādhva school of Vedānta, which was founded by Madhvācārya in the thirteenth century, and I too have arranged my doxography hierarchically, culminating with Vedānta, specifically—and not surprisingly—Mādhva Vedānta. Consequently, my interest in compiling this introduction emerges not simply from the need to address a deficiency in Western scholarship—although doing so is important—but also because I wish to provide a much-needed response, perhaps a rejoinder or even the *siddhānta* (the final view), to the history of Advaita doxographies and to the Advaita Vedānta position. With its publication, this book, *Classical Indian Philosophy*, a *navadarśana-samuccaya* (*compendium of the nine systems*), becomes part of a long lineage of Sanskrit doxographies, and the first Mādhva-oriented one.

BASIC PHILOSOPHICAL AND THEOLOGICAL ISSUES

Before one plunges into the Indian philosophical texts, it is essential to know the basic issues that were the primary concerns of classical Indian philosophies and theologies. The philosophical and religious schools extant in India, other than the Cārvāka and Abrahamic ones, all shared a belief in the mechanism of *karma*, that one's actions in earlier lives affected both one's rebirth and the events that are to occur in one's future lives. The entity that was reborn is the *jīva* (enduring self), also known as the *ātman*. One accumulates some combination of *puṇya* (meritorious *karma*) and *pāpa* (demeritorious *karma*)—popularly rendered in the West as "good" and "bad" *karma*—and is born again and again in *saṃsāra* (worldly existence).

One manifests one's *prārabdha* (latent) *karma*. That is, an individual's accumulated *karma* manifests itself until it is depleted or until more is accrued. Though the schools differed widely on the origins and precise function of these mechanisms of *karma* and *saṃsāra*, they all agreed that they existed. They also all shared an interest in ending this seemingly endless cycle, and this desire was their raison d'être. The state that sentient beings enter after being liberated from the cycle is called *nirvāṇa* in Buddhism and Jainism, and *mokṣa* and *apavarga* among the Hindu traditions. The ontological status and characteristics of *nirvāṇa* and *mokṣa/apavarga* differ vastly, and each school of thought offered methods by which adherents could break the cycle and attain the desired end.

This also required the development of elaborate ontologies (theories about what exists) and epistemologies (theories about the grounds of knowledge) that were joined intimately and inextricably with correlate soteriologies (theories about salvation). One's ontology, for example, must be in harmony with, and indexed to, one's soteriology: If one makes an epistemic claim that knowledge derives from *pratyakṣa* (perception) alone, then one's ontology must account for the existence of objects of perception. The desired end, furthermore, must follow concomitantly from these ontological and epistemological claims. The desired end (*nirvāṇa* and *mokṣa/apavarga* or otherwise) must thus be perceptible given the demands of the epistemology. Like organ systems in the human body as they work together, each component of a philosophical system must work closely with the others and all must function together as one unit. If one organ—or in this case, philosophical component—is not functioning properly or works against another, the whole system will collapse. Much debate in Indian philosophy concerns possible inconsistencies in the relations between a school's ontology and its epistemology, and so on. The drive was always to uncover flaws in what appeared to be an otherwise healthy and coherent philosophical system. The introductory sections for each school of thought in this book are thus divided to reflect the crucial importance of these categories, namely ontology, epistemology, and soteriology.

Competition between the schools of Indian philosophy involved showing that one's own system was more coherent, convincing, and easier to follow than others; in the process, the goal was to convert potential adherents. Indian philosophy developed out of an attempt to systematize the methods and to argue for their superiority. In this process there appeared a number of issues that are central to the debates between schools of Indian philosophy. These are arguments about what constitutes a *pramāṇa* (source of valid knowledge), about the mechanisms for cognition, about whether objects of perception exist independently of the mind (realism versus idealism), about the nature of universals, about the problem of causality, and about the nature and utility of language. These issues and debates are directly and indirectly illustrated in the texts included here.

SAṂVĀDA (DISCUSSION AND DEBATE); OR, "GUIDE TO THE PERPLEXED"

There are at least two basic strategies that one ought to employ when one reads Indian philosophical texts: distillation and critical evaluation. When distilling, readers should try to extract a systematic position from the text. In some cases the author of the text may have presented the materials in a systematic way, thus making distillation quite easy. In other cases, the author may have embedded the materials in narrative or other kinds of prose. To facilitate the extraction, the reader will benefit from trying to answer basic questions about the author's presuppositions: What is the epistemology, the ontology, and the soteriology that can be gleaned from the text? What is presupposed to be a *pramāṇa* (source of valid knowledge)? What is presupposed to exist? and not to exist? What is the prescribed method to obtain *mokṣa* or *nirvāṇa*? What were the detrimental cognitive habits? the advantageous ones? Who is the opponent? What is the position whose refutation is attempted? A careful reader should be able to answer these and related questions after reading each text. The same reader ought to be able to give a verbal or written systematic account of the distilled position that can be put forth to someone not at all familiar with the text or even the genre.

When one critically evaluates, one pays close to attention to the coherence of the overall system that has been presented, the coherence of arguments put forth to justify or defend the system, and the coherence of arguments made against rival traditions. This is known as *saṃvāda* (discussion and debate). Debates between the schools of Indian philosophy were formal events occurring in the presence or under the auspices of royalty. Such events were also overseen by a *sabhāpati* (judge, lit. "Lord of the meeting"), who would objectively determine the validity or success of arguments.

Madhvācārya characterizes these *prāśnikas* (arbitrators of the dispute), as wise, all-knowing, and with neither hate nor anger.[3] The *prāśnika*'s knowledge would include a close understanding of the positions of the debaters as well as the potential *tarka-doṣas* (errors in logic). When one participant was unable to respond to a criticism then a loss might be declared by the *prāśnika*. Defeat has several outcomes, including censure and even conversion! Many of the schools of Indian philosophy grew in size when rivals lost in debate and had to convert.

Consequently, much time and effort was involved in constructing arguments against rival traditions and preparing students to partake in debates, between students in the confines of the *maṭha* (monasteries) and other educational institutions, and eventually with other experts. *Maṭhas* of each of the schools of Vedānta are still places where debating is encouraged and formal and informal debates take place. Viśveṣa Tīrtha, the *svāmiji* (bishop) of the Pejāvara *maṭha* of Mādhva Vedānta, for example, allocates some of his time to lively arguments with students and visitors. These debates still occur today, although less frequently they did in medieval South Asia.

Madhvācārya holds that there are three kinds of debate: *vāda, jalpa*, and *vitaṇḍā*. *Vāda* is a debate whose purpose is the pursuit of truth. *Jalpa* is a debate whose purpose is to bring fame and glory to the competitive victor. The third kind of debate, *vitaṇḍā*, is where one participant seeks only to destroy the position of the other, yet does not reveal any position whatsoever; this form of debate is a kind of reductio ad absurdum in which victory may be achieved only by showing the incoherence of the position of one's opponent and not by either presenting or exposing one's own position for judgment. The *vitaṇḍā* method is by far the best one to employ when reading Indian philosophy as an outsider. Both *vāda* and *jalpa* methods are ideal for those who have allegiance to a particular system, whether it is Indian or not.

Madhvācārya lists a number of *tarka-doṣas* (logical errors) in his *Pramāṇalakṣaṇa*. These can be used to show *doṣas* (errors) in opponents' positions. The schools of Indian philosophy each provide accounts of these errors in their manuals on *saṃvāda* and many agree on them. There are, of course, debates about what ought to be included as a *tarka-doṣa*. Four of these are *ātmānyonyāśraya* (mutual dependence); *cakrakā* (circularity); *anavasthā* (infinite regress); and *kalpanāgaurava* (complexity, i.e., "Ockham's razor").[4] *Ātmānyonyāśraya* (sometimes *ānyonyāśraya*) involves circularity with only two members: for example: "Where is Dinesh?" "He is in my house." "Where is your house?" "Where Dinesh is." *Cakrakā* involves more than two members and concerns a dependency on the first term by the last. For example, the series *a, b, c . . . a* is a *cakrakā*. For example, if Deepak relies on Shakuntala for information about X, and Shakuntala relies on Nandita, and she, in turn, relies on Deepak, then there is a *cakrakā*. *Anavasthā* is a series with no end such as *a, b, c . . . .* One well-known example concerns a claim about the foundation upon which the world rests, namely a turtle. When the proposer of this claim is asked "What does the turtle rest on?" s/he answers, "It's turtles all the way down!" This *doṣa* is known as an *anavasthā*.[5] *Kalpanāgaurava* is the principle of the economy of thought, giving precedence to simplicity. If there are two competing explanations, the simpler one is preferable. Another important *tarka-doṣa* that is accepted by many schools is *ātmāśraya* (self-residence), in which the cause and effect are identical. For example: "Why did Curious George grab the balloons? Because he is Curious George!"

By no means is this list of *tarka-doṣas* exhaustive. As already mentioned, there are many more that could be included, such as *hetu-ābhāsas* (fallacies of inference).[6] Knowledge of these helps one to understand the rules and grounds for dispute among the schools of Indian philosophy.

SĀDHANA (ACCOMPLISHING AN EXPEDIENT)

As mentioned previously, this book is intended as an introduction to the seminal texts and issues of Indian philosophy. In this connection, one issue that has been thematized throughout these pages concerns the debate between the realists (who believe that the objects of perception have a real existence outside of the mind of the perceiver) and the idealists (who believe that these objects of perception are in some way dependent upon the mind and do not exist independently of it). Realists include the Jains, the Nyāya/Vaiśeṣika schools, and the Mādhva school of Vedānta. The idealist schools are the Yogācāra school of Buddhism as well as the Advaita school of Vedānta. This theme is reflected in debates between the Nyāya/Vaiśeṣika schools (both realist schools) and the Yogācāra school (an idealist school). To this end I have included both a selection from Śrīdhara's *Nyāya-kandalī*, a Vaiśeṣika text that has concepts referred to, and rejected by, the Yogācāra school, and a selection from the *Nyāya-vārttika* of Uddyotakara, a Nyāya text that refutes Yogācāra idealism. The theme is further exemplified in debates between the Advaita school (idealists) and the Mādhva school (realists). I have included three texts, Madhvācārya's *Māyāvādakhaṇḍana*,

Upādhikhaṇḍana, and selections from his *Viṣṇutattva(vi)nirṇaya*, that contain arguments that refute Advaita idealism.

This book is thus intended, in part, as a *sādhana* (expedient) for shedding light on this critical theme. This book will have accomplished another of its goals if its readers were to be able to reflect decisively on this issue.

NOTES

1. For more on the use of the word "philosophy" to characterize the intellectual traditions of India, see Wilhelm Halbfass, "*Darśana, Ānvīkṣikī*, Philosophy," in *India and Europe: An Essay in Understanding* (Albany: State University of New York Press, 1988), 263–286.
2. See Wilhelm Halbfass, "The Sanskrit Doxographies and the Structure of Hindu Traditionalism," in *India and Europe*, 349–368.
3. *rāgadveṣavihīnāstu sarvavidyāviśāradāḥ* | *prāśnikā iti* (Madhvācārya, *Kathālakṣaṇa* 5) (see *Sarvamūlagrantha*, ed. Prabhanjanacharya [Bangalore: Sri Vyasa Madhwa Seva Pratisthana, 1999], 18).
4. *ātmānyonyāśrayatācakrakānavasthākalpanāgauravaśrutadṛṣṭahānādayo dūṣaṇānumāḥ* (Madhvācārya, *Pramāṇa-lakṣaṇa*) (see *Sarvamūlagrantha*, ed. Prabhanjanacharya, 5). Madhvacāryā includes a fifth, *śrutadṛṣṭahā* (destruction of what is seen by what is heard), in this list. More detailed descriptions of these and other fallacies can be found in Karl Potter, *Presuppositions of India's Philosophies* (Delhi: Motilal Banarsidass, 1991). I rely upon his explanations and examples for my characterizations here.
5. Aquinas proposes the existence of God, in his "First Cause" argument, as a way to avoid the infinite regress. See Aquinas' "Five Ways," to be found in his *Summa Theologiae*, part a, 2, 3 (St. Thomas Aquinas, *Summa Theologica: Complete English Edition in Five Volumes*, trans. Fathers of the English Dominican Province [Westminister, Md.: Christian Classics, 1981], 1:13–14).
6. See Potter, *Presuppositions of India's Philosophies*, 65–78.

FURTHER READING

Ganeri, Jonardon. *Indian Logic: A Reader*. Richmond, Surrey, UK: Curzon Press, 2001.

Halbfass, Wilhelm. *India and Europe: An Essay in Understanding*. Albany: State University of New York Press, 1988.

Ingalls, Daniel H. H. *Materials for the Study of Navya-Nyāya Logic*. Delhi: Motilal Banarsidass, 1987.

King, Richard. *Indian Philosophy*. Edinburgh: Edinburgh University Press, 1999.
Matilal, Bimal Krishna. *The Character of Logic in India*. Albany: State University of New York Press, 1998.
Potter, Karl. *Presuppositions of India's Philosophies*. Delhi: Motilal Banarsidass, 1991.
Stcherbatsky, F. Th. *Buddhist Logic*, vol. 1. New York: Dover, 1962.
Vidyabhusana, Satis Chandra. *A History of Indian Logic: Ancient, Mediaeval, and Modern Schools*. Delhi: Motilal Banarsidass, 1988.

Part I. NĀSTIKA (HETERODOX) SCHOOLS

1

CĀRVĀKA

HISTORY

The Cārvāka school of Indian philosophy (also known as the Lokāyata [materialist] school) held a skeptical position asserting that matter is the only real and knowable entity. They thus maintained that *pratyakṣa* (perception) is the only *pramāṇa* (source of valid knowledge). The ultimate goal of life for this school of materialism was to maximize pleasure and to minimize pain.

Though versions of this position are timeless and it is thus virtually impossible to determine their origins, forms of skepticism were present in the *Ṛg Veda*, *Upaniṣads*, and even in the *Ramāyāṇa*.[1] Mādhavācārya, author of the *Sarvadarśana-saṃgraha* (*Compendium of All of the Systems*), considered Bṛhaspati to be the founder of the Cārvāka school. The first complete Cārvāka text is Jayarāśi Bhaṭṭa's *Tattvopaplava-siṃha* (*The Lion of Annihilation of [All] Principles*), composed in the eighth century C.E. Other than the references in earlier Hindu texts, evidence for a Cārvāka position is largely gleaned from two compendiums, Mādhavācārya's *Sarvadarśana-saṃgraha* and Haribhadra's *Ṣaḍdarśana-samuccaya* (*Compendium of the Six Systems*), in which one finds codification of the Cārvāka position.

EPISTEMOLOGY

pramāṇam tvakṣajam eva hi.

Perception is the only measure of valid knowledge.

—Haribhadra, *Ṣaḍdarśana-samuccaya* 82

In the Cārvāka position, where *pratyakṣa* is the only *pramāṇa*,[2] no other kinds of knowledge are reliable. This position stands in stark contrast with ones put forth by the other schools of Indian philosophy, which held that there were a host of other *pramāṇas*, including *śabda* (verbal testimony), *upamāna* (analogy), and *anumāna* (inference). The Cārvāka arguments center chiefly upon the validity of the components of the *anumāna*, most notably, upon the *vyāpti* (the universal concomitance). Among the schools of Indian philosophy (and exemplified in the Nyāya school), an *anumāna* is typically understood to have (at least) three component parts: the *sādhya* (the property to be proven); the *hetu* (the reason); and the *vyāpti* (the universal concomitance between the *sādhya* and the *hetu*).

The standard example that has been used to illustrate these components is the inference that where smoke is observed, one can infer that fire must also be present. "Fire-possessing" is the *sādhya* and "smoke-possessing" is the *hetu*. The *vyāpti* is the universal concomitance between fire and smoke. In this example, it is the universal that wherever one sees smoke, one can conclude that fire must also be present; hence the inference "where there is smoke, there is fire." Conclusions about particular events are drawn from the universal concomitances. The Cārvāka argument, then, is that inference is possible if and only if the *vyāpti* is graspable. The argument against *anumāna* thus hinges on the impossibility of grasping the *vyāpti*: the *vyāpti* is true only if all cases have been observed. According to the Cārvāka, it is impossible to observe all instances since these include the past and the future as well as the present. The Cārvāka will ask, for example, if the observer has seen every case where smoke and fire appear together. There may be an instance in the past (and there may be one in the future) where fire and smoke do not appear together. Given this possibility, it is impossible to infer that "wherever smoke is seen, fire is also seen." The implication from this is that there is no reliable knowledge of any universal concomitances, and hence *anumāna* is not a *pramāṇa*. *Pratyakṣa*, then, is the only *pramāṇa*. The majority of arguments put forth on behalf of the Cārvāka by Mādhavācārya revolve around what they perceive to be the fragility of the apprehension of the *vyāpti*.

ONTOLOGY

In the light of the Cārvāka epistemology, the only things that exist are ones that are perceivable. The world is made up of only four elements: *vāyu* (air), *agni* (fire), *ap* (water), and *pṛthivī* (earth). Consciousness does not stand apart from these four. In fact, consciousness emerges from their combination and ceases to be when the body ceases to be. There is, then, no eternal *ātman* (self), or even an all-pervading god to whom religious rites should be performed. This position conflicts with ones put forth by those who upheld the truth of the Vedas. To answer the question as to how things come together, the Cārvāka philosophy states that the four material elements join according to their *svabhāva* (nature). Consequently, there is no need to posit a god as the material cause of the world.

SOTERIOLOGY

It follows from the Cārvāka epistemology and ontology that there can be no knowledge of life after the body dies. There is no perpetuation of the consciousness after the body ceases to function, or even a telos other than hedonism, to maximize pleasure and to minimize pain.

THE TEXTS

The Cārvāka texts here are taken from two sources, both compendiums produced by non-Cārvākans. Mādhavācārya devotes the first section of his *Sarvadarśana-saṃgraha* to the Cārvāka tradition. Composed in the fourteenth century C.E., the *Sarvadarśana-saṃgraha* contains a short presentation of basic Cārvāka philosophy and includes several arguments and counterarguments, primarily concerning *anumāna*. The second text used here is the *Sarvasiddhānta-saṃgraha* (*Compendium of All of the Established Truths*). Likely composed after 1000 C.E., it is falsely ascribed to Śaṃkārācārya, founder of the Advaita school of Vedānta in the eighth century C.E.[3] There are no explicit arguments in this text. Rather, it is a basic presentation of the Lokāyata (Cārvāka) position.

FROM MĀDHAVĀCARYA'S *SARVADARŚANA-SAṂGRAHA*

In this school the four elements, earth, etc., are the original principles; from these alone, when transformed into the body, intelligence is produced, just as the inebriating power is developed from the mixing of certain ingredients; and when these are destroyed, intelligence at once perishes also. . . . Therefore the soul is only the body distinguished by the attribute of intelligence, since there is no evidence for any soul distinct from the body, as such cannot be proved, since this school holds that perception is the only source of knowledge and does not allow inference, etc.

The only end of man is enjoyment produced by sensual pleasures. Nor may you say that such cannot be called the end of man as they are always mixed with some kind of pain, because it is our wisdom to enjoy the pure pleasure as far as we can, and to avoid the pain which inevitably accompanies it. . . .

If you object that, if there be no such thing as happiness in a future world, then how should men of experienced wisdom engage in the *agnihotra* and other sacrifices, which can only be performed with great expenditure of money and bodily fatigue, your objection cannot be accepted as any proof to the contrary, since the *agnihotra*, etc., are only useful as a means of livelihood, for the Veda is tainted by the three faults of untruth, self-contradiction, and tautology; again the imposters who call themselves Vaidic pundits are mutually destructive, as the authority of the *jñāna-kāṇḍa* is overthrown by those who maintain that of the *karma-kāṇḍa*; and lastly, the three Vedas themselves are only the incoherent rhapsodies of knaves, and to this effect runs the popular saying:

> The *Agnihotra*, the three Vedas, the ascetic's three staves, and smearing oneself with ashes,—
> Bṛhaspati says, these are but means of livelihood for those who have no manliness or sense.

Hence it follows that there is no other hell than mundane pain produced by purely mundane causes, as thorns, etc.; the only Supreme is the earthly monarch whose existence is proved by all the world's eyesight; and the only Liberation is the dissolution of the body. By holding the doctrine that the soul is identical with the body, such phrases as "I am thin," "I am black," etc., are at once intelligible, as the attributes of thinness, etc., and self-consciousness will reside in the same subject [the body]; like the use of the phrase "my body" is metaphorical and "the head of Rāhu" [Rāhu being really all *head*]. All this has been thus summed up:

> In this school there are four elements, earth, water, fire, and air;
> And from these four elements alone is intelligence produced,—
> Just like the intoxicating power from kiṇwa, etc., mixed together;
> Since in "I am fat," "I am lean," these attributes abide in the same subject,

And since fatness, etc., resides only in the body, it alone is the soul and no other,
And such phrases as "my body" are only significant metaphorically.

"Be it so," says the opponent; "your wish would be gained if inference, etc., had no force of proof; but then they have this force; else, if they had not, then how, on perceiving smoke, should the thoughts of the intelligent immediately proceed to fire; or why, on hearing another say, 'There are fruits on the bank of the river,' do those who desire fruit proceed at once to the shore?"

All this, however, is only the inflation of the world of fancy.

Those who maintain the authority of inference accept the *sign* or middle term as the causer of knowledge, which middle term must be found in the minor and be itself invariably connected with the major. Now this invariable connection must be a relation destitute of any condition accepted or disputed; and this connection does not possess its power of causing inference by virtue of its *existence*, as the eye, etc., are the cause of perception, but by virtue of being *known*. What then is the means of this connection's being known?

We will first show that it is not *perception*. Now perception is held to be of two kinds, external and internal [i.e., as produced by the external senses, or by the inner sense, mind]. The former is not the required means; for although it is possible that the actual contact of the senses and the object will produce the knowledge of the particular object thus brought in contact, yet as there can never be such contact in the case of the past or the future, the universal proposition which was to embrace the invariable connection of the middle and major terms in every case becomes impossible to be known. Nor may you maintain that this knowledge of the universal proposition has the general class as its object, because if so, there might arise a doubt as to the existence of the invariable connection in this particular case [as, for instance, in this particular smoke as implying fire].

Nor is internal perception the means, since you cannot establish that the mind has any power to act independently toward an external object, since all allow that it is dependent on the external senses, as has been said by one of the logicians, "The eye, etc., have their objects as described; but mind externally is dependent on the others."

Nor can *inference* be the means of the knowledge of the universal proposition, since in the case of this inference we should also require another inference to establish it, and so on, and hence would arise the fallacy of an ad infinitum retrogression.

Nor can *testimony* be the means thereof, since we may either allege in reply, in accordance with the Vaiśeṣika doctrine of Kāṇada, that this is included in the topic of inference; or else we may hold that this fresh proof of testimony is unable to leap over the barrier that stopped the progress of inference, since it depends itself on the recognition of a *sign* in the form of the language used in the child's presence by the old man; and, moreover, there is no more reason for our believing on another's word that smoke and fire are invariably connected, than for our receiving the ipse dixit of Manu, etc. [which, of course, we Cārvākas reject].

And again, if testimony were to be accepted as the only means of the knowledge of the universal proposition, then in the case of a man to whom the fact of the invariable connection between the middle and major terms had not been pointed out by another person, there could be no inference of one thing [as fire] on seeing another thing [as smoke]; hence, on your own showing, the whole topic of inference for oneself would have to end in mere idle words.

Then again *comparison*, etc., must be utterly rejected as the means of the knowledge of the universal proposition, since it is impossible that they can produce the knowledge of the unconditioned connection [i.e., the universal proposition], because their end is to produce the knowledge of quite another connection, viz. the relation of a name to something so named.

Again, this same absence of a condition, which has been given as the definition of an invariable connection [i.e., a universal proposition], can itself never be known; since it is impossible to establish that all conditions must be objects of perception; and therefore, although the absence of perceptible things may be itself perceptible, the absence of nonperceptible things must be itself nonperceptible; and thus, since we must here too have recourse to inference, etc., we cannot leap over the obstacle which has already been planted to bar them. Again, we must accept as the definition of the condition, "it is that which is reciprocal or equipollent in extension with the major term though not constantly accompanying the middle." These three distinguishing clauses, "not constantly accompanying the middle term," "constantly accompanying the major term," and "being constantly accompanied by it" [i.e., reciprocal], are needed in the full definition to stop respectively three such fallacious conditions, in the argument to prove the non-eternity of sound, as "being produced," "the nature of a jar," and "the not causing audition"; wherefore the definition holds—and again it is established by the *śloka* of the great Doctor beginning *samāsama*.[4]

But since the knowledge of the condition must here precede the knowledge of the condition's absence, it is only when there is the knowledge of the condition that the knowledge of the universality of the proposition is possible, i.e., a knowledge in the form of such a connection between the middle term and the major term as is distinguished by the absence of any such condition; and on the other hand, the knowledge of the condition depends upon the knowledge of the invariable connection. Thus we fasten on our opponents as with adamantine glue the thunderbolt-like fallacy of reasoning in a circle. Hence by the impossibility of knowing the universality of a proposition it becomes impossible to establish inference, etc.

The step which the mind takes from the knowledge of smoke, etc., to the knowledge of fire, etc., can be accounted for by its being based on a former perception or by its being an error; and that in some cases this step is justified by the result is accidental just like the coincidence of effects observed in the employment of gems, charms, drugs, etc.

From this it follows that fate, etc., do not exist, since these can only be proved by inference. But an opponent will say, if you thus do not allow *adṛṣṭa* the various phenomena of the world become destitute of any cause.[5] But we cannot accept this objection as valid, since these phenomena can all be produced spontaneously from the inherent nature of things. Thus it has been said:

> The fire is hot, the water cold, refreshing cool the breeze of morn;
> By whom came this variety? From their own nature was it born.

And all this has been also said by Bṛhaspati:

> There is no heaven, no final liberation, nor any soul in another world,
> Nor do the actions of the four castes, orders, etc., produce any real effect.
> The *Agnihotra*, the three Vedas, the ascetic's three staves, and smearing oneself with ashes,
> Were made by Nature as the livelihood of those destitute of knowledge and manliness.
> If a beast slain in the *Jyotiṣṭoma* rite will itself go to heaven,
> Why then does not the sacrificer forthwith offer his own father?
> If the *Śrāddha* produces gratification to beings who are dead,
> Then here, too, in the case of travelers when they start, it is needless to give provisions for the journey.

If beings in heaven are gratified by our offering the *Śrāddha* here,
Then why not give the food down below to those who are standing on the housetop?
While life remains let a man live happily, let him feed on ghee even though he runs in debt;
When once the body becomes ashes, how can it ever return again?
If he who departs from the body goes to another world,
How is it that he comes not back again, restless for love of his kindred?
Hence it is only as a means of livelihood that Brahmans have established here
All these ceremonies for the dead—there is no other fruit anywhere.
The three authors of the Veda were buffoons, knaves, and demons.
All the well-known formulae of the *pundits, jarpharī, turpharī*, etc.,
And all the obscene rites for the queen commanded in the *Aśvamedha*,
These were invented by buffoons, and so all the various kinds of presents to the priests,
While the eating of flesh was similarly commanded by night-prowling demons.

ŚAṂKARĀCĀRYA'S *SARVASIDDHĀNTA-SAṂGRAHA*

The System of the *Lokāyatikas*

1. According to the doctrine of the *Lokāyatikas*, the ultimate principles are merely the four elements, viz. earth, water, fire, and air, and there is nothing else.

2. Whatever is arrived at by means of direct perception, that alone exists. That which is not perceivable is nonexistent, for the (very) reason that it is not perceived. And even those who maintain the (real existence of) *adṛṣṭa* (the unperceivable) do not say that what has not been perceived has been perceived.

3. If what is rarely seen here and there is taken to be the unperceivable, how can they (really) call it as the unperceivable? How can that which is always unseen, like the (ever unseen) horns of a hare, and other such things, be what is really existent?

4. In consequence of (the existence of) pleasure and pain, merit and demerit should not be here (in this connection) postulated by oth-

ers. A man feels pleasure or pain by nature, and there is no other cause (for it).

5. Who colors wonderfully the peacocks, or who makes the cuckoos coo so well? There is in respect of these (things) no cause other than nature.

6. The *ātman* (or self) is the body itself, which is characterized by such attributes as are implied in the expressions "I am stout," "I am young," "I am old," "I am an adult," etc. It is nothing else which is distinct from that (body).

7. That intelligence which is found to be embodied in the (various) modified forms consisting of the nonintelligent elements—(that) is produced in the same way in which red color is produced from the combination of betel, areca nut, and lime.

8. Higher than this world there is none. There is no *svarga* (or celestial world of enjoyment) and no hell. The world of Śiva (and other such worlds) are all invented by those who are (followers of) other (systems of thought) than (what is followed by) ourselves and are (therefore) ignorant impostors.

9. The enjoyment of *svarga* consists in partaking of sweet food here, in enjoying the company of damsels of sixteen years of age, and also in enjoying the pleasures that are derivable from the use of fine clothes, sweet scents, flower garlands, sandals, and such other things (of delicious luxury).

10. The experience of (the miseries of) hell consists (only) in the pain caused by enemies, by injurious weapons, by diseases and other causes of suffering. The final beatitude of *mokṣa* is, however, death (itself); and that consists in the cessation of (breath, the principal vital air).

11. Therefore it is not proper on the part of a wise man to take (any) trouble on account of this (final beatitude). It is only a fool that becomes thin and worn out to dryness by performing penances, and by fasting, etc.

12–15½. Chastity and other such (cunning) conventions have been invented by clever weaklings. Gifts of gold and of lands, etc., the enjoying of sweet dinners on invitation, are all the devices of persons who are poor and have stomachs that are (ever) lean with hunger. With respect to temples, houses for the distribution of drinking water to travelers, tanks, wells, pleasure-gardens, and other such devices—only travelers praise them daily, (but) not others. The ritual of *Agnihotra*, the three

Vedas, the (ascetic's) triple staff, the smearing of one's self with ashes are all (merely) means of livelihood to those who are destitute of intelligence and energy: so opines Bṛhaspati.

By adopting only those means which are seen (to be practical), such as agriculture, the tending of cattle, trade, politics, and administration, etc., a wise man should always (endeavor to) enjoy pleasures (here) in this world.

NOTES

1. For example, *Ṛg Veda* 8.70.2, 8.71.8, 10.38.3; *Bṛhadāraṇyaka Upaniṣad* 4.5.13; *Rāmāyaṇa Ayodhyā khaṇḍa* 108.17.
2 While Jayarāśi did not accept *pratyakṣa*, Purandara (seventh century C.E.) accepted a limited use of the *anumāna*. See John M. Koller, "Skepticism in Indian Thought," *Philosophy East and West* 27.2 (1977): 155–164.
3. Wilhelm Halbfass, *India and Europe* (Albany: State University of New York Press, 1988), 350.
4. This refers to an obscure *śloka* of Udayanācārya, "Where a reciprocal and a nonreciprocal universal connection (i.e., universal propositions which severally do and do not distribute their predicates) relate to the same argument (as, e.g., to prove the existence of smoke), there that nonreciprocating term of the second will be a fallacious middle, which is not invariably accompanied by the other reciprocal of the first." Thus "the mountain has smoke because it has fire" (here fire and smoke are nonreciprocating, as fire is not found invariably accompanied by smoke though smoke is by fire), or "because it has fire from wet fuel" (smoke and fire from wet fuel being reciprocal and always accompanying each other); the nonreciprocating term of the former (fire) will give a fallacious inference, because it is also, of course, not invariably accompanied by the special kind of fire, that produced from wet fuel. But this will not be the case where the nonreciprocating term *is* thus invariably accompanied by the other reciprocal, as "mountain has fire because it has smoke;" here, although fire and smoke do not reciprocate, yet smoke will be a true middle, because it is invariably accompanied by heat, which is the reciprocal of fire.
5. *Adṛṣṭa*, i.e., the merit and demerit in our actions, which produce their effects in future births.

FURTHER READING

Chatterjee, Satischandra, and Dhirendramohan Datta. *An Introduction to Indian Philosophy*. Calcutta: University of Calcutta, 1939.

Dasgupta, Surendranath. *A History of Indian Philosophy*, vol. 1. Cambridge: Cambridge University Press, 1922.

Franco, Eli. *Perception, Knowledge, and Disbelief: A Study of Jayarāśi's Scepticism*. Delhi: Motilal Banarsidass, 1994.

Halbfass, Wilhelm. *India and Europe: An Essay in Understanding*. Albany: State University of New York Press, 1988.

Hiriyanna, M. *Outlines of Indian Philosophy*. Great Britain: George Allen and Unwin Ltd., 1932.

King, Richard. *Indian Philosophy*. Edinburgh: Edinburgh University Press, 1999.

Koller, John M. "Skepticism in Indian Thought." *Philosophy East and West* 27.2 (1977): 155–164.

Riepe, Dale. *The Naturalistic Tradition in Indian Thought*. Seattle: University of Washington Press, 1961.

2

BUDDHISM

HISTORY

Buddhism was and is centered chiefly upon ridding adherents of bad cognitive habits that lead to *duḥkha* (suffering) and rebirth. The tradition was founded by Siddhārtha Gautama in the sixth (or perhaps the fifth) century B.C.E. After attaining enlightenment in Bodhgaya, Siddhārtha became known as *Buddha* (one who is awakened). The Buddha spoke, and his words were first memorized and then later recorded by his followers. Disputes about the accuracy of his words led to the first schisms and then to an immense variety of doctrines and practices (most notably the Theravāda and Mahāyāna schools of Buddhism)—each claiming to represent the authentic words of the Buddha. There were disputes even within the Mahāyāna tradition itself, leading to two schools, namely the Yogācāra and Madhyamaka schools of Buddhism.

The texts that are ascribed to the Buddha are known as the *Pīṭakas* (baskets), in reference to the method by which the original palmleaf manuscripts were preserved and transported. There were three varieties of *Pīṭakas*: the *Abhidharma Pīṭakas* (analysis of *mātrkā* [lists] of the teachings from the *Sūtras*); the *Sūtra Pīṭakas* (a collection of discourses); and the *Vināya Pīṭakas* (rules for monastic discipline).

BUDDHISM IN A NUTSHELL

The Buddha taught a series of interconnected ideas and practices. He first taught that there were four noble truths:

1. There is suffering (*duḥkha*).
2. It has a source (*samudāya*).

3. It can end (*nirodha*).
4. There is a path (*marga*) that leads to the end of suffering.s

The path to end all suffering is eightfold:

1. Right views.
2. Right intention.
3. Right speech.
4. Right action.
5. Right livelihood.
6. Right effort.
7. Right mindfulness.
8. Right concentration.

There is suffering in part because there is an attachment to the false belief that things are permanent. The Buddha thus teaches *sarvam anityam*, "all things are transient." Take for example a new and unmarked book, such as this one. After it has been read religiously, its pages may begin to tear and the binding may become worn. The reader may feel sad because the book is no longer new. According to the Buddha's teachings, though, this sadness is avoidable if one accepts that the book, like all things, changes and will eventually wear out and deteriorate. The Buddha applied this principle, that all things are transient, to the (false) belief that there is an eternally existent and immutable *ātman* (self). This position, that everything lacks a self, is known as *anātman*, the no-self doctrine. Instead, what is called the *ātman* is merely five *skandhas* (aggregates) of physical and mental forms: *rūpa* (form), *vedanā* (feeling), *samjñā* (perception), *saṃskāras* (thought formations), and *vijñana* (sensory consciousness).

The Buddha also taught that the interconnectedness of his ideas is reflective of an interconnectedness that pervades the universe itself. Consequently, the reasons one is born in the cycle of birth and rebirth are not singular. There is, then, no "first-cause" that accounts for *duḥkha*. And although the Buddha posits a pattern of dependent origination (*pratītyasamutpāda*) that gives rise to suffering, each component can itself be connected to an infinite number of other causal possibilities.

The Mahāyāna school of Buddhism adds to this *upāya* (expedient pedagogical methods[1]) by which Buddhas and *boddhisattvas* (ones destined to be enlightened) may adapt their teachings and behaviors as per the requirements of their audience. This powerful, pragmatic pedagogical practice allowed the *bodhisattvas* to offer provisional teachings[2] to eager students.

SOTERIOLOGY

As already mentioned, ridding oneself of bad cognitive habits will prevent further rebirth and suffering. One can achieve this state by embracing the four noble truths and following the eightfold path. This state outside of birth and rebirth is known in Buddhism as *nirvāṇa*. *Nirvāṇa* is outside of language and consequently cannot be characterized or described, given the inherent limitation of language.

THE TEXT

Included here is the first discourse, known as the *Dharmacakrapravartana Sūtra* (*Sūtra on Setting in Motion the Wheel of Dharma*), that the Buddha purportedly gave on the four noble truths after obtaining enlightenment. His audience was five men, all of whom became his first monastic disciples. There are many different versions of this discourse and the one used here is the Sanskrit version taken from the *Mahāvastu* (*The Great Story*). It was completed by the second century B.C.E. and is regarded as a product of the Mahāsāṅghika school of Buddhism.

DHARMACAKRAPRAVARTANA SŪTRA

Thus have I heard. On one occasion the Exalted One was staying in Benares, in the Deer Park at Ṛiṣivadana. There the Exalted One addressed the venerable five monks, saying, "Monks." "Lord," said they in reply. Then the Exalted One said to the monks, "There are these two extremes to which a man who has gone forth to the religious life is liable. What two? There is the addiction to sensual enjoyment among the pleasures of sense, which is loutish, common, un-Aryan, profitless, not conducing to *brahma*-life in the future, to disgust with the world, to passionlessness, to cessation, to the state of the recluse, to enlightenment, and to *nirvāṇa*. Then there is addiction to mortification of the self, which is evil, un-Aryan, and profitless. These, monks, are the two extremes to which a man who has taken up the religious life is liable. Avoiding these two extremes, monks, by the Tathāgata's[3] Aryan *dharma* and discipline is the middle course, which is the way of the Buddhas, and confers insight, conduces to calm, to disgust with the world, to passionlessness, to cessation, to the state of a recluse, to enlightenment, and to *nirvāṇa*."

"And what, monks, is this middle course fully awakened to by the Tathāgata in his Aryan *dharma* and discipline, which confers insight and knowledge and conduces to calm, to disgust with the world, to passionlessness, to cessation, to the state of a recluse, to enlightenment, and to *nirvāṇa*? It is the Aryan eightfold Way, that is to say, right belief, right purpose, right endeavor, right action, right living, right speech, right mindfulness, right concentration. This, monks, is the middle course fully awakened to by the Tathāgata in his Aryan *dharma* and discipline, which confers insight and conduces to calm, to disgust with the world, to passionlessness, to cessation, to the state of a recluse, to enlightenment, and to *nirvāṇa*.

"Now, monks, there are these four Aryan truths. What four? They are the Aryan truth of ill, the Aryan truth of the uprising of ill, the Aryan truth of stopping of ill, and the Aryan truth of the course that leads to the stopping of ill."

"And what, monks, is the 'Aryan truth of ill'? It is this, namely, that birth is ill, old age is ill, disease is ill, death is ill, association with what is not dear is ill, separation from what is dear is ill, failure to get what one wants and seeks is ill, body is ill, feeling is ill, perception is ill, the *samṣkāras* are ill, consciousness is ill, in a word all the five *skandhas* of grasping at material things are ill. This, monks, is the Aryan truth of ill."

"Then what is the 'Aryan truth of the uprising of ill'? That it is the craving which leads to further existence and which is bound up with the passion for pleasure, finding delight in this and that—this, monks, is the Aryan truth of the uprising of ill."

"Then what is the 'Aryan truth of the stopping of ill'? That it is utter extinction of this craving which is bound up with the passion for pleasure, finding delight in this or that; it is passionlessness, cessation, self-sacrifice, renunciation, and surrender. This, monks, is the Aryan truth of the stopping of ill."

"Then what is the 'Aryan truth of the course that leads to the stopping of ill'? That it is the Aryan eightfold way, namely, right belief, right purpose, right speech, right action, right living, right endeavor, right mindfulness, and right concentration—this, monks, is the Aryan truth of the course that leads to stopping of ill."

"From the truth 'This is ill,' by whole-hearted attention to things unheard of before, there arose in me knowledge, vision, understanding, wisdom, intelligence, sagacity, and insight, and light appeared."

"From the truth 'This is the uprising of ill,' by whole-hearted attention to things unheard of before, there arose in me knowledge, vision, understanding, wisdom, intelligence, sagacity, and insight, and light appeared."

"From the truth 'This is the stopping of ill,' by whole-hearted attention to things unheard of before, there arose in me knowledge, vision, understanding, wisdom, intelligence, sagacity, and insight, and light appeared."

"From the truth 'This is the course that leads to the stopping of ill,' by whole-hearted attention to things unheard of before, there arose in me knowledge, vision, understanding, wisdom, intelligence, sagacity, and insight, and light appeared."

"At the thought that this Aryan truth of ill must be thoroughly known, by whole-hearted attention to things unheard of before, there arose in me knowledge, vision, understanding, wisdom, intelligence, sagacity, and insight, and light appeared."

"At the thought that this which is the Aryan truth of the uprising of ill must be given up, by the whole-hearted attention to things unheard of before there arose in me knowledge, vision, understanding, wisdom, intelligence, sagacity, and insight, and light appeared."

"At the thought that this which is the Aryan truth of the stopping of ill has been realized, by whole-hearted attention to things unheard of before, there arose in me knowledge, vision, understanding, wisdom, intelligence, sagacity, and insight, and light appeared."

"At the thought that this which is the Aryan truth of the course leading to the stopping of ill has been made-to-become, by whole-hearted attention to things unheard of before, there arose in me knowledge, vision, understanding, wisdom, intelligence, sagacity, and insight, and light appeared."

"And, monks, as long as I did not with perfect insight fully know these four truths, which are threefold and of twelve modes, as they really are, so long could I not claim to be thoroughly awakened to the supreme perfect enlightenment, so long did knowledge not arise in me, and so long did I not realize an unshakeable freedom of heart. But when, monks, I did with perfect insight fully know these four truths, which are threefold and of twelve modes, as they really are, then was I aware that I had awakened to the supreme perfect enlightenment; knowledge then came to me, and I realized unshakeable freedom of heart, and freedom through intuitive wisdom."

Thus did the Exalted One speak while he was staying in Benares in the Deer Park at Ṛiṣivadana.

NOTES

1. Thanks to Mark Siderits for this phrasing; see Mark Siderits, *Buddhism as Philosophy* (Aldershot: Ashgate, 2007), 139.
2. I am indebted to Richard King for this phrase; see Richard King, *Indian Philosophy* (Edinburgh: Edinburgh University Press, 1999), 96.
3. Tathāgata ("One who has thus gone/One who has thus arrived") is another name for the Buddha.

FURTHER READING

Harvey, Peter. *An Introduction to Buddhism: Teachings, History, and Practices*. Cambridge: Cambridge University Press, 1990.

King, Richard. *Indian Philosophy*. Edinburgh: Edinburgh University Press, 1999.

Rahula, Walpola. *What the Buddha Taught*. New York: Grove Press, 1959.

Robinson, Richard H., Willard L. Johnson, and Thinisasaro Bikku. *Buddhist Religions: A Historical Introduction*. Belmont, Calif.: Thomson, 2005.

Siderits, Mark. *Buddhism as Philosophy*. Aldershot: Ashgate, 2007.

Williams, Paul, and Anthony Tribe. *Buddhist Thought: A Complete Introduction to the Indian Tradition*. New York: Routledge, 2000.

3

YOGĀCĀRA BUDDHISM

HISTORY

According to the Yogācāra school of Buddhism, all perception is *cittamātra* (mind-only). The Yogācāra (practice of yoga) school thus asserts that the belief that the objects of perception exist independently of the mind of the perceiver is a false one and leads to suffering. The Yogācāra school, a tradition of Mahāyāna Buddhism, has its roots in the fourth century C.E. in the *Saṃdhinirmocana Sūtra* (*Sacred Text Which Reveals What Is Hidden*). Its most well known proponents are Asaṅga and Vasubandhu (both fifth century C.E.). According to the tradition, Asaṅga was the older brother of Vasubandhu. Asaṅga's *Yogācara-bhūmi* (*Stages of the Yogic Path*), *Abhidharma-samuccaya* (*Summary of Metaphysics*), and *Mahāyāna-saṃgraha* (*The Summation of the Mahāyāna*) were the first systematic analyses of the tradition. Vasubandhu wrote a *bhāṣya* (commentary) on his brother's *Abhidharma-samuccaya* as well as two short pieces, the *Viṃśatikā Kārikā* (*Twenty Verses*) and *Triṃśikā Kārikā* (*Thirty Verses*), that were defenses of his idealistic, anti-substance ontology.

EPISTEMOLOGY

As evidenced by the arguments put forth by Asaṅga and Vasubandhu, it seems that they accept *anumāna* (inference) as a *pramāṇa* (source of valid knowledge). Neither, however, offers an account of the *pramāṇas* in his work. The *Madhyāntavibhāga* (attributed to Asaṅga) and the *Madhyāntavibhāga-bhāṣya* (attributed to Vasubandhu) state that they accept three *pramāṇas*. Sthiramati's subcommentary lists the three as *pratyakṣa* (perception), *anumāṇa*, and *āgamas* (tradition).

ONTOLOGY

The Yogācāra school holds that all that is perceived is *cittamātra* (mind-only). To this end they deny the existence of all things that are perceived and even the coherence of the theory that the universe is composed of atoms, as exemplified in Vaiśesika atomism. Much of their effort consists in defending their idealist and anti-substance ontology and in explaining the working of *vijñāna* (consciousness) itself. To this end they posit the *ālayavijñāna* (storehouse consciousness), which serves as a repository for the *bījas* (seeds) left by past *karma*. The *bījas* mature into "consciousness events" that are perceived. The objects that are perceived are, however, merely cognitive representations (*vijñāptimātra*) and do not have enduring counterparts outside of the mind. Typically one perceives that there are objects that are different from the perceiving subject; hence reality seems to be dual.

Reality, moreover, is divisible into *trisvabhāva* (three natures) of experience: *parikalpita svabhāva* (the constructed or imagined nature); *paratantra svabhāva* (the dependent nature); and *parinispanna svabhāva* (the perfected realm). Adherents must pass through these stages en route to enlightenment.[1]

SOTERIOLOGY

As already mentioned, jettisoning bad cognitive habits will prevent further rebirth and suffering. Disciplined meditative practices lead to the rejection of these unwanted cognitive habits (including attachment to the *cittamātra* doctrines) and, eventually, to *parinispanna svabhāva*, a state of nonduality, where there is neither subject nor object. There is merely a flow of perceptions, empty of enduring entities. Hence, the Yogācāra explain this state as one of *śūnyatā* (emptiness).[2]

THE TEXT

Included here is the entirety of Vasubandhu's *Viṃśatika Kārikā* (*Twenty Verses*) and *Vṛtti*, his self-commentary. It consists of arguments against Vaiśeṣika atomism, and attempts to draw parallels between illusions and perceived reality.

VASUBANDHU'S *VIMŚATIKA KĀRIKĀ* AND *VṚTTI*

In the Great Vehicle, the three realms of existence are determined as being perception-only. As it is said in the *sūtra*, "The three realms of existence are *citta*-only." *Citta*, *manas*, consciousness, and perception are synonyms. By the word "*citta*," *citta* along with its associations is intended here. "Only" is said to rule out any (external) object of sense or understanding.

> All this is perception-only, because of the appearance of nonexistent objects,
> just as there may be the seeing of nonexistent nets of hair by someone afflicted with an optical disorder. 1

Here it is objected:

> If perception occurs without an object,
> any restriction as to place and time becomes illogical,
> as does nonrestriction as to moment-series[3]
> and any activity which has been performed. 2

What is being said? If the perception of visible, etc., arises without any object of visible, etc., why is it that it arises only in certain places, and not everywhere, and even in those places, why is it that it arises only sometimes, and not all the time? And why is it that it arises in the moment-series of all that are situated in that time and place, and not just in the moment-series of one, just as the appearance of hair, etc., arises in the moment-series of those afflicted by an optical disorder, and not in the moment-series of others? Why is it that the hair, bees, etc., seen by those afflicted by an optical disorder don't perform the functions of hair, etc., while it is not the case that other hair, etc., don't perform them? Food, drink, clothes, poison, weapons, etc., that are seen in a dream don't perform the functions of food, etc., while it is not the case that other food, etc., don't perform them. An illusory town does not perform the functions of a town, because of its nonexistence, while it is not the case that other towns don't perform them. Therefore, with the nonbeing of an object, any restriction as to place and time, any restriction as to moment-series, and any activity which has been performed, would be illogical.

Reply:

> No, they are not illogical, because
> Restriction as to place, etc., is demonstrated as in a dream. 3a

Now how is this? In a dream, even without an (external) object of sense or understanding, only certain things are to be seen: bees, gardens, women, men, etc., and these only in certain places, and not everywhere. And even there in those places, they are to be seen only sometimes, and not all the time. In this way, even without an (external) object of sense or understanding, there may be restriction as to place and time.

> And nonrestriction as to moment-series is like with the *pretas*.[4] 3b

The phrase "is demonstrated" continues to apply here (to make the verse read: "And nonrestriction as to moment-series is demonstrated as with the *pretas*"). How is it demonstrated?

> In the seeing of pus-rivers, etc., by all of them. 3c

all together. A "pus-river" is a river filled with pus. Just as one says "a ghee pot." For all the *pretas* who are in a similar situation due to a similar retribution for action, and not just one of them, see a river filled with pus. With the expression "etc." rivers full of urine and feces, guarded by men holding clubs or swords, and other such perceptions, are included also. Thus, nonrestriction as to moment-series in regard to perceptions is demonstrated even with an (external) object of sense or understanding being nonexistent.

> And activity which has been performed
> is just like being affected in a dream.[5] 4a

A case of "being affected in a dream" is like where semen is released even without a couple's coming together. So, by these various examples, the fourfold restriction as to place and time, and so on, is demonstrated.

> And as in a hell-state[6]
> all of these 4b

are demonstrated. "In a hell-state" means "among those experiencing a hell-state." How are they demonstrated?

> In the seeing of hell-guardians, etc.,
> and in being tormented by them. 4c

Just as "the seeing of hell-guardians," etc., by those experiencing a hell-state (and with the expression "etc." the seeing of dogs, crows, moving mountains, and so on is included) is demonstrated with a restriction as to place and time for all those experiencing a hell-state, and not just for one of them, and just as their torment inflicted by them is demonstrated through the sovereignty of the common retribution for their individual actions, even though the hell-guardians, and so on, are really nonexistent. So the fourfold restriction as to place and time is to be known as demonstrated in yet another way.

Objection: But for what reason is the existence of hell-guardians, dogs, and crows (experienced in hell-states) not accepted?

Reply: Because they are illogical. For to assume that these kinds of hell-beings have an external existence is not logical. This is so because they don't feel the sufferings there themselves, or if they tormented each other mutually, there would be no difference in situation between those experiencing a hell-state and the hell-guardians, and if they mutually tormented each other, having equal make-ups, sizes, and strengths, there would be no fear in those experiencing a hell-state, and since they couldn't stand the burning suffering of standing on a ground made of heated iron, how could they be tormenting others? And how could there be an arising of those not experiencing a hell-state, together with those who are?

Objection: How is this? The arising of animals in a heaven-state may occur, so in the same way, there may be the arising of hell-guardians, etc., which have the distinct qualities of animals or *pretas* in hell-states.

Reply:

> There is no arising of animals in hell-states, as there is in heaven-states,
> nor is there any arising of *pretas*,
> since they don't experience the sufferings that are engendered there. 5

Those animals that arise in heaven-states experience all the pleasure that is engendered there because of (past) actions bringing pleasure to their environment. But hell-guardians, etc., don't experience hellish suffering in the same way. So the arising of animals (in hell-states) is not logical, and neither is the arising of *pretas* there.

An opinion: Then it's because of the actions of those experiencing a hell-state that special material elements arise, which have special qualities as to color, make-up, size, and strength, and are cognized as hell-guardians, etc. That's why they are constantly transforming in various ways, and appear to be shaking their hands, etc., in order to instill fear, just as mountains that look like sheep appear to be coming and going, and just as thorns in forests of iron silk-cotton trees appear to be bowing down and rising up again. And yet it isn't that (these phenomena) aren't arising.[7]

Reply:

> If the arising and transformation of material elements due to the actions of those accepted,
> why isn't (such arising and transformation) of a consciousness accepted? 6

Why is a transformation of consciousness itself due to (past) actions not accepted, and why instead are material elements constructed? And furthermore,

> It's being constructed that the process of impressions from actions takes place elsewhere than does its effect,
> and it is not being accepted that it exists there where the impressions take place: Now what is your reason for this? 7

Because it is through their action that such an arising and transformation of material elements is constructed for those experiencing a hell-state, and inasmuch as impression through actions enter together into their consciousness-series, and not anywhere else, why is it that that effect is not accepted as being such a transformation of consciousness taking place just where the impressions themselves do?[8] What is the reason for an effect being constructed where there is no process of impression?

(You may say): By reason of scriptural authority. If consciousness were only the appearance of visible, etc., and there were no (external) objects of visible, etc., the existence of the sense-fields of visible, etc., would not have been spoken of by the Exalted One.

Reply:

> This is no reason,
> because speaking of sense-fields of visible, etc., was intended for those to be introduced to Dharma,
> just as in the case of spontaneously generated beings.[9] 8

It's just like in the case where spontaneously generated beings were discussed by the Exalted One. This was done with intention of indicating the nondiscontinuity of the *citta*-series in the future.[10] "There is neither a sentient being or a self, but only events along with their causes," has been stated by the Exalted One. Thus, statements were made by the Exalted One regarding the existence of the sense-fields of visible, etc., with an intention directed at people to be introduced to the Dharma. And what was the intention there?

> Because their appearances continue as perceptions,
> because of (consciousnesses') own seeds,
> the Sage spoke in terms of states of twofold sense-fields. 9

A perception with the appearance of visibles arises through a special transformation (in the consciousness-series). In respect to such a perception, the Exalted One spoke in terms of the sense-field of the eye and of visibles, in respect to the seed and the appearance that arises, respectively. In the same way, a perception with the appearance of tactile sensations arises through a special transformation (in the consciousness-series). In respect to such a perception, the Exalted One spoke in terms of the sense-fields of the tactile body and tactile sensations, in respect to the seed and the appearance that arises, respectively.[11]

This is the intention.

> What is the advantage of teaching with such an intention?
> In this way, there is entry into the selflessness of personality. 10a

If the sense-fields are taught in this way, people will enter into an understanding of the selflessness of personality. The group of six consciousnesses evolves because of duality. But when it is known that there is not any one seer (any one hearer, any one smeller, any one taster, any one toucher), or any one thinker, those to be introduced to Dharma through the selflessness of personality will enter into an understanding of the selflessness of personality.

> And in yet another way, this teaching is entry into the selflessness
> events 10b

"And in yet another way," etc., is in reference to how the teaching of perception-only is entry into the selflessness of events, when it becomes known that this perception-only makes an appearance of visibles, etc., arise, and that there is no experienced event with the characteristics of visible, etc. But if there isn't an event in any way, then perception-only also isn't, so how can it be demonstrated? But it's not because there isn't an event in any way that there is entry into the selflessness of events. Rather, it's

> in regard to the constructed self. 10c

It is selflessness in reference to a constructed self—i.e., all those things that constitute the "own-being" believed in by fools—that is the constructed with its "objects apprehended" and "subject apprehendors," etc., and not in reference to the ineffable Self, which is the scope of the Buddhas.[12] In the same way one penetrates the selflessness of perception-only itself in reference to a "self" constructed by another perception,[13] and through this determination of perception-only there is entry into the selflessness of all events, and not by a denial of their existence.[14] Otherwise, there would be an object for this other perception because of a perception itself (i.e., either "perception-only" or "the perception of self" would be a real object), there would be at least one perception that has an object consisting of another perception, and the state of perception-only wouldn't be demonstrated, because of the perception's state of having objects.[15]

But how is it to be understood that the existence of the sense-fields of visible, etc., was spoken of by the Exalted One not because those things that singly become sense-objects of the perceptions of visible, etc., really exist, but rather with a hidden intention? Because

> A sense-object is neither a single thing,
> nor several things,
> from the atomic point of view,
> nor can it be an aggregate (of atoms).
> So atoms can't be demonstrated. 11

What is being said? The sense-fields of visibles, etc., which consists (in a moment) of a single sense-object of a perception of visibles, etc., is either a unity, like the composite whole constructed by the Vaiśeṣikas, or it is several things, from the atomic point of view, or it is an aggregation of atoms. Now, the sense-object can't be a single thing, because one can nowhere apprehend a composite whole that is different from its component parts. Nor can it be plural, because of atoms, since they can't be apprehended singly.[16] Nor does an aggregation of atoms become a sense-object, because an atom as one entity can't be demonstrated, either.

How is it that it can't be demonstrated?
Because through the simultaneous conjunction of six elements,
the atom has six parts. 12a

If there is a simultaneous conjunction of six elements in six directions, the atom comes to have six parts.[17] For that which is the locus of one can't be the locus of another.

If there were a common locus for the six,
the agglomeration would only be one atom. 12b

It might be maintained that the locus for each single atom is the locus of all six elements. But then, because of the common locus for all of them, the agglomeration would be only one atom, because of the mutual exclusion of occupants of a locus. And then no agglomeration would become visible.[18] Nor, for that matter, can atoms join together at all, because of their state of having no parts. The Vaibhāṣikas of Kashmir say, "We aren't arguing such an absurdity. It's just when they're in aggregation, that they can join together." But the question must be asked: Is then an aggregation of atoms not an object different from the atoms themselves?

When there is no conjunction of atoms,
how can there be one for their aggregations?
Their conjunction is not demonstrated,
for they also have no parts. 13

So the aggregation themselves can't mutually join together either. For there is no conjunction of atoms, because of their state of having no parts. That is to say, such a thing can't be demonstrated. So even in the case of aggregation, which does have parts, its conjunction becomes inadmissible (because there can be no aggregation of atoms unless individual atoms conjoin). And so the atoms as one entity can't be demonstrated. And whether the conjunction of atoms is accepted or isn't,

(To assume) the singleness of that which has divisions
as to directional dimensions, is illogical. 14a

For one atom, there may be the directional dimension of being "in front," for another, of being "on the bottom," and if there are such divisions as to directional dimensions, how can the singleness of an atom, which partakes of such divisions, be logical?

> Or else, how could there be shade and blockage? 14b

If there were no divisions as to directional dimensions in an atom, how could there be shade in one place, light in another, when the sun is rising? For there could be no other location for the atom where there would be no light.[19] And how could there be an obstruction of one atom by another, if divisions as to directional dimensions are not accepted? For there would be no other part for an atom, where, through the arrival of another atom, there would be a collision with this other atom. And if there is no collision, then the whole aggregation of all the atoms would have the dimensions of only one atom, because of their common locus, as has been stated previously.

It may be argued: Why can't it be accepted that shade and blockage refer to an agglomeration, and not to a single atom?

Reply: But in that case, is it being admitted that an agglomeration is something other than the atoms themselves?

Objector: No, that can't be admitted.

> If the agglomeration isn't something other,
> then they can't refer to it. 14c

If it is not accepted that the agglomeration is something other than the atoms, then shade and blockage can't be demonstrated as occurring in reference to the agglomeration only. This is simply an attachment to mental construction. "Atoms" or "aggregations": what's the point of worrying with those, if "their basic characteristics of being visible, etc.," are not refuted?

What then is their characteristics? That they are in a state of being sense-objects of the eye, etc., in a state of being blue, etc. It is just this which should be investigated. If a sense-object for the eye, and so on, is accepted in the form of blue, yellow, etc., then are these one entity, or several? Now what follows from this? The flaw inherent in assuming their severalness has already been discussed (in relation to the arguments on atomic aggregation).

> If their unity existed, one couldn't arrive at anything gradually,
> there couldn't be apprehension and nonapprehension simultaneously

there couldn't be separate, several, developments,
and there would be no reason for the non-seeing of the very subtle. 15

If one entity as a sense-object for the eye, with no separations, and no severalness, were constructed, then one couldn't arrive at anything gradually on the Earth: that is, there could be no act of going. For, even with placing down a foot once, one would go everywhere. There could be no apprehension of a nearer "part of something" and a nonapprehension of a more removed "part," simultaneously. For a concurrent apprehension and nonapprehension of the same thing isn't logical. There would be no special development for species that are separate, such as elephants, horses, etc., and since they would all be one in that case, how could their separation be accepted? And how can they be accepted as single, anyway, since there is the apprehension of an empty space between two of them? And there would be no reason for the non-seeing of subtle water-beings, since they would be visible in common with the more apparent.

An otherness in entities is constructed if there is a division of characteristics, and not otherwise, so when speaking from the atomic point of view, one must by necessity construct divisions, and it cannot be demonstrated that they (the atoms) are in any way one kind. With their unity undemonstrated, visibles', etc.'s, state of being sense-objects of eye, etc., is also undemonstrated, and thus perception-only *is* demonstrated.

If the existence and nonexistence of objects of sense or understanding are being investigated by force of the means-of-cognition (direct perception, inference, appeal to reliable authority), direct perception must be recognized as being the most weighty of all means-of-cognition. But with an object of sense or understanding not existing, how can there be any cognizing that can be termed "direct perception"?

Cognizing by direct perception is like a dream, etc., 16a

For it is without an object of sense or understanding, as has been made known previously.

And when it occurs, the object is already not seen,
so how can it be considered a state of direct perception? 16b

When a cognition through direct perception arises in the form "This is my direct perception," the object itself is already not seen, since this distinguishing takes place only through a mental consciousness, and the visual consciousness has already ceased by that time, so how can its being direct perception be accepted? This is especially true for a sense-object, which is momentary, for that visible, or taste, etc., has already ceased by that time.[20] It may be said that nothing which hasn't been experienced (by other consciousnesses) is remembered by the mental consciousness, and that this takes place by necessity as it is brought about by the experience of an object of sense or understanding, and that those can be considered to be a state of direct perception of sense-objects, visible, etc., in this way. But this remembering of an experienced object of sense or understanding is not demonstrated, either. Because

> It has been stated how perception occurs with its appearance. 17

It has already been stated how perceptions in the shape of eye-consciousnesses, etc., arise with the appearance of an object, even without there being any (external) object of sense or understanding.

> And remembering takes place from that 17b

"From that" means "from the perception." A mental perception arises with the discrimination of a visible, etc., when that appearance is linked with memory, so an experience of an (external) object can't be demonstrated through the arising of a memory.

Objection: If, even when one is awake, perception has sense-objects which weren't, like in a dream, then people would understand their nonbeing themselves. But that isn't the case. So it's not that the apprehension of objects is like in a dream, and all perceptions are really without an (external) object.

Reply: This argument won't bring us to the cognition you wish because

> Somebody who isn't awake doesn't understand the nonbeing
> of the visual sense-objects in a dream. 17c

Just as people when they are asleep in a dream have their faculties concentrated on impressions of appearances of discriminations that appear differently than they do later, and, as long as they aren't awake, don't understand the nonbeing of objects of sense and understanding that weren't, just so when they become awakened by the attainment of a supermundane knowledge free from discriminations, which is the antidote to these (discriminations), then they truly understand the nonbeing of these sense-objects through meeting with a clear worldly subsequently attained knowledge.[21] So their situations are similar.

Objection: If, through a special transformation of "their own" moment-series, perceptions with the appearance of (external) objects of sense or understanding arise from beings, and not through special objects themselves, then how can any certainty as regards perceptions be demonstrated from association with bad or good friends, or from hearing about the existent and nonexistent events,[22] since there can exist nether association with the good or bad, nor any real teaching?

Reply:

> The certainty of perception takes place mutually,
> by the state of their sovereign effect on one another. 18a

For all beings there is certainty of perception through a mutual sovereign effect of perceptions on one another, according to circumstances.[23] "Mutually" means "each affecting the other." So one special perception arises within a moment-series through a special perception within the moment-series, and not because of a special object.

Objection: If a perception is without an (external) object, just like in a dream, even for those who are awake, why is it that in the practice of the beneficial and unbeneficial there won't be an equal result from desirable and undesirable efforts, for those who are asleep and those who aren't?[24]

Reply: Because

> *Citta* is affected by torpor in a dream,
> so their results are different. 18b

This is the reason, not the existing being of an (external) object.

Objection: If all this is perception-only, there can't be body or speech for anybody. So how can the dying of sheep who have been attacked by shepherds take place? If their dying takes place without the shepherds having done anything, how can the shepherds be held responsible for the offense of taking life?

Reply:

> Dying may be a modification resulting from a special perception by
> another,

just like the losses of memory, etc., may take place through the mental control of spirits, etc. 19

Just as there may be modifications in others, such as loss of memory, the seeing of dreams, or being taken possession of by spirits, by the mental control of psychic powers, as in the case of Sāraṇa's seeing dreams through Mahā-Kātyāyana's mental force, or, as in the case of the vanquishing of Vemacitra through mental harming coming from the forest-dwelling seers.[25] In the same way, through the force of a special perception of another, a certain modification of the aggregate-series, destroying its life-force, may arise, through which dying, which is to be known as a name for a discontinuity in the aggregate-series taking part in an organism, takes place.

Or else, how was it that the Daṇḍaka forest became empty because of the anger of seers? 20a

If it isn't accepted that the dying of being can occur through the force of a special perception in others, how is it that the Exalted One, in order to demonstrate that mental harm constitutes a great offense, questioned Upāli, when he was still a householder, as follows : "Householder! Through what agency were the Daṇḍaka, Mataṅga, and Kaliṅga forests made empty and sacred, as has been reported?," and Upāli replied, "I heard that it happened through the mental harming of seers, Gautama."

If not, how could it be demonstrated that mental harm constitutes a great offense? 20b

If this situation were constructed as not taking place through a mental harming, and it were to be said that those sentient beings that were living in that forest were destroyed by nonhuman spirits that had been propitiated as if they were seers, how could it be demonstrated by this passage that mental harm through mental action is a greater offense than bodily or verbal harm?[26] This passage demonstrates that the dying of so many sentient beings came about only through a mental harming.

Objection: But if all this is perception-only, do those who understand the *cittas* of others really know the *cittas* of others, or don't they?

Reply: What about this?

Objector: If they don't know them, how can they be "those who understand the *cittas* of others"?

Reply: They know them.

The knowledge of those who understand others' *cittas* is not like an object.
And how is this? As in the case of a knowledge of one's own *citta*. 21a

Objector: And how is that knowledge (of one's own *citta*) not like an object?

Reply:

Because of nonknowledge, as in the case of the scope of Buddhas. 21b

It's just like in the case of the scope of Buddhas, which comes about through the ineffable Self. Thus both of these knowledges, because of their inherent nonknowledge, are not like an object, because it is through the state of an appearance of something which appears differently than it does later that there is a state of non-abandonment of the discrimination between object apprehended and subject apprehendor.[27]

Though perception-only has unfathomable depth, and there are limitless kinds of ascertainments to be gained in it,

I have written this demonstration of perception-only according to my abilities,
but in its entirety it is beyond the scope of *citta*. 22a

It is impossible for people like me to consider it in all its aspects, because it is not in the range of dialetics. And in order to show by whom it is known entirely as a scope of insight, it is said to be

the scope of Buddhas. 22b

In all its modes, it is the scope of Buddhas, Exalted Ones, because of their lack of impediment to the knowledge of everything that can be known in all aspects.

NOTES

1. Mario D'Amato, "Three Natures, Three Stages: An Interpretation of the Yogācāra *Trisvabhāva*-Theory," *Journal of Indian Philosophy* 33 (2005): 203.
2. I rely upon Paul Williams here for this language; Paul Williams, *Mahāyāna Buddhism: The Doctrinal Foundations* (New York: Routledge, 1989), 85.

3. "There would be no restriction as to place and time of objects perceived" means that any object of sense or understanding would arise anywhere and at any time if there were no definite external object to which it corresponded. "Nor would there be nonrestriction as regards consciousness-series perceiving them" means that if there were no definite external object, it couldn't happen that all consciousness-series in a given place and time see the same object. Of course Vasubandhu will deny that the latter is true at all, since there are always various ways of perceiving "the same sequence." And the restriction as to place and time for objects of sense and understanding does not depend on a definite external object, as it is a principle operating even in the perceptions taking place in dreams.
4. The *pretas* are "the hungry ghosts" of traditional Buddhist lore, who undergo special sufferings because of past unbeneficial actions. All of them will see the same pus-rivers, etc., even though others won't: another indication that experienced reality may be totally mentally created.
5. The objector is saying that an external object of consciousness is proved by "action's being performed." This means, for instance, that food that is tasted while awake has the activity of nourishing, while "food" that is tasted in a dream is not really food, as it does not nourish the organism. Vasubandhu says that this argument is not foolproof, because when a man has a sexual dream, the biological function of releasing semen is performed in this case.
6. The hell-states will be reduced by Vasubandhu to afflicted events existing only in the consciousness-streams of those experiencing them.
7. Hallucinations exist as much as anything else does, since they are perceptions.
8. Residual impressions take place in consciousness. Retribution is a fruition or maturation of impressions, and thus should take place in the consciousness-series only.
9. "Spontaneously generated beings" are those that arise all at once, with all their organs neither lacking nor deficient. They do not have to undergo embryonic stages or any other development. Traditionally, gods, hell-beings, and the intermediate existences between one full life-series and the next (the *bardo* of the *Bardo-Thōdol,* or *Tibetan Book of the Dead*) are considered to be "spontaneously generated beings" (cf. Kośa III 9 b–c). We have seen that Vasubandhu in *The Twenty Verses* denies the existence of special hell-beings, and "god-states" are for him again only special transformations of consciousness.
10. As regards "intermediate existences" between lives, he says that they aren't really born yet, but only in the process of being born (*Kośa* III, ad 10–end). In the deeper perspective of Vasubandhu's *Explanation of Dependent Origination* and the *Tibetan Book of the Dead*, every life-stream consists of an alternating series of "life" and "death," i.e., there is dying and being again in every moment. In that sense, every "dying moment" is an intermediate existence. But then it also no longer had the traditional characteristic of a "spontaneously generated being." Vasubandhu here assumes that the category of "spontaneously generated hu-

man beings" really doesn't exist, and that the Buddha spoke of them, and in particular of spontaneously generated intermediate existence, only to demonstrate the nondiscontinuity of the *citta*-series. Without the assumption of a spontaneously generated intermediate existence, people might assume that there is a discontinuity in *citta* between one life and the next, including the one life, next one, next one, next one, next one, etc., that is going on in each successive moment.

11. As far as what we directly experience is concerned, a "seed" and perception become manifest in what we term "seeing a visible." "The visible seen" is really a reflection of the "seed," i.e., an impression on consciousness; the visual consciousness is a special transformation in the consciousness-series affected by that "seed."
12. The completely signless perception of Buddhas is here seen to be equivalent with the Universal Self of the *Upaniṣads*. The recognition of their fundamental oneness is rare in Buddhist writing. The selflessness of events and personalities does not of course refer to this Universal Self, which Vasubandhu might more usually call "Emptiness" or "the Ground of all events." It refers rather to any fixed particular individualizing force.
13. "One" sees the selflessness of perception-only when "one" has seen that the "self" previously constructed by another perception is void. Actually, the use of the pronoun "one" is inaccurate, and does not occur in Sanskrit, where the verbs need have no subjects. It has been adopted here as the least pernicious pronoun, but should not be taken too literally. In other words, the phrase "one sees" really stands for "there is a new consciousness-moment of seeing in a psychophysical complex." "One," as used here and subsequently in these translations, is not numerically "one."
14. This is an important difference. It is not that anything is being denied. It is just that any particular unchanging characters by which we could delimit events and personalities don't exist.
15. If perception-only is not self-dissolving, "perception-only" would be an object of perception, and perception-only wouldn't be demonstrated. Obviously, "perception-only" is itself perception-only, and not a fixed object.
16. In Vaiśeṣika, atoms are absolutely imperceptible.
17. Any collision of one atom with another, any atom's being in a positional relation to one another, implies that the atom has parts, and thus is not really an atom.
18. Since the atom is imperceptible, if the locus for an aggregation of atoms is common for all of them, then this aggregation, as taking up only the place of one atom, would only be one atom itself, and hence imperceptible.
19. The arising of shade is explainable only if there is blockage of one material complex by another. Now this becomes atomically impossible, since the mutual resistance of materialities is possible according to an atomic theory only where atoms collide. And the collision of atoms implies parts of atoms.
20. A mental consciousness that becomes aware of a visible depends on previous

visual consciousness. But since all events are momentary, and the mental consciousness registers the visible after the visual consciousness has arisen, the visual consciousness is already past by that time, thus "cognizing a visible" is not strictly speaking "direct perception."

21. "A supermundane knowledge" is a perception free from mental marks and dualities, "pure perception." It is followed by "a clear, worldly, subsequently attained knowledge," where "objects" are again seen plurally, but are no longer conceptually clung to, since characteristics that would warrant dividing them off from one another are seen to be constructed.
22. If everything perceived is equally a transformation of consciousness, then what are the criteria by which one can distinguish the beneficial, unbeneficial, the existent, and the nonexistent?
23. Here it is seen that each perception influences the next, and the only basis for certainty of perception is the consistency of these influences.
24. If all perception is without a clear external object, then why is it that beneficial and unbeneficial acts committed in a dream don't have the same retributory effect as those committed while awake?
25. The objector is saying that if everything is perception-only, then only mental actions exist, and bodily and verbal actions have no reality. In that case, he says, when a shepherd kills a sheep, we can't really call him responsible for a death, because that bodily action wasn't real. Vasubandhu has already evolved an answer to this objection in *A Discussion for the Demonstration of Action,* where the ethical nature of an act is traced to the beneficiality of the "agent's" volition. The shepherd faces retribution for unbeneficial action as soon as the volition to kill arises. But then another volition, that "which sets into agitation," which puts the materiality-aggregate into action, must occur for there to be what is conventionally called "a bodily act." "A bodily act" is thus really, according to Vasubandhu, "an act of volition affecting the body," and the killing of the sheep is strictly speaking result of this volition.

    Instead of reiterating this argument, Vasubandhu here focuses upon another point: that death may come about through special mental forces (i.e., perceptions) of "another." However, this does not seem to be an answer to the objector's question. The objector is asking how one can call the shepherd responsible for a bodily act if there is no bodily act; Vasubandhu is replying that death can result from a mental act, which seems besides the point. However, Vasubandhu's does emphasize again the organic interrelationship of the consciousness- and materiality-aggregates. (It is by the way not inconsistent to continue to speak of a materiality-aggregate in the context of "perception-only," since the materiality-aggregate are those events which are perceived primarily by the tactile consciousness. Here, one consciousness-aggregate is stated to have a radical effect on another psychophysical complex.) Vasubandhu cites two canonical stories to back up his assertion. Sāraṇa, the son of King Udayana of Vatsa, became a pupil of Mahā-Kātyāyana, one of the Buddha's chief disciples.

Mahā-Kātyāyana and Sāraṇa together journeyed to Ujjain, in the kingdom of Avanti. There, King Pradyota of Avanti suspected Sāraṇa of having relations with his wives. Though the charge was unfounded, Pradyota had Sāraṇa beaten until he was streaming with blood. When released, Sāraṇa asked Mahā-Kātyāyana to absolve him from his monastic vows. He wanted to go to his father and levy an army against Pradyota. (The hostility between the kingdoms of Avanti and Vatsa under Pradyota and Udayana had some history behind it. Udayana had already spent some time as a prisoner of Pradyota, and had only been released because of the love between Udayana and Vāsavadattā, the daughter of Pradyota. This is the theme of Bhāsa's famous drama, *Pratijñāyaugandharāyaṇa.* However, Sāraṇa apparently felt that his father's forces were equal to those of Pradyota in a fair fight, since on that previous occasion, Pradyota had captured Udayana by means of a ruse.) Mahā-Kātyāyana refused to release Sāraṇa from his vows, and instead preached to him about the unbeneficiality of violent action. When Sāraṇa remained obdurate, Mahā-Kātyāyana waited until he was asleep, and then affected his dreams by his own mental powers. He made Sāraṇa see in a dream a huge battle, in which Pradyota was victorious. Sāraṇa himself was led away for execution. On the way to death, he met Mahā-Kātyāyana, and begged him for forgiveness. In order to show him that this was only a dream, Mahā-Kātyāyana made rays of light come out of his right arm. This story is told in detail in Kumāralāta's *Kalpanāmaṇḍatikā*, XII, story no. 65. (This text used to known as Aśvaghoṣa's *Sūtrālaṅkāra;* cf. Sylvain Levi, "Aśvaghoṣa, le *Sūtrālaṅkāra* et ses sources," *Journal Asiatique*, 1908, II, pp 149 ff.) In the second story alluded to by Vasubandhu, Vemacitra, king of the Asuras, decided to pay no respect to a group of virtuous seers who were living together in leaf-huts in a great forest. He came to them with his shoes on, his sword hanging at one side, and his canopy of state held over him. After he left, the seers decided that danger might come to them from him, unless he was led to see the limitation of his powers in comparison with theirs. Using their special powers, those seers, "as quickly as a strong man might stretch out his bent arm, or bend his arm stretched out, vanished from their leaf-huts and appeared before Sambara." They asked him for a safety-pledge, but Vemacitra arrogantly refused, telling them, "Terror is all that I do give." The seers then replied: "And dost thou only peril give / to us who ask for safety-pledge? / Lo! Then, accepting this from thee, / May neverending fear be thine! / According to the seed that's sown, / So is the fruit ye reap therefrom." Then they disappeared from his presence, and reappeared in their forest huts. That night, Vemacitra was tormented by terrible nightmares three times. These came directly from the forest seers' mental powers. According to Buddhaghoṣa, he was afflicted by terrible dreams thereafter, and finally became constantly terrified even when awake. This story is told in the *Saṃyutta-Nikāya* (I, XI, 225–227), and expanded in Buddhaghoṣa's *Sārathappakāsini* (comment on I, XI).

26. Violent mental act toward another's mental series carries more weight than a physical or verbal violence. For physical or verbal violence can be borne with

forbearance, but a deliberate alteration of the consciousness-series of another may make even equanimity impossible.

27. The nondual awareness of enlightened ones, and the empathetic insight into another's *citta*, are not knowledges in the sense of apprehending "an object," but rather represent the free flow of consciousness. The apprehension of an "object" always implies the presence of an appearance that is abandoned in these two kinds of awareness. Thus, these "knowledges" are really nonknowledges, because a specific object is not known within them.

FURTHER READING

Anacker, Stefan. *Seven Works of Vasubandhu: The Buddhist Psychological Doctor.* Delhi: Motilal Banarsidass, 1984.

Chatterjee, Ashok Kumar. *The Yogācāra Idealism.* Delhi: Motilal Banarsidass, 1962.

D'Amato, Mario. "Three Natures, Three Stages: An Interpretation of the Yogācāra *Trisvabhāva*-Theory." *Journal of Indian Philosophy* 33 (2005): 185–207.

Griffiths, Paul J. *On Being Mindless: Buddhist Meditation and the Mind-Body Problem.* La Salle, Ill.: Open Court, 1986.

King, Richard. *Indian Philosophy.* Edinburgh: Edinburgh University Press, 1999.

Robinson, Richard H., Willard L. Johnson, and Thinisasaro Bikku. *Buddhist Religions: A Historical Introduction.* Belmont, Calif.: Thomson, 2005.

Siderits, Mark. *Buddhism as Philosophy.* Aldershot: Ashgate, 2007.

Waldron, William S. *The Buddhist Unconscious: The Ālaya-Vijñana in the Context of Indian Buddhist Thought.* London: RoutledgeCurzon, 2003.

Williams, Paul. *Mahāyāna Buddhism: The Doctrinal Foundations.* New York: Routledge, 1989.

Williams, Paul, and Anthony Tribe. *Buddhist Thought: A Complete Introduction to the Indian Tradition.* New York: Routledge, 2000.

4

MADHYAMAKA BUDDHISM

HISTORY

The Madhyamaka (middling) school, a tradition of Mahāyāna Buddhism, propounds that *dharmas* (here taken to mean "all things") are *śūnya* (empty) of *svabhāva* (independent existence/essence). The Madhyamaka school thus explains that seeing entities as anything but mental constructs leads to *duhkha* (suffering). Since it was founded by Nāgārjuna and his disciple Aryadeva in the second century C.E., the methods of the Madhyamaka school have made a tremendous impact on the development of Buddhism in Tibet (as Svātantrika and Prāsaṅgika Buddhism) and in Japan (as Zen Buddhism).

Nāgārjuna composed a number of texts, including the *Mūlamadhyamaka-kārikā* (*Fundamental Verses on the Middle*), which was commented upon by Candrakīrti (600–650 C.E.) in his *Prassanapāda*. The *Prassanapāda* became an integral component in the curriculum of Tibetan Buddhist universities. Nāgārjuna's enigmatic style has made his work open to various interpretations. Ironically, in his *Vigrahavyāvartanī* (*Averting the Arguments*) he claims not to have a *pratijñā* (thesis).

EPISTEMOLOGY

Nāgārjuna claims not to have a *pratijñā*, and this includes, of course, statements concerning the *pramāṇas* (sources of valid knowledge). In fact, much of his *Vigrahavyāvartanī* is a critique of *pramāṇa* theory itself. His critique has led some to suggest that Nāgārjuna is positing a radical form of skepticism even more extreme than that of the Cārvāka school.

Nāgārjuna states in his *Mūlamadhyamaka-kārikā* that there are two levels of truth: *lokasaṃvṛtisatya* (conventional truth) and *paramārthasatya* (ultimate truth). These levels of truth, or even reality, are not opposed to one another. Rather, they are mutually dependent on one another. Although things are certainly *śūnya* in *paramārthasatya*, they nonetheless functioned in *lokasaṃvṛtisatya*.

ONTOLOGY

Nāgārjuna holds that *dharmas* are *śūnya* (empty) of *svabhāva*. His argument is directed toward the Abhidharma teachings in which attempts were made to systematize Buddhism. These systematizations "provided a categorisation of the various types of mental and physical processes (*dharmas*)."[1] According to the Abhidharma, these *dharmas*, which were "ultimately real impartite entities," had *svabhāva* (independent existence).[2] It was against this ontology that Nāgārjuna directed part of his attack. Since all entities lack independence then it follows that they are also causally dependent. Furthermore, *śūnya* is thus *pratītyasamutpāda* (dependently originated). From this, Nāgārjuna also states that ultimately neither *sat* (existence) nor *asat* (nonexistence) makes sense, as they reek of *svabhāva* (here used as "essences").

SOTERIOLOGY

Ridding oneself of bad cognitive habits will prevent further rebirth and suffering. One needs to realize that all things are *śūnya*. This includes *nirvāṇa*, which must be equated with *saṃsāra* (rebirth), which also is *śunya*. Of course, *śūnya* too must be empty of *śūnyatā* (emptiness). One attains a proper understanding by closely examining all other positions and finding their internal flaws. This *prasaṅga* method is a reductio ad absurdum style of argumentation that thus uses the presuppositions of the opponent to show that their thesis is flawed. In this way, the Mādhyamika is not attached to a position but must merely refute others'.

THE TEXT

Included here is Nāgārjuna's *Vigrahavyāvartanī* (*Averting the Arguments*). I have not included the *vṛtti* (commentary) that Nāgārjuna himself wrote. The *Vigrahavyāvartanī* consists of arguments against the Abhidharma position that *dharmas* have *svabhāvas*. It begins with arguments offered by an opponent against Nāgārjuna. The opponent is reacting to what appears to be Nāgārjuna's claim that "*dharmas* are *śūnya* (empty) of *svabhāva*." Twenty arguments are put forth, followed by Nāgārjuna's reply.

NĀGĀRJUNA'S *VIGRAHAVYĀVARTANĪ*

Part I. The Arguments of the Opponents

1. If self-existence (*svabhāva*) does not exist anywhere in any existing thing,

Your statement, [itself] being without self-existence, is not able to discard self-existence.

2. But if that statement has [its own] self-existence, then your initial proposition is refuted;

There is a [logical] inconsistency in this, and you ought to explain the grounds of the difference [between the principle of validity in your statement and others].

3. Should your opinion be that [your statement] is like "Do not make a sound," this is not possible;

For in this case by a [present] sound there will be a [future] prevention of that [sound].

4. If [your statement] were that: "This is a denial of a denial," that is not true;

Thus your thesis, as to a defining mark (*lakṣaṇata*)—not mine—is in error.

5. If you deny existing things while being seen by direct perception,

Then that direct perception, by which things are seen, also does not exist.

6. By [denying] direct perception inference is denied, as also Scripture and analogy,

[As well as] the points to be proved by inference and Scripture and those points to be proved by a similar instance (*dṛṣṭānta*).

7. The people who know the modes of the *dharmas* know [there is] a good self-existence of good *dharmas*.

As to the others, the application is the same.

8. There is a self-existence of liberation in those [*dharmas*] mentioned as liberative modes of *dharmas*.

Likewise, there is that which is nonliberative, etc.

9. And, if there would be no self-existence of *dharmas*, then that would be "non–self-existence";

In that case the name (*nāma*) would not exist, for certainly there is nothing without substance [to which it refers].

10. If [one asserts:] That which is self-existent exists, but the self-existence of the *dharmas* does not exist,

One should give the explanation concerning that of which there is self-existence without *dharmas.*

11. As there must be a denial of something that exists, as [in the statement:] "There is not a pot in the house,"

That denial of yours which is seen must be a denial of self-existence that exists.

12. Or if that self-existence does not exist, what do you deny by that statement?

Certainly, the denial of what does not exist is proved without a word!

13. Just as children erroneously apprehend that there is "non-water" in a mirage,

So you would erroneously apprehend a nonexisting thing as deniable.

14. If this is so, then there is the apprehension, "what is apprehended" and the one who apprehends,

Also the denial, "what is denied" and the one who denies—six all together.

15. However, if the apprehension, "what is apprehended" and the one who apprehends do not exist,

Then is it not true that denial, "what is denied," and the one who denies do not exist?

16. If denial, "what is denied," and the one who denies do not exist,

Then all existing things as well as the self-existence of them are proved [since you have eliminated their denial].

17. Because of non-self-existence there is no proof of any grounds [of knowledge]; whence are your grounds?

There is no proof of a "point" possible for you if it has no grounds.

18. If the proof of your denial of a self-existent thing is not a result of grounds of knowledge,

Then my affirmation of the existence of a self-existent thing is proved without grounds.

19. Or if you maintain: "The real existence of grounds is such that it is a non-self-existent thing (*asvabhāva*)"—this is not justified;

Because no thing whatever in the world exists lacking its own nature (*niḥsvabhāva*).

20. When it is said: The denial precedes "what is denied," this is not justified.

[Denial] is not justified either later or simultaneously. Therefore self-existence is real.

Part II. Nāgārjuna's Reply to the Arguments of the Opponents

21. If my thesis does not bear on the totality of causes and conditions, or on them separately,

Is not emptiness proved because of the fact that there is no self-existence in existing things?

22. The "being dependent nature" of existing things: that is called "emptiness."

That which has a nature of "being dependent"—of that there is a non–self-existent nature.

23. Just as a magically formed phantom could deny a phantom created by its own magic,

Just so would be that negation.

24. This statement [regarding emptiness] is not "that which is self-existent"; therefore, there is no refutation of my assertion.

There is no inconsistency and [thus] the grounds for the difference need not be explained.

25. [Regarding] "Do not make a sound"—this example introduced by you is not pertinent,

Since there is a negation of sound by sound. That is not like [my denial of self-existence].

26. For, if there is prevention of that which lacks self-existence by that which lacks self-existence,

Then that which lacks self-existence would cease, and self-existence would be proved.

27. Or, as a phantom could destroy the erroneous apprehension concerning a phantom woman that:

"There is a woman," just so this is true in our case.

28. Or else the grounds [of proof] are that which is to be proved; certainly sound does not exist as real.

For we do not speak without accepting, for practical purposes, the workaday world.

29. If I would make any proposition whatever, then by that I would have a logical error;

But I do not make a proposition; therefore I am not in error.

30. If there is something, while being seen by means of the objects of direct perceptions, etc.,

[It is] affirmed or denied. That [denial] of mine is a nonapprehension of non-things.

31. And if, for you, there is a source [of knowledge] of each and every object of proof,

Then tell how, in turn, for you there is proof of those sources.

32. If by other sources [of knowledge] there would be the proof of a source—that would be an "infinite regress";

In that case neither a beginning, middle, nor an end is proved.

33. Or if there is proof of those [objects] without sources, your argument is refuted.

There is a [logical] inconsistency in this, and you ought to explain the cause of the difference [between the principles of validity in your statement and others].

34. That reconciliation of difficulty is not [realized in the claim:] "Fire illumines itself."

Certainly it is not like the nonmanifest appearance of a pot in the dark.

35. And if, according to your statement, fire illumines its own self,

Then is this not like a fire which would illumine its own self and something else?

36. If, according to your statement, fire would illumine both its "own self" and an "other self,"

Then also darkness, like fire, would darken itself and an "other self."

37. Darkness does not exist in the glow of a fire; and where the glow remains in an "other individual self,"

How could it produce light? Indeed light is the death of darkness.

38. [If you say:] "Fire illumines when it is being produced," this statement is not true;

For, when being produced, fire certainly does not touch (*prāpnoti*) darkness.

39. Now if that glow can destroy the darkness again and again without touching it,

Then that [glow] which is located here would destroy the darkness in "every corner" of the world.

40. If your sources [of knowledge] are proved by their own strength (*svatas*), then, for you, the sources are proved without respect to "that which is to be proved";

Then you have a proof of a source, [but] no sources are proved without relation to something else.

41. If, according to you, the sources [of knowledge] are proved without being related to the objects of "that which is to be proved,"

Then these sources will not prove anything.

42. Or if [you say]: What error is there in thinking, "The relationship of these [sources of knowledge to their objects] is [already] proved"?

[The answer is:] This would be the proving of what is proved. Indeed "that which is not proved" is not related to something else.

43. Or if the sources [of knowledge] in every case are proved in relation to "what is to be proved,"

Then "what is to be proved" is proved without relation to the sources.

44. And if "what is to be proved" is proved without relation to the sources [of knowledge],

What [purpose] is the proof of the sources for you—since that for the purpose of which those [sources] exist is already proved!

45. Or if, for you, the sources [of knowledge] are proved in relation to "what is to be proved,"

Then, for you, there exists an interchange between the sources and "what is to be proved."

46. Or if, for you, there are the sources [of knowledge] being proved when there is proof of "what is to be proved," and if "what is to be proved" exists when

The source is proved, then, for you, the proof of them both does not exist.

47. If those things which are to be proved are proved by those sources [of knowledge], and those things which are proved

By "what is to be proved," how will they prove [anything]?

48. And if those sources [of knowledge] are proved by what is to be proved, and those things which are proved

By the sources, how will they prove [anything]?

49. If a son is produced by a father, and if that [father] is produced by that very son [when he is born],

Then tell me, in this case, who produces whom?

50. You tell me! Which of the two becomes the father, and which the son—

Since they both carry characteristics of "father" and "son"? In that case there is doubt.

51. The proof of the sources [of knowledge] is not [established] by itself, not by each other, or not by other sources;

It does not exist by that which is to be proved and not from nothing at all.

52. If those who know the modes of the *dharmas* say that there is good self-existence of good *dharmas,*

That [self-existence] must be stated in contradistinction to something else.

53. If a good self-existence were produced in relation to [something else],

Then that self-existence of the good *dharmas* is an "other existence." How, then, does [self-existence] exist?

54. Or if there is that self-existence of good *dharmas,* while not being related to something else,

There would be no state of a spiritual way of life.

55. There would be neither vice nor virtue, and worldly practical activities would not be possible;

Self-existent things would be eternal because that without a cause would be eternal.

56. Regarding [your view of] bad, "liberative," and undefined [*dharmas*], there is an error;

Therefore, all composite products (*saṁskṛta*) exist as noncomposite elements (*asaṁskṛta*).

57. He who would impute a really existing name to a really existing thing

Could be refuted by you; but we do not assert a name.

58. And that [assertion]: "The name is unreal"—would that relate to a real or a nonreal thing?

If it were a real thing, or if it were a nonreal thing—in both cases your entire proposition is refuted.

59. The emptiness of all existing things has been demonstrated previously;

Therefore, this attack is against that which is not my thesis.

60. Or if [it is said]: "Self-existence exists, but that [self-existence] of *dharmas* does not exist"—

That is questionable; but that which was said [by me] is not questionable.

61. If the denial concerns something real, then is not emptiness proved?

Then you would deny the non–self-existence of things.

62. Or if you deny emptiness, and there is no emptiness,

Then is not your assertion: "The denial concerns something real" refuted?

63. Since anything being denied does not exist, I do not deny anything;

Therefore, [the statement]: "You deny"—which was made by you—is a false accusation.

64. Regarding what was said concerning what does not exist: "The statement of denial is proved without a word,"

In that case the statement expresses: "[That object] does not exist"; [the words] do not destroy that [object].

65. Regarding the great censure formerly made by you through the instance of the mirage—

Now hear the ascertainment whereby that instance is logically possible.

66. If that apprehension [of the mirage] is "something which is self-existent," it would not have originated presupposing [other things];

But that apprehension which exists presupposing [other things]—is that not emptiness?

67. If that apprehension is "something which is self-existent," with what could the apprehension be negated?

This understanding [applies] in the remaining [five factors: "what is apprehended," the one who apprehends, the denial, "what is denied," and the one who denies]; therefore that is an invalid censure.

68. By this [argument] the absence of a cause [for denying self-existence] is refuted—on the basis of the similarity [with the foregoing]:

Namely, that which was already said regarding the exclusion of the instance of the mirage.

69. That which is the cause for the three times is refuted from what is similar to that [given] before;

Negation of cause for the three times affirms emptiness.

70. All things prevail for him for whom emptiness prevails;

Nothing whatever prevails for him for whom emptiness prevails.

NOTES

1. Richard King, *Indian Philosophy* (Edinburgh: Edinburgh University Press, 1999), 84.
2. Thanks to Mark Siderits for this phrasing; see Mark Siderits, *Buddhism as Philosophy* (Aldershot: Ashgate, 2007), 111.

FURTHER READING

Bhattacharya, Kamaleswar. *The Dialectical Method of Nāgārjuna*. Delhi: Motilal Banarsidass, 2005.

Burton, David F. *Emptiness Appraised: A Critical Study of Nāgārjuna's Philosophy*. London: Curzon, 1999.

King, Richard. *Indian Philosophy*. Edinburgh: Edinburgh University Press, 1999.

Robinson, Richard H., Willard L. Johnson, and Thinisasaro Bikku. *Buddhist Religions: A Historical Introduction*. Belmont, Calif.: Thomson, 2005.

Siderits, Mark. *Buddhism as Philosophy*. Aldershot: Ashgate, 2007.

Westerhoff, Jan. *Nāgārjuna's Madhyamaka: A Philosophical Introduction*. Oxford: Oxford University Press, 2009.

Williams, Paul. *Mahāyāna Buddhism: The Doctrinal Foundations*. New York: Routledge, 1989.

5

JAINISM

HISTORY

Na hu pāṇvahaṃ anujāṇe muccejja kayāi savvadukkhāṇaṃ | evāriehiṃ akkhāyaṃ jehiṃ imo sāhudhammo pannatto.

One should not permit (or consent to) the killing of living beings; then he will perhaps be delivered from all misery.

—*Uttarādyayana Sūtra* 8.8[1]

Jainism was and is centered chiefly upon limiting, and eventually eliminating, the amount of *hiṃsā* (violence) that one commits. *Ahiṃsā* (nonviolence) is the preeminent obligation for Jains and is achievable through severe austerities. Jainism rejects the entire tradition of the Vedas and, like Buddhism, offers an alternative to the sacrificial and hierarchical world envisioned in the Vedas.

Jains believe that there were twenty-four *tīrthaṅkaras* (bridge-builders) in each half-cycle of time, each of whom attained *nirvāṇa* (liberation from the cycle of birth and rebirth) through rigorous ascetic practices focused upon *ahiṃsā*. Vardhamāna Mahāvīra, purportedly alive in the sixth and fifth centuries B.C.E., was the twenty-fourth of these *tīrthaṅkaras*, also known as *jinas* (victors), who succeeded in conquering their passions, annihilating their accumulated *karma*, and breaking out of *saṃsāra* (the cycle of birth and rebirth). Mahāvīra thus cannot be said to be the founder of the tradition, because he is the latest in a lineage of teachers.

The Mahāvīra did not offer a systematic philosophical system. According to the tradition, though, his discourses were recorded and transmitted somewhat loosely as a body of texts known as the *āgamas*. The *Kalpa Sūtra* is one of the earliest *āgamas* and is a biography of the Mahāvīra and his predecessors and also contains some references to monastic codes and regulations. Jainism eventually split up into the Śvetāmbara (white-clad) and Digambara (sky-clad) traditions, and each has its own body of canonical texts. The two schools disagree on the importance of male renunciants wearing clothing on the path to *nirvāṇa*. The Digambara school holds that male renunciants must abandon all possessions, including clothing, to obtain *nirvāṇa,* while the Śvetāmbara holds that they may possess (and wear) clothing.

Umāsvāti (fourth or fifth century C.E.) composed the *Tattvārtha Sūtra* (*Mnemonic Rules on the Meaning of the Reals*), which is the first attempt to systematize the Jain teachings. This text is held to be authoritative by both schools. Kundakunda (second or third century C.E.)[2] is prominent in the Digambara tradition and composed, among others, the *Samayasāra* (*Essence of the Doctrine*). Haribhadra Sūri (770 C.E.)[3] is perhaps the most prolific Jain author. More than 1,400 texts are attributed to this Śvetāmbara monk, including the *Ṣaḍdarśana-samuccaya* (*Compendium of the Six Systems*). Hemacandra (1089–1172 C.E.) is also well known for sustaining the Śvetāmbara tradition and wrote the *Yogaśastra* (*Treatise on Behavior*).

EPISTEMOLOGY

Jains believe that every *jīva* (sentient being) is omniscient and pure.[4] *Jñāna* (knowledge) is thus an essential characteristic of the *jīva*. Accumulated *karma* obfuscates the clarity of the *jīva*. Jainism accepts two different kinds of knowledge: *aparokṣa jñāna* (immediate knowledge), and *parokṣa jñāna* (mediate knowledge). *Aparokṣa jñāna*, which is through the *jīva*, is threefold: *avadhi* (clairvoyance), *manaḥparyāya* (telepathy), and *kevala* (unlimited and absolute knowledge). If one rids oneself of accumulated *karma* one can return to the *kevala* state. *Parokṣa* knowledge is twofold: *mati* (inferential) and *śruta* (via words). *Mati* is further subdivided into *pratyakṣa* (perception), *smṛti* (remembering), *sanjñā* (or *pratyabhijñā*) (recognition), and *tarka* (or *anumāna*) (reasoning). Not surprisingly, the knowledge of the Mahāvīra is *kevala*.

In the light of the belief that knowledge is obscured by the influx of *karma*, Jains believe that the judgment of those who are not *kevala* is flawed. It is for this reason that they propose *anekantavāda* (the doctrine of many-sidedness) and the accompanying *syādvāda* (doctrine of "may be"). The Jains believe that only partial truths are available to those who do not possess *kevala-jñāna*. They suggest that there are seven *nayas* (modes) from which to consider an object. *Naya* is relational knowledge, knowledge from one perspective, and is thus limited. Several judgments can thus be relatively true when they are taken from different points of view. *Anekantavāda*, the position that each thing has an infinite number of characteristics, is a corollary to this position. *Syādvāda* is an application of this epistemology that suggests that all judgments are conditional. It gives rise to *saptabhaṅgi-naya* (the sevenfold application of "may be"), namely that

1. Somehow, S is P.
2. Somehow, S is not-P.
3. Somehow, S is both P and not-P.
4. Somehow, S is indescribable.
5. somehow, S is P and is indescribable.
6. Somehow, S is not-P and indescribable.
7. Somehow, S is P and not-P and indescribable.

This Jain epistemic position is reflected in the well-known parable of the blind men and the elephants that has its origins in both Jainism and Buddhism: Several blind men interact with an elephant for the first time. One holds a leg and describes the elephant as being like a tree. Another holds its side and states that it is like a great wall. Sill another holds on to the elephant's tail and claims that elephants are like snakes and so on. The elephant is thus the combination of these different, infinite, and limited perspectives. Jain epistemology thus emphasizes the multiplicity and relativity of views.

ONTOLOGY

The Jains propose a universe that is both realistic and pluralistic. It is separable into five *astikāyas* (collection of existents): *jīvas* (sentients), *pudgala* (matter), *ākāśa* (space), *dharma* (motion), and *adharma* (rest) (the Digambara tradition adds *kāla* [time] to this list). *Pudgala, ākāśa, dharma*, and *adharma* are categorized as *ajīva* (nonsentient). Jains further believe that *karma* is actual matter that, in its undifferentiated form, exists throughout *ākāśa*. Undifferentiated *karma* is attracted to the body (*āsrava*) through the volitional activities of *jīvas*. Once bound to the body (*bandha*), the *karma* particles mature and manifest in relation to the activity that brought it about. The accumulated *karma* accounts for the seemingly endless birth and rebirth in *saṃsāra.*

SOTERIOLOGY

The primary directive for a Jain is to observe the practice of *ahiṃsā.* In so doing one can stop and eventually reduce the amount of *karma* that one attracts. All activities are oriented around this goal of *saṃvara* (stoppage of *karmic* influx) and *nirjarā* (disassociation of *karmas*). Right action entails following the five *mahāvratas* (great vows): *ahiṃsāvrata* (refraining from causing injury); *satya* (refraining from false speech); *asteya* (refraining from theft); *brahmavarta* (refraining from illicit sexual activities); and *aparigrahavrata* (limiting one's possessions). Monastic Jains follow these vows to a higher degree than lay Jains.

Through *tapas* (asceticism), a Jain practitioner can reduce and eliminate the accumulation of *karma*, can return to a state of omniscience (*kevala-jñāna*), and will no longer be born in *saṃsāra* (the cycle of birth and rebirth).

THE TEXTS

The first selection is from the *Yogaśāstra* of Hemacandra, which is a systematic account of Śvetāmbara Jain doctrine. Hemacandra was a court scholar and historian in Gujarat who was aligned with several kings of the Caulukya dynasty. The *Yogaśāstra* was written for Kumārapāla, who was one of these kings. The first three chapters, included here, address the *ratnatraya* (three jewels) of Jainism, namely *darśana* (correct belief), *jñāna* (correct knowledge), and *cāritra* (correct conduct). In chapter 2 one finds a polemic against the Hindu text *Manusmṛti* and Vedic sacrifice. The text also offers a very clear characterization of how the ideas and practices of Jainism ought to be implemented.

The second selection is from Samantabhadra's *Āptamīmāṃsā* (*Critique of an Authority*). Very little is known about Samantabhadra (600 C.E.). Samantabhadra demonstrates that *ekantavāda* (the position accepting only one aspect) is flawed. He does so by appealing to *anekantavāda*. These sections contain a critique of the belief that the universe is pervaded by a nondualism, a critique of the belief that things are permanent, and a critique of the notion that things are governed by difference.

FROM HEMACANDRA'S *YOGAŚĀSTRA*

Chapter 1. *Homage to Mahāvīra*

1. I bow down to Mahāvīra, the protector [of all living beings], the [omniscient] lord of ascetics, the enlightened who has eliminated the multitude of [inner] enemies which [otherwise] are difficult to eradicate, such as attachment.

2. I bow down to Lord Śrī [Mahā]vīra, [who remained] mentally indifferent toward [the malevolent] snake [Caṇḍa]Kauśika and [the devoted] king of gods, [Indra], when they touched his feet.

3. Blessed are the eyes of the [spiritual] victor, Śrī [Mahā]vīra, slightly wet with tears [and] with pupils dejected out of compassion even for people who have done offense [to him, like the hostile god, Saṅgamaka].

4. By the excessive pleadings from his majesty, King Kumārapāla of the Caulukya dynasty, this Yoga-Upaniṣad, or Handbook on Yoga (*Yogaśāstra*), is composed [by me, Hemacandra,] having acquired [knowledge] from the ocean of scriptures, from the tradition of a good teacher, and from personal experience.

YOGA; OR, THE THREE JEWELS

5. *Yoga* is [like] a sharp-edged axe for the tangle of creepers of all calamities. It is a supernatural means for [attaining] the happiness of liberation without [the use of] medical herbs, spells or Tantric [teachings].

6. Just as a multitude of dark and dense clouds [vanish] due to a forceful wind, [the results of] even the most evil deeds obviously dissolve by [the power of] *yoga*.

7. Just as a quick [burning] fire [reduces] a pile of firewood [into ashes] within a moment, [the practice of] *yoga* destroys [instantaneously the results of] evil deeds although accumulated over long time.

8. Moreover, the splendor of this "Yogic dance" [transforms] the [seven] magic powers—phlegm, excrement, secretion, "touch" and "every [part of the body]"—into remedies and [develops also] miraculous powers [such as] the acquisition of an undivided sense-organ.

9. The fortune of the blossoming flowers of the [fabulous] wishing tree of *yoga* consists of [supernatural attainments, such as] walking in the air, the ability of curse and favor, extraordinary perception, and mind-reading.

10. Praise the greatness of *yoga*! Bharata, [for example], the descendant of universal sovereignty [and] the ruler [of the six continents] of Bharata[-kṣetra], obtained omniscience [due to the practice of it].

11. Rejoicing in supreme bliss [at the sight of her enlightened son Ṛṣabha], Marudevā [instantaneously] attained the highest state (i.e., liberation) by means of *yoga*, although [she in her] previous [lives] had not [even] been able to obtain the religious teachings (*dharma*).

12. *Yoga* is an extended hand for such [a person] as Dṛḍhaprahāri, who is the guest of hell, having [committed] the sins of killing a brahmin, a woman, an embryo, or a cow.

13. At that time [when Dṛḍhaprahāri and others commited their sins], who would not desire [that kind of] *yoga* which [even] protects a malevolent person [like] Cilātīputra, who is intent on doing [all kinds of] evil deeds, [such as killing a woman]?

14. Let the man whose ears have not been pierced by the needle of the syllables *yoga*, and whose life is [thus] worthless, be deprived of birth as a man!

15. Liberation is the foremost among the four goals [of human objectives (*puruṣārtha*)], the means of which is *yoga*. This [*yoga*, which also is designated] the three jewels (*ratnatraya*), consists of [correct] knowledge, faith, and conduct.

16. Here [in this Jaina system], the wise define correct knowledge as the understanding, either in detail or in brief, of the [seven] principles as they really are.

17. [To have] a liking for [these] principles, explained by the Jina, is the definition of true faith. That [faith] arises either spontaneously, or [indirectly], through the knowledge of [one's] teacher.

18. [Proper] conduct is defined as the abandonment of all blameworthy activities. That [proper conduct] has been described as fivefold because of the division into the vow of non-harm and so forth.

THE PROPER CONDUCT OF A MENDICANT

19. Non-harm, truthfulness, honesty, continence, and propertylessness, coupled with [their] five respective exercises, lead to liberation.

20. The fact that one does not use violence against the life of mobile and immobile beings through activities [proceeding from] heedlessness, that is, according to [our tradition] (*mata*), the vow of non-harm.

21. The vow of truthfulness amounts to [upholding] a pleasant, accurate, and truthful speech. That [truth] which is unpleasant and unsuitable is not truthful even though it is true.

22. The vow of honesty [simply] means not taking that which is not granted [by its owner]. Material wealth is the "external life" of men. Consequently, [if] someone takes that [wealth] away, those [external lives of men] are taken away.

23. The eighteen kinds of continence consist, according to [our tradition], in abandoning [all] desires pertaining to celestial [beings] and bearers of gross bodies, [humans as well as animals], in mind, speech, and body, whether one enjoys them oneself, approves of their enjoyment, or makes others enjoy them.

24. Propertylessness consists in abandoning obsessional desires with respect to any object, because obsessional desires contribute to the mind's bewilderment, even when nothing is present.

25. When [these five] great vows are gradually practiced by virtue of their five respective exercises, who will they not lead to the imperishable state?

26. The wise should constantly practice [the vow of] non-harm by carefully (1) protecting the mind, (2) accepting alms, (3) picking up [things and putting them down], (4) walking, and [finally] (5) [only] consuming food and drink [properly] examined.

27. One should practice the [great] vow of truthfulness by continuously avoiding [speaking non-truth] for the sake of (1) entertainment, (2) greed, (3) fear, [and] (4) anger, [and] by (5) [cultivating] thoughtful speech.

28–29. The exercises of [the great vow of] honesty include (1) explicitly asking for [permission to] use a dwelling, (2) repeatedly asking [permission to use] a dwelling, (3) only to make use of a dwelling of a certain size, (4) asking those following the same [religious] rules [and who already are occupying a certain place] for [permission to use] a dwelling, and (5) to consume food and drink [only after] having obtained the consent [of one's teacher].

30–31. One should practice [the great vow of] continence by avoiding (1) houses, seats, and dwellings occupied by women, eunuchs, and animals, (2) tales about passionate women, (3) memories of earlier sexual enjoyments [as a householder], (4) casting a covetous eye in the direction of the "pleasant parts" of a woman and adorning the body, and [finally] (5) by avoiding extravagant and immoderate eating [which will awaken the passions].

32–33. The five exercises of [the great] vow of "nothingness" [or propertylessness] are defined as (1–5) the abandonment of vehement obsessional desire in relation to the objects of the five senses, which are [so] enchanting, [i.e.] when there is a pleasant touch, taste, smell, form, and sound. [One should also] completely avoid hatred when these [five sense objects] are not pleasing to the mind.

34. Alternatively, the foremost among mendicants define proper conduct as that conduct which is purified by the five kinds of carefulness and the three kinds of control.

35. The five kinds of care concern [the mendicant's] (1) walk, (2) speech, (3) begging, (4) receiving and rejecting, and (5) his excretory functions. The three kinds of control depend on the restraint of the three [kinds of] activity[: mental, verbal, and physical].

36. (1) [Care with respect to] walking consists, according to virtuous people, in that [the mendicant] when he travels on remote paths, kissed by the rays of the sun, should watch his step for the sake of the protection of living beings.

37. (2) When one's speech is restrained and humane, because it is free from imperfection, [then] that is said to be pleasant to mendicants whose speech is controlled.

38. (3) When a mendicant receives food that is completely unspoiled by the 42 defects of begging[-food], [then] that is defined as care in accepting alms.

39. (4) When he chooses or rejects seats, etc., having carefully inspected [them] and brushed away [living beings], [then] that is called care in receiving a seat.

40. (5) When a holy man carefully empties out phlegm, urine, feces, and the like, on a spot free from living beings, that is [defined as] care in excretory functions.

41. (1) A mind which is free from the net of mental constructions [connected with sorrowful and cruel meditation], well established in equanimity, and resting in itself, that has been declared as control of mind by the wise.

42. (2) When one remains silent, avoiding [every means of communication], such as gestures, moderating one's choice of words, that is called control of speech here [in the Jaina doctrine].

43. (3) When the body of an ascetic remains immobile as he dwells in [the posture called] "abandoning the body," even in the case of a supernatural attack, [this] is said to be control of the body.

44. Another form of control of the body amounts to controlling one's movements while lying, sitting, rejecting, receiving, walking about, and standing still.

45. These [five forms of carefulness and three kinds of control] are traditionally called "the eight mothers," because they bring up, protect, and purify the holy men's "body" of [proper] conduct.

46. The [proper] conduct defined [above] applies completely to enlightened mendicants. For the householders who profess themselves adherents of the [ethical] norms of the mendicants, it is only partially [valid].

THE PROPER CONDUCT OF A LAYMAN

47–56. (1) One who is legitimately endowed with wealth, (2) who puts in action the conduct of a gentleman, (3) who is married to [a person] from a family of the same moral conduct [as his own], but from another lineage, (4) who is afraid of evil, (5) who practices the well-established conduct of the country, (6) who never criticizes [others], especially not kings, (7) whose residence is neither too exposed nor too hidden, located in a good neighborhood, and free from too many front doors, (8) who is in the company with [those] of virtuous conduct, (9) who honors his parents, (10) who avoids overpopulated places, (11) who does not get involved in anything reproachable, (12) who makes sure that his expenditure accords with his income, (13) who assumes a dress according to [his] wealth, (14) who is endowed with the eight qualities of intelligence, (15) who listens to the religious preaching daily, (16) who does not eat when [he is] not hungry, (17) and [who eats] with mindfulness at [an appropriate] time, (18) who cultivates the three groups [of human objectives (*puruṣārtha*): *dharma, artha,* and *kāma*] without their coming into mutual conflict, (19) who treats a guest, a holy man, and a poor man respectfully, [according to their status], (20) who, on the one hand, is always impartial, and, on the other, (21) is partial with respect to [the good] qualities [within man], (22) who avoids improper behavior with regard to time and place, (23) who knows his strength and weaknesses, (24) who respects virtuous and learned persons, (25) who supports those who deserve to be supported, (26) who is far-sighted, (27) discriminative, (28) grateful, (29) loved by people, (30) modest, (31) compassionate, (32) gentle, (33) [and] intent on doing good to others, (34) who is devoted to removing the group of the six internal enemies of the body, [such as lust and anger], (35) and who has reduced to subjection his (lit. "the collection of") senses, [such] a householder [endowed with these 35 qualities] fulfils [his] duty (*dharma*).

Chapter 2. Orthodoxy and Heterodoxy

1. As far as a householder is concerned, the roots of orthodoxy are the five minor vows, the three virtuous [vows], [and] the four educational vows. [These twelve vows progressively bring him closer to the life of a mendicant.]

2. Orthodoxy consists in recognizing the deity as the [true] deity, the teacher as the [proper] teacher, and the teaching as the correct teaching.

3. Heterodoxy, as opposed to [orthodoxy], consists in mistaking an idol for a [true] deity, a false teacher for a [proper] teacher, and a heresy for a [correct] teaching.

4. God is [that] *arhat* and supreme Lord who is omniscient, who has conquered defects such as attachment [and aversion], who is worshiped in the three worlds [by gods, demons, humans, and so forth], and who explains things as they really are.

5. If one is in possession of one's senses, one should meditate upon Him, worship Him, regard Him as [one's only] refuge, [and] one should only follow his teaching.

6. Such deities [as Śiva, Viṣṇu, and Brahmā] who are faulted by blemishes such as attachment to women, weapons, and rosaries, [respectively], and who are given to controlling and favoring [people], cannot lead [anyone] to liberation.

7. How could those [deites], who [themselves] have lost their composure by excitements such as dancing, gaiety, and music, be able to lead their followers to the peaceful state [of liberation]?

8. Wise men who observe the [five] great vows, who live only on alms, who are established in equanimity, [and] who preach the [Jaina] religion, are considered [true] teachers.

9. Those who desire everything [material from their devotees], who enjoy everything, [including alcohol, honey, and meat], who lay hold of [every worldly possession], who do not live in celibacy, [and] who preach a false [doctrine]—these are, however, not [reckoned as true] teachers.

10. Those who are [deeply] involved in [worldly matters of] business and administration, how can they help others to cross [the ocean of worldly existence]? One who is himself a [poor] beggar is not able to make someone else a [rich] master.

11. *Dharma* has its name because ["religion"] rescues human beings from bad destinies [such as that of an infernal being or animal]. The omniscient [Jina] has explained that [this *dharma*, consisting of] self-control, etc., is tenfold [and] leads to liberation.

12. A statement without a human source is simply impossible. If it were possible then the words would have no authority, because the authority [or reliability] of words, of course, always depends on a competent author.

13. If one accepts the so-called *dharma*, which is transmitted by heretics and which is tainted by [notions of] violence, etc., [then that will be] the cause of one's wandering from [one] existence [to the other].

14. If [as in the Vedas] a God can be [a person] with attachment, a teacher can be a noncelibate, and the teaching can be without compassion—alas! [then] poor mankind is doomed.

15. Orthodoxy is correctly defined by virtue of [the following] five characteristics: (1) tranquility [as a result of stilling the passions], (2) desire [for liberation], (3) disgust [with mundane existence], (4) compassion [for all living beings], and (5) acceptance [of the Jaina doctrine as the true creed, even in the presence of other opinions].

16. [Orthodoxy] is also said to have five "ornaments": (1) firmness [in one's belief], (2) illumination [of the Jaina religion], (3) devotion, (4) familiarity with the Jaina doctrine, and (5) frequentation of the places [of birth, consecration, enlightenment, and final death] of the Jinas [by the fourfold community of monks, nuns, laymen, and laywomen].

17. [The following] five [faults] may, [however], considerably contaminate orthodoxy: (1) doubt, [total or partial, calling in question the entire creed or a particular dogma], (2) desire [for one, or for all other doctrines than Jainism], (3) hesitation [about the value of the results of various human activities or repugnance for the filthy and sweaty bodies of Jaina ascetics], (4) praise of adherents of other creeds, and (5) acquaintance [with adherents of other creeds].

18. The Jinas have defined the five minor vows—non-harm, etc.—as the dissociation, [according to convenience, capacity and circumstance], from gross forms of [mental, verbal, and physical] harm, [performed either by oneself or indirectly through another person].

19. Having realized the consequences of [past] violence, such as loss of limbs, leprosy, and paralysis, an innocent, wise person, should avoid intentionally harming [any] mobile being.

20. Happiness [such as the enjoyment of food, drink, a garland of flowers, and ointment] and unhappiness [such as that resulting from the experience of murder, bondage, and death] are pleasing and displeasing, [respectively], to all beings, just as it is to oneself. One should, [therefore], not *deliberately* do harm to another person that is unwelcome to oneself.

21. A lay disciple who desires liberation and who understands the principle of harmlessness should not use meaningless violence, even against immobile beings [such as earth-, water-, fire-, and air-bodies as well as plant beings, having only one sense, that of touch].

22. A human being who is willing to give away even his kingdom in payment of his bloodthirstiness cannot atone for the sin arising for such a murder, even if the entire world is given [as a gift].

23. One who kills [and] desires the meat of harmless animals in the forest who feed on air, water, and grass, how would he be distinguished from a dog?

24. Alas! He who suffers even from being wounded on his body by [a blade of] *kuśa* grass, how can he kill innocent beings with [his] "sharp" weapons?

25. Those who perform cruel deeds in order to provide for their own, [egoistic], temporary pleasure, bring complete dissolution to the body of other human beings.

26. If a person is hurt merely by being told that he will die, how would he feel by the time he is actually being killed with cruel weapons?

27. It is stated [in the scriptures (*āgama*) that the universal monarchs], Subhūma and Brahmadatta, who both were devoted to cruel meditation, were sent to the seventh [and worst] hell because of murder.

28. It is better to be a person [born] with paralysis [and] devoid of hands, feet. and a proper body, than as an assailant with all limbs intact.

29. Violence can [only] be for destruction. Even though—[as in] the well-known [case of Yaśodhara]—it was performed for the sake of

removing obstacles [or] conceived as the proper duty of the family, it [still] brought destruction on the family.

30. On the other hand, he is superior who even abandons hereditary violence, like [the warrior (*kṣatriya*)] Sulasa, the son of Kālasaukarika.

31. If one does not give up violence, controlling [the senses], paying respect to deities and teachers, [indulging in] charity, studying [religious scriptures, etc., or practising] austerity, all is without result; [neither is bad *karma* destroyed nor is good acquired].

32. Alas! The unsuspecting, dull-witted world of men is made to fall into the region of hell by brutal and bloodthirsty [men] who preach the code of violence.

MANUSMṚTI: A SCRIPTURE OF VIOLENCE

33. [According to Manu], "Brahmā himself created the animals merely for the sake of sacrifice, which is for the prosperity of the entire world. Therefore, violence in relation to sacrifice is not [real] violence."

34. "Medicinal herbs, beasts, trees, [other] animals, and birds, which are killed for the sake of sacrifice, later on become reborn in high [birthplaces]."

35. "Manu has stated that, at the 'honey-mixture' sacrifice, animals are to be killed as offerings to the manes and the gods, not on any other [occasion]."

36. "If a brahmin who knows the essence of the Veda kills animals for these purposes [stated above], he himself, as well as the sacrificed animals, reach the highest realm" [, according to Manu].

37. Those cruel performers [of sacrifice] who composed the scripture that openly recommends violence, to which hell will those—the worst of all nihilists—go?

38. "Rather a wretched materialist, who openly condemns [the Vedas], than [the demon] Jaimini, who hides behind the ascetic guise of the Vedic testimony."

39. Those who, devoid of pity, hurt [other] beings, either under the pretext of making an oblation to a deity, [like Bhairava or Caṇḍikā], or under the disguise of sacrifice, will go to the most cruel hell.

40. Having repudiated [this Jaina] teaching (*dharma*) that has been bestowed on the world as a source of stilling [the passions and the senses], [cultivating] a [pleasant] behavior as well as compassion [for all living beings], alas! even violence has been proclaimed by the dull-witted as the [true] religion.

41. "I [Manu] will now thoroughly explain how that oblation which is intended to last for a long period, and that which is intended to last forever, are to be given to the *manes*, according to the [prescribed] rules:"

42. "The *manes* of the people are pleased for a month when presented correctly with sesamum, rice, barley, black gram, water, root [vegetables, and] fruit."

43. "By [offering them] the meat of fish, deer, sheep, and fowl, [they are pleased for] two, three, four, and five months, [respectively]."

44. "By [feeding them] the meat of he-goat [and the meat from the following species of deer:] Pṛṣata, Eṇa, and Rurava, [they are pleased for six, seven, eight, [and] nine months, [respectively]."

45. "By [offering them the meat of] wild boar and buffalo, they remain content for ten months, whereas the meat of hare and tortoise [makes them satisfied for] eleven months."

46. "By [offering] an oblation made out of cow's milk, rice, and sugar, [they remain content for] one year, [whereas] by [presenting them with] the meat of rhinoceros, [they are] content for twelve years."

47. According to the [Hindu] law-books (*smṛti*), violence, which is performed by dull-witted persons in order to satisfy the *manes*, is responsible for a bad destiny [such as hell—not only for a good destiny as said above]. [Accordingly, the authors of these scriptures contradict themselves].

48. He who gives protection to living beings, for him, there is also no *fear* of living beings. Whatever gift is given, a corresponding effect is established.

49. What a tragedy that murderers, [such as the Hindu] gods, [Śaṅkara, Yama, Viṣṇu, Śiva, and Kumāra], armed with a bow, a staff, a [discus-shaped] wheel and a sword, a trident, and a spear, [respectively], even are worshiped and thought of as gods!

50–51. Non-harm is like the beneficent mother of all living beings, a channel of ambrosia in the desert of *saṃsāra*, a line of rain-showers over the forest fire of misery, [and] a supreme remedy for those suffering from the disease of wandering from one existence [to the other].

52. Long life, excellent beauty, good health [and], praiseworthiness, these are all the rewards of doing no harm, and besides that, [non-harm] grants [you all] desires.

53. Knowing [that defects such as] murmuring, stammering, deafness, and diseases of the mouth are the consequences of falsehood, one

should give up [speaking] untruth [in the form of] *kanyālīka*, and so forth.

54. The five [kinds] of gross lies that one should not speak are untruth about (1) [beings with two legs or feet, such as] a girl, [a boy, or a man], (2) [animals with four legs, such as] a cow [an ox, and a buffalo], (3) [entities without legs that grow in] the soil, [such as trees], [untruth told for the sake of] (4) making away with a pledge, (5) and bearing false witness.

55. That which the entire mankind opposes, that which is considered as betrayal of confidence, and that which is opposed to merit, that is proclaimed as untruth.

56. Out of untruth [comes] unreliability, distrustfulness, and a place in hell. Therefore, falsehood should be avoided.

57. A wise man should also not speak untruth even due to negligence, [doubt, or ignorance], because that which grants you good fortune [will then be destroyed], just as huge trees are split by a whirlwind.

58. [Certain] faults, such as enmity, regret, and distrust, result from speaking untruth, just as diseases [result] from [consuming] unwholesome food.

59. By the power of telling lies, living beings are born to live among *nigodas* and animals, and afterward as hell-beings.

60. One should not tell a lie out of fear [of death], or out of respect, like the monk Kālika [did]. He who tells [a lie] goes to hell, like king Vasu.

61. On the other hand, even though a statement may be true, it should not be spoken if it causes affliction to others. [This is] because, even if it is accepted [by all the people] in the world, Kauśika was sent to hell [on account of making such a statement].

62. Birth in [hells], such as Raurava [and Maharaurava], results from telling even "white" lies. Alas, alas! What will be the destiny of those who distort the words of the Jina?

63. Those who say [that] truth alone is the foundation of both knowledge and conduct, the earth is purified by the dust of their feet.

64. Ghosts, spirits, snakes, and so on, are unable to offend those who do not tell a lie and whose great [inner] wealth is the vow of truthfulness.

65. Having known the consequences of taking what is not given [to one by its rightful owner, such as] ill fortune, servitude, slavery, mutilation, [and] poverty, one should refrain from gross [forms of] stealing.

66. An intelligent man should not, at any cost, take [property] that is not given to him [but] belonging to others, [whether it consists of pick-

ing up things that have] fallen [from a carriage, etc., things kept and] forgotten [somewhere], lost [things, or things that have been] kept for the owner for storage or as a deposit.

67. The moment one robs [property] belonging to another, one also bereaves oneself of everything, viz. [one's] religion, courage, steadfastness, intelligence, as well as this and the next world.

68. When [a person] is being killed, temporary suffering arises only for [that] particular [person], whereas when someone is robbed of [his] wealth, [many people], including his son and grandson, [will suffer] for [the rest of their] life.

69. Here [in this world], the fruit of the tree [called] "the sin of theft" is death, bondage, etc., whereas in the world hereafter, the result is the experience of hell.

70. A person [who has committed theft] is as if pierced by [that] theft [and] will never attain a sound state during the day or the night, while asleep or awake, ever.

71. Friends, sons, wives, brothers, and parents do not, even for a moment, want to be associated with a thief, just as [they do not want to be associated] with a barbarian.

72. Even if one is a relative of the king, like [the frog] Maṇḍika, one will be punished [if one commits] theft. [On the other hand], a thief like Rauhiṇeya, who quit stealing, may even enjoy heaven.

73. Let alone an attempt to rob the entire property of another, one must not even try to take a blade of grass which is not given [to one].

74. Wealth comes [all by itself] to those who are pure-hearted [and] who abstain from taking the wealth of others, [just like a girl who] chooses [her husband all by] herself.

75. For those who practice the [vow of] honesty, disasters depart, good renown prevails, [and] the pleasures of heaven draw near.

76. When the wise man has realized the consequences of noncontinence, [such as becoming] an eunuch [or being] castrated, he should remain content with his own wife, in other words, he should avoid all other women.

77. Who will indulge in sexual intercourse that is pleasant only in the beginning [but] utterly terrible in its consequence, similar to the [red fruit] Kiṃpāka[, which is sweet in taste but fatally poisonous]?

78. Tremor, sweating, fatigue, swooning, giddiness, self-disgust, weakness, and [fatal] diseases, such as pulmonary consumption, occur as the consequences of sexual intercourse.

79. Extremely subtle collections of life are produced in the mechanical contrivance of the birth canal, where they die being crushed [by the phallus]. Therefore one should abandon sexual intercourse.

80. [According to the *Ratirahasya,* these collections of life consist of] subtle [forms of] insects of low, middle, and high power, which are generated in the blood within the birth canal, [and] which produce itching corresponding to their kind.

81. He who seeks to combat the fever of lust by copulation with a woman [is like he who] expects to extinguish a fire by throwing ghee [into it].

82. It is better to embrace a burning iron-pillar than to enjoy the thighs of a woman being a door to hell.

83. The moment a fair-eyed woman puts a foot in the heart of even virtuous people, she definitely ruins the collection of good virtues [in them].

84. Who will enjoy women whose innate faults are deceitfulness, cruelty, unsteadiness [of mind], [and] a predilection for bad habits?

85. It is possible to reach to the end of the ocean, but it is not possible to reach the end of the bad conduct of women, who are by nature crooked.

86. When women with beautiful buttocks are given to bad conduct, they will, in a moment, seduce even their husband, son, father, [or] brother into improper activity that even may endanger [their] life.

87. Woman is the seed of creation, the illuminator of the path to the gate of hell, the root of sorrow, the source of deceit, [and] the mine of [various kinds of mental and physical] suffering.

88. Prostitutes, who have one thing in mind, say something else, and do something quite different, how can they be a cause of happiness?

89. Who would kiss the mouth of a prostitute, which has been kissed by countless pimps, which is mixed with liquor, and which smells of raw meat, like leftover food.

90. Prostitutes who have taken everything, [including] all the money, from [their] lover, even wish to rip his clothes off as he leaves.

91. One who is under the rule of prostitutes, always enjoying [their] bad company, does not respect either gods, teachers, friends, or relatives.

92. One should abandon a harlot who even places lepers on a par with the god of love due to [her] longing for money, but who, on the other hand, is without affection and displays feigned love.

93. Laymen ought to make love to their wives without even being attached, not to speak of [being attached to] other women who are a storehouse of all [kinds of] evil.

94. A woman who shamelessly enjoys her paramour, having neglected her [own] husband, how can one have confidence in her [or] in [any] other woman [for that matter]?

95. Just as an animal near a slaughter-house is unhappy, one who is mentally retarded, afraid [of the woman's husband, the king, etc.], [or] miserable, [sleeping and sitting in ruined temples, etc.], finds no pleasure in indulging in love-making with another woman.

96. One should refrain from the [whole] act of approaching other women. It creates doubt about [one's] life, it causes great enmity, and it is against both worlds[: heaven and earth].

97. The adulterer [in this life] obtains bondage, which robs him of all his possessions [and leads to] mutilation. Furthermore, at death, [he will be reborn in one of] the dreadful infernal regions.

98. How can a man who continuously makes an effort to protect his own wife, have intercourse with another woman, even though he knows it [creates] suffering?

99. Even Rāvaṇa, who conquered the whole world with his valor, brought ruin upon his family [and] went to hell because of his desire to enjoy [sexual intercourse with] other women.

100. One should give up women belonging to other [men], even if every part [of their body] is beautiful, pure, and the abode of elegance and wealth, and [even if they are] skilful in all the arts.

101. How much can we praise the eminent Sudarśana, who remained in a spotless state of mind even when other women approached him.

102. Women should, [on the other hand], leave other men alone, even if they are the king of kings in wealth, [like Kubera], or the god of love in beauty, [like Kāmadeva], just as Sītā left Rāvaṇa alone.

103. Those men and women whose minds are attached to the wives [or husbands] of others are [re]born as hermaphrodites and animals, and will [encounter] repeated misfortunes in life after life.

104. When one practices [the vow of] continence, which is the essence of [the correct] conduct [of laymen and mendicants] and which is the single cause of [achieving] the supreme reality [of liberation], one is worshiped [in mind, body, and speech] even by those who are worshiped by others, [such as gods, demons, and kings].

105. As a result of the practice of continence, men obtain long life, well-shaped [bodies], strong constitutions, luminousness, and great potency.

106. Once [a layperson] has understood that discontentedness—distrust and involvement—results from possessiveness [and] is the cause of suffering, he should limit [his] possessions.

107. Due to a great amount of possessions, a human being definitely sinks into the ocean of existence, like a huge [overloaded] ship. One should, therefore, avoid [owning too many] possessions [which are the cause of hell].

108. Similar to dustlike *trasa* creatures there is not a single virtue in [possession], but the defects are big as a mountain, and they demoralize.

109. Even latent enemies, such as attachment and aversion, come into existence due to attachment [to possessions], just as even the mind of a mendicant becomes fickle due to [contact with] those whose [minds] are agitated.

110. Involvement is the cause of *saṃsāra*, and the cause of it is ownership. A lay disciple should therefore gradually decrease [his] wealth.

111. The objects of the surrounding world rob a man who is subjected to attachment, fire in the form of passion burns [him], [and] beasts in the form of women obstruct [him].

112. Sagara, [the second Cakravartin], was not content with [his 60,000] sons, Kucikarṇa with [his] property in cattle, Tilakaśreṣṭhī with [his storage of] grain, [and king] Nanda was not [satisfied with] heaps of gold.

113. Mendicants who are possessed by the demon of ownership will give up even the wealth coming from the kingdom of equanimity, including austerities and learning.

114. There is no happiness, either for the king of gods, or for the universal monarchs, who possess discontentedness, but there is for an [ordinary] person, like Abhaya[kumāra], who possesses contentedness.

115. One who has contentedness as his ornament, for him there is wealth at hand, the wish-fulfilling cow follows him, and the gods become his servants.

Chapter 3. The Three Virtuous Vows

1. When one does not transgress a territory that exists within the ten directions, [then] that constitutes the first virtuous vow, called *digvirati*.

2. This virtuous vow [of *digvirati*] also applies to the householder, who is as [dangerous as] a heated iron-ball, because it prevents him from killing mobile and immobile beings.

3. He who has taken [the vow of] *digvirati* has thereby formed an embankment against the ocean of greed, which [otherwise] rushes in and attacks all humanity.

4. When one decides, according to one's ability, what number of [things] should be enjoyed once, and what number of [things] should be enjoyed repeatedly, [then] that [constitutes] the second virtuous vow, [called] *bhogopabhogamāna.*

5. *Bhoga* is that which is only to be enjoyed once, like food and a garland. *Upabhoga* is that which is to be enjoyed again and again, such as a woman, [a house, a bed, a seat, and a vehicle].

6–7. One should abstain from [consuming] (1) liquor, (2) meat [from animals living on the earth, in the water, or moving in the air, as well as skin, blood, fat, and marrow], (3) butter [from the cow, buffalo, goat, or a mixture of these], (4) honey [from the *makṣika, bhramara,* and *kauttika* bee], (5–9) the five kinds of tree pods, (10) food containing infinite bodies, (11) unknown fruit, (12) [food eaten] at night, (13) pulses mixed with raw milk products, (14) rice that has fermented, (15) curds kept for more than two days, and (16) tainted food.

8. (1) Just as through bad luck even a rake [may lose his] wife, one may lose one's senses merely on account of drinking liquor.

9. Evil people, whose minds have gone beyond control because of the consumption of liquor, alas! they mistake their mother for their mistress and their mistress for their mother.

10. He whose mind is disturbed by liquor does not know the difference between himself and others. [Such] a fool makes himself a master and his master his servant.

11. A drunken person rolls about like a carcass on the crossroad [and] dogs urinate in [his] mouth, assuming the opened mouth to be a hole.

12. A person who is given to the pleasure of drinking liquor sleeps naked on the crossroad and exposes, with the greatest ease, [even his most] secret intentions.

13. [A person's] beauty, fame, intelligence, and wealth vanish by imbibing liquor, just as paintings with many colors are discolored by soot.

14. A drunk person dances like a man possessed, as it were, by a spirit, laments loudly, as if taken by grief, and rolls about on the ground, as if suffering from a burning fever.

15. Liquor is comparable to poison since it produces looseness of body, weakens the senses, and creates a long spell of swooning.

16. Judgment, [self-]control, knowledge, truth[fulness], purity [of conduct, and] compassion, all are extinguished by liquor, just as a haystack is [extinguished] by a spark of fire.

17. Liquor is the cause of [all] defects and calamities. One should, therefore, avoid liquor, just as a person who is afflicted with disease [should avoid] unsuitable food.

18. (2) He who desires to eat meat by killing living beings uproots the root of the tree of religion called compassion.

19. He who is always greedy for food [in the form of] meat, [and yet] desires to be compassionate, [is like a person who] wants to grow a plant in a burning fire.

20. One who kills for meat, one who sells it, one who prepares it, one who eats it, one who approves [of your buying it], [and] one who gives [it away], are [all] definitely killers, [even] according to Manu.

21. [According to Manu], "one who approves of [the killing of an animal], one who dissects it, one who kills it, one who sells and buys [the meat], one who prepares it, one who serves it, and one who eats it, [all] are killers."

22. "Without doing harm to living beings, meat cannot be procured. Moreover, murder is not something that leads to heaven. Therefore, [even Manu recommends you to] abandon meat."

23. Those who eat the meat of other [living beings] in order to satisfy their own flesh, they are definitely murderers [themselves], since without a consumer [there can be] no killer.

24. Who will undertake such an evil [activity] for the sake of this miserable body in which even delicious food may become excrement, and ambrosia, urine.

25. Those wicked fellows who declare that there is no fault in eating meat, they have made hunters, eagles, wolves, tigers, and jackals their teachers.

26. "Manu gives [the following] derivation [of the word 'meat']: 'The one whose meat I eat here [in this life], he is going to eat me in the next. This is the real meaning of the word "me-eat".'"

27. The mind of one who is addicted to the enjoyment of meat, like an evil-minded spirit, is [always] engaged in [thoughts of how] to kill each and every being.

28. Those who eat meat, even [though] there are divine edibles available, eat poison, having abandoned ambrosia.

29. There is no religion for one who is pitiless, [and] how can there be compassion for someone who eats meat? [However], one who is desirous of meat does not know this, for if he did know, he would not prescribe it.

30. Some [people] do not only eat meat themselves out of great ignorance, but they even serve it to gods, *manes*, and [visiting] mendicants, arguing as follows:

31. [According to Manu], "One is not guilty [of sin] if one eats meat—whether one has bought it, produced it [by killing an animal], or received it from others—[as long as] one has worshiped the gods [and] the *manes* [with it]."

32. One should not ingest even [as little as] a small slice of meat, even if it has been consecrated by [the chanting of] *mantras,* since (*hi*) even a small drop of poison results in the destruction of [one's] life.

33. Which intelligent man will eat meat, which immediately [after the killing of the animal] is blemished by a continuous flow of infinite numbers of living beings formed into a solid mass, and which is like provisions on the road leading to hell?

34. (3) Within 48 minutes after [the butter is separated from the buttermilk], it becomes the breeding ground for extremely subtle life [where they grow]. Butter should, therefore, not be consumed by the wise.

35. If there is [so much] evil in the killing of a single being, who would eat butter, which is full of life?

36. (4) Who will eat honey, which is produced by the killing of numerous living beings [and] which is disgusting like saliva?

37. One who eats honey, which is manufactured by the destruction of tens of thousands of tiny beings, is worse than butchers who kill [comparatively] few living beings.

38. Religious people should not eat honey, which consists of the leavings of [matter] which bees spit out, having drunk the nectar from the interior of one flower after the other.

39. Even if taken as a medicine, honey is the cause of hell, [just as] the swallowing of even a small quantity of poison leads to death.

40. Ah! Honey is [conventionally] said to be sweet by [its] unenlightened consumers. [In reality, however,] hellish pain results from eating [it].

41. Alas! Honey, which is produced by destroying living beings spewed from the mouth of bees, is considered holy [and even] used in the lustration of the god [by people such as the Śaivites].

42. (5–9) One should not consume fruit of [the following five fig] trees crawling with a multitude of worms: *Udumbara*, Banyan, *Plakṣa*, Crow-*udumbara*, and the Pipal [or the Indian Fig Tree].

43. Even if one is weak due to hunger, [or] unable to obtain other food, a pious [Jaina] should not eat fruit coming from [these] five fig trees.

44–46. (10) Every moist bulb and each sprout, [the tree] *Snuhī*, Lavanī-tree bark, Cardamom, *Girikarṇikā*, *Śatāvarī*, *Śatāvarī*, sprouted [pulses or grains], *Guḍūcī*, the pleasant Tamarind, beetroot, *Amṛtavallī*, *Sūkara-valla*, [and plants] with infinite bodies [growing outside of India and] mentioned in the scriptures, as well as other unknown [plants], should be diligently avoided by those who are compassionate [and] who have an incorrect view of reality, [maintaining that plants do not have a Self].

47. (11) An intelligent person should eat fruit known to himself or to others, [but] he should keep away from prohibited or poisonous fruit.

48. (12) One should not, at any occasion, eat food after sunset, which may be contaminated by [the touch of] arbitrarily roaming [spirits], such as ghosts and goblins, or by other [evil spirits].

49. Who would eat at night where creatures, [such as insects, ants, and flies], may imperceptibly have fallen into the food, [one's] sight being obstructed in the pitch-dark night?

50–52. The obvious disadvantages for all [those who have an incorrect view of reality and] eat at night are for example that an ant fallen into the sauce destroys the intelligence, a louse causes dropsy, a fly makes one vomit, a spider [causes] leprosy, thorn and pieces of wood cause a sore throat, a scorpion perforates the palate, and resin and hair bring about stammering.

53. One should not thoughtlessly eat even insentient [food] at night [since it may contain] minute, invisible organisms [such as *kunthu*]. Even by those who have obtained omniscience eating at night is not held in [high] esteem.

54. He who knows the rules [according to the scriptures] should not, at any time, eat after sunset. Even [ordinary people] being outside [of the Jaina teaching] are of the opinion that food consumed at night is not [real food] to be consumed.

55. Those conversant with the Vedas declare that the sun is full of the splendor of the three Vedas, [*Ṛg*, *Sāma*, and *Yajur Vedas*], [and] all auspicious actions are purified by its beams.

56. Oblation to [the fire], bathing, offerings to the *manes*, worshiping the gods, and in particular, eating at night, are illicit.

57. As everyone knows, night [begins] at the eighth part of the day when the sun grows dim (i.e., three hours prior to sunset), [and] one should not eat at night.

58–59. [As it is stated in the *Devīpurāṇa*:] "In the morning the gods eat, at midday the seers, in the afternoon the *manes*, in the evening [demons, such as] *daityas* and *dānavas,* and in the twilight the demigods and *rākṣasas.* Such food is always good for the family. Having passed all [these] appropriate mealtimes, [food] enjoyed at night is a 'non-meal.' "

60. [According to Āyurveda,] when the light from the sun vanishes, the heart lotus and the navel lotus contract. One should, therefore, not eat at night. [Another reason is that, due to the absence of light,] one may consume tiny creatures.

61. How can those dull-witted persons who enjoy nightly meals, which have been in contact with multitude of living beings, be distinguished from demons (*rākṣasa*)?

62. He who goes on eating day and night, he is clearly a simple animal [though] without horns and a tail.

63. Listen! He who is aware of the defects resulting from eating at night avoids eating during the first and last 48 minutes of the day. That is wholesome intake of food.

64. If one has not made a vow not to eat at night, one eating by day will not enjoy the real result [of such abstention]. Without something said, no profit.

65. Those imbecile persons who only eat at the night, [and] not during the day, [are like those who] reject a ruby and accept glass.

66. Those who at their own will would rather eat when it is night are [like those who] sow rice on saline soil even though a [water] tank is available.

67. Because of eating at night, one is reborn as an owl, or a crow, or a cat, or a vulture, or a pig, or a serpent, or a scorpion, or a lizard.

68. It is told [in the *Rāmāyaṇa*] that Lakṣmaṇa, having disregarded other oaths, was forced to swear the oath of not eating at night by [his wife] Vanamālā.

69. He who permanently renounces eating at night is blessed [and] will definitely spend half of his life fasting.

70. No one except an omniscient person is able to tell all the advantages for those who abstain from eating during nighttime.

71. (13–16) Subtle organisms are observed by the omniscient in pulses with raw milk products, [rice that has fermented, curds kept for more than two days, and tainted food]. Therefore these are to be avoided.

72. [To sum up:] Those who are devoted to Jainism should renounce fruits, flowers, leaves, and other [things] that are mixed with living beings, as well as [things which are] joined or attached [with sentient beings].

73–74. That which [not only] stands opposed to purposeful violence with respect to the body, etc., but which [also] repudiates meaningless violence, [such as] brooding or harming oneself or others, offering harmful advice, facilitating destruction, [and] careless conduct, that constitutes the third virtuous vow.

75. Brooding over killing an enemy, becoming a king, ruining a town, setting fire, flying, etc., should not exceed 48 minutes.

76. Harmful advice, such as "break in the oxen," "plough the fields," "castrate the horse," is not suitable, unless it is a question of being helpful [to sons, brothers, ploughmen, etc., and should not be given out of mere talkativeness].

77. [A lay disciple] who is compassionate toward other living beings should not procure harmful [things], such as carts, ploughs, swords, bows, pestles, mortars, and bellows, [unless] it is a question of being helpful.

78–80. A wise man should abandon careless conduct, such as out of curiosity listening to concerts, watching dance [displays] and theatrical representations [without a religious theme], [as well as] being fond of [reading] books on sexual love, being addicted to gambling, liquor, [and dicing]. [He should furthermore renounce] entertainment, such as sporting in the water, playing with swings, [watching] animal fights [between cocks, etc.], [nursing] enmity toward the sons, etc., of [one's] enemy, idle talk about food, women, [one's] country, and king. [He should also] not sleep the whole night, except due to illness [and] fatigue from walking.

81. Inside the temple of the Jinendra [he should avoid] sport, laughing loudly, spitting, sleeping, disputing, gossiping, and [consuming any of] the four kinds of food.

82. *Sāmāyikavrata* is known as that [state of] equanimity which [a person attains] who has abandoned self-depreciating and cruel thoughts and [all] faulty actions for a period of 48 minutes.

83. Even for a firm-minded householder who is established in the vow of *sāmāyika,* [accumulated] *karma* is destroyed, as was the case of Candrāvataṃsaka.

84. The limitation [set] in the *digvrata* for a person is furthermore shortened for a day or a night. This is called *deśāvakāśikavrata.*

85. On the four holy days [one should perform asceticism], such as fasting, suspend blameworthy activities, practice continence, [and] abandon [bodily care], such as bathing. [This is called] *poṣadhavrata.*

86. Even householders who practice the meritorious, [but] difficult, *poṣadhavrata,* like the father of Culanī, are praiseworthy.

87. Offerings alms, [such as] the four kinds of food, bowls, clothing, and a place to stay to a [mendicant] guest, is called *atithisaṃvibhāgavr ata.*

88. Take notice of [the example of] the calf-herd by name Saṅgamaka, who acquired an astonishing [amount of] wealth through [presenting] gifts to mendicants.

89. When the [minor] vows are infracted, they are not for the good [of a lay disciple]. Therefore one should abstain from the infractions—five for each [minor] vow.

90. (1) [Keeping cattle and children in] captivity out of anger, (2) skinning, (3) overloading [cattle or humans], (4) beating, and (5) depriving [someone] of food [and drink], etc., these are declared [to be the infractions] with respect to [the minor vow of] non-harm.

91. (1) [Spreading of] false information, (2) sudden calumniating, (3) revealing [somebody else's] secret, (4) revealing a trusted secret, and (5) [producing] forged documents, [these are the infractions] with respect to [the minor vow of] truthfulness.

92. (1) [Giving] a thief [one's] consent, (2) receiving stolen goods from him, (3) transgressing [the limits of] the enemy's kingdom, (4) producing a counterfeit, and (5) [using] false measures, [these are the infractions] pertaining to the minor vow of honesty.

93. (1) Intercourse with a woman [temporarily] taken [as a wife], (2) intercourse with an unmarried woman, (3) match-making, (4) excessive sex indulgence, and (5) amorous play [with limbs other than the organs of sexual enjoyment], these are considered [the infractions] pertaining to the minor vow of continence.

94. Exceeding the limits set for (1) grain and other foodstuffs [by packing several individual items together], (2) for household chattels [by counting several individual items as one single unit], (3) [for

bipeds and quadrupeds, such as] cows [by disregarding their offspring when counting them], (4) for land and houses [by incorporating several items into one lot], and (5) for gold and silver [by not counting donated goods], [these are the infractions] pertaining to [the minor vow of] non-possession.

95. For one who has taken [the minor] vow [of limiting one's possessions, the following] five kinds [of infractions] are not allowed: [Exceeding the limits set for grain, etc.,] by (1) packaging together, (2) [postponing one's] interest [to a later date], (3) [not counting] the womb(s) [or the young ones for a certain period], (4) joining [utensils in order to keep the total number of items below the set limit], and (5) [pretending] to give [property away to one's wife, for example].

96. (1) Forgetfulness, going beyond the limits in an (2) upward, (3) downward, (4) and horizontal direction, and (5) expanding the limits of the area of movement, these are the five infractions with respect to the [minor] vow of restraining [movement in a given] direction.

97. These [are the infractions] connected with the vow of restricting the things that may be enjoyed once and those which may be enjoyed frequently: (1) [consuming] sentient things, (2) [consuming what is] connected [with sentient things], (3) [consuming food which is] mixed [with sentient things], (4) [consuming what has been conserved by] fermentation, and (5) consuming [food that is] not properly cooked.

98. These [five infractions described above] are concerned with the renunciation of food, whereas the cruel activities [listed below] are concerned with [one's] occupation. In the following, the 15 impure occupations which one should avoid [are described:]

99–100. (1) Livelihood from charcoal, (2) forest, (3) carts, (4) transport fees, (5) [hewing and] digging; trade in (6) [animal byproducts such as] ivory, (7) lac [and similar substances], (8–9) men, animals, anything liquid, and forbidden foodstuffs, (10) destructive articles; work involving (11) milling, (12) mutilation, (13) breeding and rearing, (14) the use of fire, [and] (15) the use of water. These are the fifteen [occupations which] one should avoid.

101. (1) Livelihood by use of charcoal [includes] making coal [out of fire], construction of ovens, being a potter, an ironsmith, and a goldsmith, as well as the burning [performed] by a blacksmith and a brickmaker.

102. (2) Sale of cut or uncut timber, leaves, shoots and fruits, [making of flour] from pounding [in a mill], and grinding of grains [between two stones], is called livelihood by use of the forest.

103. (3) Construction of carts [or] parts of them, driving them and selling them, is called "livelihood by use of cart."

104. (4) [To earn one's livelihood] by transporting goods in a cart, [or on the back of] oxen, buffaloes, camels, donkeys, mules, [and] horses, [such a] profession is called livelihood by carts.

105. (5) Excavating [artificial] pools and wells, etc., quarrying of rocks, [or] making a living by any other work pertaining to the earth, [such as the ploughing of fields], is called livelihood from [hewing and] digging.

106. (6) [Obtaining] ivory, [tail-]hairs [of yaks, etc.], claws [of owls, etc.], bones (i.e., shells) [of conches, etc.], pelts [of antelopes, etc.], [and] feathers [of geese] in abundance, from mobile beings for the sake of [earning one's] living is called livelihood in [animal byproducts such as] ivory.

107. (7) Sale of destructive [things such as] lac, red arsenic, indigo, *dhātakī*, borax, etc., is called trade in lac—an abode of evil.

108. (8–9) Sale of butter, fat, honey, liquor, etc., [is called] trade in alcohol, [etc., whereas] sale of men and animals [is called] trade in [creatures that have] hair.

109. (10) Trade in life-destructive articles, such as the poison [aconite], weapons, [such as swords], iron [implements, such as spades and] ploughs, mechanical devices, [such as water-wheels], and yellow orpiment of arsenic, etc., is called trade in toxic substances.

110. (11) [Livelihood by mechanically] crushing sesamum seed, sugarcane, mustard seed, castor-oil beans in a watermill, etc., and working with oil from leaves, is called [work involving] milling.

111. (12) Nose-piercing, branding, castration, docking, cutting off the ear and dew-laps, is called [work involving] mutilation.

112. (13) [The breeding and keeping of destructive animals and birds, such as] nightingales, parrots, cats, dogs, cocks, peacocks, and the rearing of a female slave for profit, is known as work involving breeding and rearing.

113. (14–15) The work involving the use of fire is twofold, either out of habit, or out of considering it to be a meritorious act. Draining the water from a lake, a river, a pond, etc., [is called] work involving the use of water. [All are bad occupations].

114. [The infractions] related to [the third virtuous vow, called] *anarthadaṇḍa*, include (1) the bringing together of harmful implements, [such as a plough, a pounder, and a cart], (2) superfluity of luxuries, (3) talkativeness, (4) buffoonery, [and] (5) libidinous speech.

115. (1–3) Misdirection of body, speech, and mind [during meditation], (4) instability [with respect to the practice of equanimity], and (5) forgetfulness [of it], are defined as [the infractions] related to the vow of *sāmāyika*.

116. (1) Sending a servant for something from outside [of the set area], (2) having something brought from outside, (3) communicating by throwing objects [and thereby attracting the attention of someone outside of the prescribed area], (4) communicating by making sounds, and (5) communicating by making signs [to someone outside the area, constitute the infractions] pertaining to the vow of limiting the area of one's movement.

117. (1–3) Excreting or making one's bed without examining and sweeping the spot, (4) disrespect [toward the *poṣadhavrata*], and (5) forgetfulness [of having undertaken it], are [the infractions] related to [the vow of] *poṣadha*.

118. (1) Throwing [alms] on sentient beings, (2) covering [alms with sentient beings], (3) transgressing the appointed time, (4) jealousy in almsgiving, (5) pretending that the alms belong to others, these are defined [as the transgressions] pertaining to the fourth educational vow.

119. Thus, one who is firm in [the twelve] vows and with devotion strews his wealth in the seven "fields," including [images, temples, scriptures, male mendicants, female mendicants, laymen, [and] laywomen], and one who out of compassion [strews his wealth on] the oppressed, [such a person] is said to be an exceptional layman.

120. He who does not strew existing wealth, which is external and impermanent, into [these seven] fields, how can such a wretch [ever hope to be able to] practice the conduct [of a mendicant], which is difficult to realize?

121. [The exceptional layman] should get up [before dawn] at the [auspicious] moment [called] Brāhma, reciting the praises to the [five] highest venerables[: the *arhats* or the Jinas, the perfected beings (*siddha*) who have attained liberation (*mokṣa*), the mendicant leaders of the Jaina order (*ācārya*), the mendicant preceptors (*upādhyāya*), and all the Jaina mendicants (*sādhu*)], and he should ponder over [the questions]: What is my *dharma*? What is my family [duty]? What are my vows?

122. [Having made himself] pure [through mouth-rinsing, tooth-cleaning, tongue-scraping, bathing, [and] having [externally and internally] worshiped the deity (i.e., the Jina) with flowers, oblations, and hymns of praise, [on the shrine] in [his] house, and having renounced [certain food-stuffs], according to his ability, he should go to the temple.

123. Having entered there, he should, according to the rite, circumambulate the Jina three times, clockwise, [then], having worshiped him with flowers, etc., he should eulogize [him] with excellent hymns of praise.

124. Then, in the presence of a teacher, the purified [layman] discloses, with great devotion, [what temporary rules he has taken in the early morning concerning] the renunciation of certain foods.

125–126. When he sees the [teacher], he should immediately rise from his seat to receive [him], [and] when he comes near, he should with folded hands in front of the forehead offer his seat [to him]. [Then he himself] receives a seat [and] with great devotion, he performs the ritual salutation [of the monk]. When [the monk] leaves [the temple], [then he may also] follow. This is considered "honoring of the teacher."

127. Then, having returned [from the temple and] gone to his own place, a wise [layman] should, in a manner that does not conflict with his religious duties, take care of his business.

128. After [work] he should perform the noon worship (*pūja*) and, having had his lunch, he should study the "mysteries" of the texts together with those who know them.

129. Then, having once more worshiped the divine [Jina] at the time of sunset, and having performed the [six] mandatory duties, [such as confession (*pratikramaṇa*)], he should study the scriptures.

130. Then, at the proper time, the lay devotee, who is purified by remembering the deity and the teacher, should take a light sleep, generally avoiding sex.

131. After having slept, he should contemplate the real nature of a young woman's limbs, reflecting upon [the manner in which] Sthūlabhadra and other saints abstained from such an attachment [to the female body].

132. [He should think of] women as bags of leather made up of sinews that are pleasant to look at from outside, but [inside] filled with feces, impurities, marrow, phlegm, nerves, and bones.

133. If one incorrectly mistakes the inner for the outer of the woman's body, then one should save this [body as food] for vultures and jackals.

134. [One should think that,] if the god of love desires to gain victory over the entire world, why does this dull-witted [god use a woman as his weapon] and not a weapon made of a peacock's feather [which is not that full of excrement, etc., and not that difficult to obtain].

135. Alas! The whole world is harassed by this god of love, [resulting in wretched lamentation of gods, such as Brahmā, Viṣṇu, and Śiva]. One

should, therefore, think [after waking up]: "I shall uproot this thought, which is the source of all this [embracement and adoration of women]".

136. Whatever obstructing fault that may exist, [such as attachment, anger, and pride,] he should think of [its] remedy[, such as detachment, friendliness, and humility]. He does so by delighting in teachers who are free from [such] defects.

137. [The layman] who is firmly convinced that worldly existence is miserable for all living beings should, for the sake of [all] these [people], seek liberation, which has the nature of happiness.

138. [After relinquishing sleep, he should also think of] those blessed [lay-followers], like Kāmadeva, who were praised even by the Tīrthaṅkaras, and who kept to their vows even when they were subject to attacks.

139. [In Jainism], where the Jina is the deity, compassion the teaching, and the teachers those who lead you to the goal, who of unbewildered intelligence would not praise having this as the true religion?

140. [One should cultivate desires such as:] I do not want to be a Universal Monarch if I cannot have the Jina and his *dharma*. I do not mind even if I become a slave or a poor man, [as long as I may be] consecrated in the teaching of the Jina.

141. When shall I resort to the conduct of a mendicant, who is free from attachment, whose clothes are [all] old, whose body is smeared with dust, and whose mode of livelihood is like that of a bee?

142. When shall I be able to put an end to existence, abandoning the company of people of evil conduct, touching the dust of the feet of the teacher (i.e., being in his company), and practicing *yoga*?

143. When shall I be able to stand in meditation at midnight outside of the city, like a pillar, with the bulls brushing their shoulders against me[, thinking I am just a pillar]?

144. When will the leaders of the herd smell my mouth, [taking me to be a lifeless thing, when I am] seated in the woods, in the lotus posture, with the young of deer resting in my lap?

145. When shall I become someone who does not distinguish between an enemy and a friend, grass and a woman, gold and a stone, jewel and clay, liberation and worldly existence?

146. Thus one should [cultivate] desires that are the root of the creeper of supreme bliss, in order to climb the ladder of the fourteen stages of purification to the abode of liberation.

147. Even a householder who carefully observes the [prescribed] conduct regarding day and night, and who adheres to proper conduct, according to what has been said [above], will be purified.

148–152. If one is unable to perform the [six] mandatory duties, [and] if death is imminent, having undertaken [the vow of] ritual death by fasting (*saṃlekhanā*), he [then] takes new restraints. [For the implementation of ritual death], he should go where the Tīrthaṅkaras were born, renounced the world, [reached] enlightenment, and died. If he cannot go there, [he may carry out the ritual,] either in his own house, in the forest, or in a level place free from insects. Having renounced the four kinds of food, and concentrating on the holy litany, he should worship [the Jina, etc.,] [and] take refuge in the four refuges. He who is besprinkled with the ambrosia of liberation (*samādhi*) has no anticipation left, either in this world or in the next, either in life or in death. Fearless of any calamities or afflictions (*parīṣaha*), devoting himself to the worship of the Jina, he should attain death [while in meditation ([*samādhi*]-*maraṇa*), like the lay-follower Ānanda.

153–154. Having reached [heaven], he rejoices for eons as the king of the gods, or in any other superior position, as a result of the excellent rewards of [his] accumulated merits. Then, coming out of heaven, he will be reborn as a human, and having experienced [a kind of] enjoyment that is very hard to obtain, being detached [from the world, like Bharata], [and] being pure-hearted, he attains liberation within eight lifetimes.

155. Thus in brief I have explained the three proper jewels without which nobody can attain liberation.

FROM SAMANTABHADRA'S *ĀPTAMĪMĀṂSĀ*

Oneness and Separateness

24. If one maintains that things are possessed of the character "absolute nonduality," then too one would be contradicting the observed distinction between an act and the various factors-of-action connected with this act (in their capacity as the doer, object, instrument, etc., of this act); for certainly a thing cannot be produced out of itself.

25. (On maintaining the position in question) there will be no duality of the types of act (in the form of good and evil types), no duality of the types of fruit yielded by an act (in the form of happy and unhappy types), no duality of the planes of existence (in the form of this world and the world beyond), no duality of knowledge and ignorance, no duality of bondage and liberation (*mokṣa*).

26. If the doctrine of nondualism is established with the help of a probans there ought to be there the duality of probans and proban-

dum; if the doctrine is established without the help of a probans why should not the (rival) doctrine of dualism be established through a mere movement of lips (alternatively, on the mere authority of scriptural texts)?

27. There can be no nondualism without dualism being already there, just as there can be no pseudo-probans without a probans being already there; certainly, the denial of a word-denoted entity never makes sense except when the entity sought to be denied is a real something.

28. On the other hand, if one maintains that things are possessed of the character "absolute separateness," then there arises the following difficulty. Two things (sought to be declared separate) ought to be nonseparate from separateness itself (which will be an undesirable contingency for one who is out to repudiate all nonseparateness). Certainly, if separateness is separate from the things in question it should not be genuine separateness that is conceived as a quality residing in more than one object (and hence nonseparate from the objects acting as its seat).

29. If the reality of oneness (as characterizing many things) is repudiated one cannot legitimately speak of the phenomena—all genuine without a shadow of doubt—like series (of successive entities), aggregate (of simultaneous entities), similarity (between any two entities), rebirth.

30. If cognition does not share with the thing cognized even the universal character "being," both cognition and the thing cognized turn out to be something nonentitative. Certainly, in the absence of cognition how can our opponent speak of the thing cognized—whether external or internal?

31. Certain other people are of the view that words denote universal characters without possessing the capacity to describe a real particular object (distinguished by its own specific characters); and since they (on the other hand) declare the universal characters to be something nonentitative they are forced to conclude that all verbal utterance whatsoever is a falsity.

32. The enemies of the logic of *syādvāda* can also not maintain that the two (viz. "absolute nonduality" and "absolute separateness") characterize one and the same phenomenon, for such a position will be self-contradictory. And if they maintain that the phenomena that are there are absolutely indescribable, then even to say that a phenomenon is indescribable becomes an impossibility on their part.

33. Oneness and separateness as unrelated to each other are both something fictitious on account of the two sets of considerations (that

have already been offered). As a matter of fact, one and the same phenomenon is characterized by both oneness and separateness just as one and the same probans is characterized by a number of essential features (enumerated by the logicians).

34. All the phenomena of the world are one with each other insofar as they all share the universal character "being" while they are separate from each other insofar as each of them has got its own root-substance, etc. (i.e., its own root-substance, place, time, form); this is just as the speaker sometimes intends to emphasize the identity of an effect with its appropriate cause while sometimes he intends to emphasize their mutual difference (alternatively, this is just as the speaker sometimes intends to emphasize the oneness of a valid probans while sometimes he intends to emphasize its numerous essential features).

35. It is only in the case of the existing qualifications—and not the nonexisting ones—of a qualificand-possessed-of-innumerable-attributes that those who are so desirous (that is, who are desirous of emphasizing this qualification rather than that) intend to speak of this qualification and not to speak of that.

36. Difference and nondifference that are taken cognizance of by the authentic sources of knowledge are verily real and no mere appearances. On your showing, they coexist in one and the same body without coming in conflict with each other, while they become primary or secondary depending on the speaker's intention.

Permanence and Transience

37. If one maintains that things are possessed of the character "absolute permanence," then too one cannot account for the process of transformation. And when there is already an absence (i.e., an impossibility) of agentship, how can one thing be treated as an authentic source of knowledge and another thing the result yielded by this source?

38. It might be maintained that an authentic source of knowledge or an agent reveals the *vyakta* (lit. "manifest"—meaning the manifest phenomena allegedly the products of a root-substance called *prakṛti* that is therefore alternatively designated *avyakta*, or nonmanifest), just as a sense-organ does its object, and that this source of knowledge and this agent are both something permanent. But what thing can be treated as capable of undergoing a transformation on the showing of those who have not embraced the doctrine taught by you?

39. If an effect is something absolutely existent it cannot be a produced entity—just as *puruṣa*, i.e., soul (on the Sāṅkhya philosopher's

showing), is not. On the other hand, to posit the possibility of a thing undergoing transformation goes counter to the thesis that things are possessed of the character "absolute permanence."

40. Those who do not accept your (spiritual) leadership are incapable of accounting for the virtuous and sinful acts, for rebirth, for the fruits of the acts performed, for worldly bondage and liberation (*mokṣa*).

41. If one maintains that things are possessed of the character "absolute momentariness," then too rebirth, etc., remain an impossibility. Certainly, in the absence of phenomena like recognition, etc., how can there be the production of an effect, and (consequently) how can there be the reaping of fruits of the acts performed?

42. If an effect is absolutely nonexistent, then it should rather never be produced just as sky-flower is never produced; then there should rather be no fixed rule that this material cause will bring about that effect; and then there should rather be no confident feeling that this effect will be forthcoming out of that cause.

43. There can obtain no relationship of cause-effect, etc., between two entities that are (utterly) separate from one another, their mutual separateness in its turn being due to the absence of a persistent element running through the two; this is just as there is (on the momentarist's own showing) no relationship of cause-effect, etc., between two entities that belong to two different series. Moreover, there is in fact nothing like a "series" apart from the members constituting this series.

44. It might be pleaded that "series" is just a word that has been attributed in common to things that are in fact different and that therefore its employment is a case of mere usage. But why should a meaning yielded by mere usage be not a falsity? Moreover, the chief meaning of a word cannot be dubbed as a meaning yielded by mere usage, while there can be no occasion for usage unless the word concerned has got a chief meaning.

45–46. One might argue: "It is the case with any and every alleged characteristic of an entity that we are not entitled to give verbal expression to any of the following four alternatives as to the relationship between this characteristic and this entity: (i) this characteristic belongs to this entity; (ii) this characteristic does not belong to this entity; (iii) this characteristic both belongs and does not belong to this entity; (iv) this characteristic neither belongs nor does not belong to this entity. Consequently, we can also not say about a series whether it is one with its members or different from them (or both or neither)." To this we reply: "In that case you can make assertion not even to the effect that we are not entitled to give verbal expression to the four alternatives in question. Moreover, an entity that is allegedly devoid of all characteristics whatsoever is really a nonentity, for such an entity can act neither as a qualificand nor as a qualifier."

47. It is only a really existing entity-denoted-by-a-word that—when proposed to be a possessor of the root-substance, etc. (i.e., root-substance, place, time, form), that are not its own root-substance, etc.—can be subjected to a negative assertion. On the other hand, an alleged entity that is really but a nonentity can be subjected neither to a positive assertion nor to a negative one.

48. What is devoid of all characteristics whatsoever, let that be an indescribable nonentity (as posited by our rival). On the other hand, a real entity (as posited by us), too, can be treated as a nonentity when the procedure (of attributing characteristics to it) is reversed (i.e., when it is proposed that this entity possesses characteristics that are not in fact its own characteristics).

49. If all characteristics whatsoever are indescribable why is it that our rival himself goes on to speak of certain characteristics (which according to him belong to reality)? If it is replied that this kind of talk is but a mere usage, it turns out to be but a falsity, for such a thing (i.e., what is a mere usage) is just the opposite of truth.

50. We ask whether the reality is thus (being declared to be) indescribable because our rival is incapable of describing it, or because it does not exist, or because our rival has no knowledge about it. Of these the first and third alternatives should not be acceptable to our rival. Why then does he resort to camouflage and not clearly state his position (viz. that the reality is indescribable because it does not exist)?

51. On our rival's position the mind that kills has not willed to kill, one that has willed to kill does not kill, one that suffers bondage has neither willed to kill nor killed, one that attains liberation (*mokṣa*) has not suffered bondage.

52. Since it is our rival's position that destruction is causeless, he should be ready to concede that the killer is not the cause of killing and that the (celebrated) eightfold path is not the cause of liberation (*mokṣa*) conceived (by our rival himself) in the form of a destruction of the series of mental states.

53. It might be maintained that the activity of a cause is required in order to bring into existence a dissimilar effect (i.e., an effect dissimilar from the one that had occurred at the same place but at the immediately preceding moment). But then the relation of this cause should be

the same to both the coming into existence of the effect in question and the going out of existence of the effect of the preceding moment, for the two processes (viz. the coming into existence of the effect in question and the going out of existence of the effect of the preceding moment) are not different from one another; this is just as the entities that are internally connected do not have different causes.

54. Thus on our rival's position the series and the aggregates, being mere usages, turn out to be something nonentitative (strictly speaking, unoriginated); of such alleged entities there can certainly be no continuation, origination, and cessation, just as there can be no continuation, etc., of the horns of a donkey.

55. The enemies of the logic of *syādvāda* can also not maintain that the two (viz. "absolute permanence" and "absolute momentariness") characterize one and the same phenomenon, for such a position will be self-contradictory. And if they maintain that the phenomena that are there are absolutely indescribable, then even to say that a phenomenon is indescribable becomes an impossibility on their part.

56. A real is something permanent, because it is subject to recognition while the (indispensable) uninterruptedness of an object of recognition cannot be accidental; at the same time, a real is something momentary because it is different at different times. In the absence of these features (viz. permanence and momentariness) in a real there would arise the undesirable contingency of one state of cognition never being replaced by another one. This is your position.

57. An entity neither originates nor ceases so far as its universal character is concerned, for the continuation of this universal character is an obvious fact; on the other hand, an entity originates as well as ceases so far as its particular characters are concerned. This is how on your position a real entity is characterized by the coexistence of origination, etc. (i.e., of origination, cessation, continuation).

58. The production of an effect is the same thing as the destruction of the cause of this effect, for the two (i.e., the production of an effect and the destruction of the cause of this effect) are invariably found to go together even if they are mutually distinguishable through their respective definitions. And inasmuch as there is here a continuation of the concerned universal character, etc. (i.e., of the concerned universal character, the concerned numerical identity, the concerned inherent capacity, and so forth), the two are not independent of each other, an independence that would have reduced them to the status of (a nonentity like) sky-flower.

59. When there occur three phenomena (viz. that of destruction [of a jar], that of production [of potsherds], and that of continuation [of gold]), three persons (viz. one desirous of getting a jar, one desirous of getting potsherds, and one desirous of getting gold) respectively experience three feelings (viz. that of sorrow, that of joy, and that of neutrality); and such a behavior on their part is well established.

60. One who has taken a vow to feed himself on nothing save milk does not partake of curd, one who has taken a vow to feed himself on nothing save curd does not partake of milk, while one who has taken a vow not to partake of any dairy product partakes of neither milk nor curd; hence it follows that a real entity is possessed of three characters (viz. origination, cessation, and continuation).

Difference and Identity

61. If one maintains that an effect is absolutely distinct from its cause, a quality is absolutely distinct from the thing qualified by this quality, and a universal is absolutely distinct from the particular possessing this universal(, one would be faced with the following difficulties).

62. An effect cannot reside in what are many, for it is possessed of no parts; alternatively, one would be forced to concede that this effect is itself of the form of a number of entities (which is an undesirable contingency). Or one might concede that this effect is possessed of parts, but then it will no more be a single entity (which again is an undesirable contingency). These are the difficulties that a certain non-Jaina position has to face on the question of the mode of an effect's residence in its cause.

63. On the rival's position it should be possible for an effect to occupy a place and a time that are different from those of its cause, just as two externally connected physical substances may occupy two different places and two different times. Nay, since both an effect and its cause are corporeal entities it should never be possible for them to occupy one and the same place.

64. It might be pleaded that there obtains the relation of substratum–superstratum between two entities that are related through *samavāya*-relation and that therefore they cannot exist in independence from each other. To this we reply that it is not proper to posit a relation that is supposed to relate two entities by existing alongside them but which is itself not related to them (a description that fits the *samavāya*-relation posited by the rival in question).

65. Since a particular universal as well as the *samavāya*-relation exist in their entirety in some one entity (acting as their substratum), it follows that they ought to exist nowhere else inasmuch as an entity to act as their substratum can be available nowhere else; but then what happens (to the universal in question and to the *samavāya*-relation) when an old entity perishes or when a new entity comes into existence?

66. On the rival's position there obtains absolutely no relation between a universal and the *samavāya*-relation, nor is the entity alleged to be the substratum of both related to either; thus all these three (viz. the universal in question, the *samavāya*-relation, and the entity in question) turn out to be nonentities like sky-flower.

67. If one maintains that an effect is absolutely nondistinct from atoms (that are to act as its cause), then there arises the difficulty that these atoms should remain as much unrelated after their mutual conjunction (that is to give rise to the effect in question) as they were in the early state of mutual disjunction; moreover, in that case the four basic elements (viz. earth, water, fire, air) will turn out to be but illusory appearances.

68. And when their effects (viz. the basic elements earth, water, fire, air) thus turn out to be illusory appearances, these atoms themselves follow suit, for the nature of cause is inferred from that of its effect. Again, in the absence of all cause and all effect there also do not exist qualities, universals, etc., supposedly residing in a cause or an effect.

69. If an effect and its cause are declared to be one, then either of them must be nonexistent; but then the other partner too must be nonexistent inasmuch as the two invariably go together. Moreover, in that case (i.e., if an effect and its cause are declared to be one) the twoness of an effect and its cause will remain unaccounted for; and if it is said that this twoness is a mere usage, it turns out to be but a falsity.

70. The enemies of the logic of *syādvāda* can also not maintain that the two (viz. "absolute distinctness" and "absolute nondistinctness") characterize one and the same phenomenon, for such a position will be self-contradictory. And if they maintain that the phenomena that are there are absolutely indescribable, then even to say that a phenomenon is indescribable becomes an impossibility on their part.

71–72. A substance and its mode are one with each other insofar as they are invariably found to go together, insofar as a substance is found to undergo transformation that is peculiar to itself, insofar as a substance is a possessor of such capacities as it is found to exercise. On the other hand, they are also different from each other insofar as they have got different designations, different numerical properties, different definitions, different utilities, and so on and so forth; however, they are not different from each other in an absolute fashion.

NOTES

1. Hermann Jacobi, *Gaina Sutras*, part II: *The Uttaradhyayana Satra, The Satraritanga Sutra* (Delhi: Motilal Banarsidass, 1995); Jarl Charpentier, *The Uttarāyayanasūtra: Being the First Mūlasūtra of the Svetāmbara Jains* (Delhi: Ajay Book Service, 1980), 93–94.
2. See Paul Dundas, *The Jains*, 2nd ed. (London: Routledge, 2002), 107, for more on Kundakunda's dating.
3. Ibid., 132–134, for more on Haribhadra's dating.
4. The term *ātman,* not *jīva*, was used in the oldest canonical texts and by some Digambara writers.

FURTHER READING

Dundas, Paul. *The Jains.* 2nd ed. London: Routledge, 2002.

Jaini, Padmanabh S. *The Jaina Path of Purification.* Berkeley: University of California Press, 1979.

Malvania, Dalsukh, and Jayendra Soni. *Jain Philosophy, Part 1.* Delhi: Motilal Banarsidass, 2007.

Matilal, Bimal K. *The Central Philosophy of Jainism (Anekānta-Vāda).* Ahmedabad: L. D. Institute of Indology, 1981.

——. "The Jaina Contribution to Logic." In *The Character of Logic in India,* ed. Jonardon Ganeri and Heeramann Tiwari, 127–139. Albany: State University of New York Press, 1998.

Padmarajiah, Y. J. *A Comparative Study of the Jain Theories of Reality and Knowledge.* Delhi: Motilal Banarsidass, 1963.

Shah, Nagin J. *Jaina Theory of Multiple Facets of Reality and Truth.* Delhi: Motilal Banarsidass, 2000.

Sharma, Chandradhar. *A Critical Survey of Indian Philosophy.* London: Rider, 1960.

Part II. FIVE ĀSTIKA (ORTHODOX) SCHOOLS

6

NYĀYA

HISTORY

The Nyāya system holds that *mokṣa* (liberation) from *saṃsāra* (the cycle of birth and rebirth) is brought about through knowledge of the material world. For this reason, they believe that one must first have a complete understanding of what constitutes knowledge and how it is obtained. Such knowledge is soteriologically efficacious. While its sister school, Vaiśeṣika, offers a detailed ontology, the Nyāya school offers a corresponding and complementary epistemology. In addition to producing texts on specific epistemic issues, the Nyāya school put forth manuals for debate in which they addressed theories about syllogism and rhetoric.

Akṣapāda Gautama (250–450 C.E.) is the purported author of the *Nyāya Sūtras*, the foundational text for the school. This text seems to be a compilation of several texts with a variety of authors, thus making Gautama's authorship uncertain. The *Nyāya Sūtras* gave rise to two well-known commentaries: Vātsyāyana's *Nyāya-bhāṣya* (ca. 350–450 C.E.) and Uddyotakara's *Nyāya-vārttika* (sixth century C.E.). Jayanta Bhaṭṭa's *Nyāyamañjari* (ca. 900 C.E.) is an independent treatise in which the author examines Buddhist and Mīmāṃsā theories. The Navya-Nyāya (new-logic) school had emerged from the Nyāya school by the fourteenth century, when Gaṅgeśa authored his *Tattvacintāmaṇi* (*The Jewel of Reflection on Reality*). Gaṅgeśa and his followers put forth new and refined methods for argumentation.

EPISTEMOLOGY

The Nyāya school accepts four *pramāṇas* (sources of valid knowledge): *pratyakṣa* (perception), *anumāna* (inference), *upamāna* (comparison), and *śabda* (testimony). Among these, *pratyakṣa* is believed to be the principal *pramāṇa* since all others are dependent upon it.

The presentation of *anumāna* in the *Nyāya Sūtras* became the standard form of inference found among the schools of South Asian philosophy. The customary example that has been used to illustrate the components of the inference is the conclusion that there is fire on the mountain if smoke is observed. Gautama breaks the syllogism down into five components:

1. *pratijñā* (proposition): This mountain has fire.
2. *hetu* (reason): Because it has smoke.
3. *udāharaṇa* (example): Wherever there is smoke, there is fire, just as in a kitchen.
4. *upanaya* (application): This mountain is smoky.
5. *nigamana* (conclusion): Therefore, this mountain has fire.

The inference must contain the following four terms:

1. The mountain is the *pakṣa* (the subject).
2. "Fire possessing" is the *sādhya* (property to be proven).
3. "Smoke-possessing" is the *hetu* (use here different from that above).
4. The kitchen is the *sapakṣa* (a similar instance confirming the concomitance).

The *vyāpti* is the universal concomitance (here, between fire and smoke). In this example, it is the universal that wherever one sees smoke, one can conclude that fire must also be present. Hence the inference, "where there is smoke, there is fire."

Several chapters of the *Nyāya Sūtras* are devoted to in-depth analyses of the *hetvābhāsas* (types of fallacious reasoning) and other errors that can occur in the composition of an *anumāna* as well as the rules for argument. These include the types of debates and the context within which they take place. The *Nyāya Sūtras* were, in part, a dialectical handbook.

Gautama proposed sixteen topics that must be known by aspirants. These are *pramāṇas* (sources of valid knowledge); *prameyas* (valid objects of knowledge); *saṃśaya* (doubt); *prayojana* (purpose); *dṛṣṭānta* (example); *siddhānta* (established tenet); *avayava* (members); *tarka* (reasoning); *nirṇaya* (ascertainment); *vāda* (discussion); *jalpa* (wrangling); *vitaṇḍā* (cavil); *het-*

vābhāsa (fallacious reasoning); *chala* (quibble); *jāti* (futility); and *nigrahasthāna* (occasion for rebuke).

ONTOLOGY

According to the realist Nyāya school, the universe is real and objects exist whether they are perceived or not. The Nyāya school accepts the categories proposed by their Vaiśeṣika counterparts, although these are here subsumed under *pramāṇa* and *prameya*. There are, then, *ātman* (self), *śarira* (body), *indriyas* (senses), *arthas* (object of the senses), *buddhi* (consciousness), *manas* (inner sense organ), *pravṛtti* (activity), *doṣa* (fault), *pretyabhāva* (rebirth), *phala* (fruit), *duḥkha* (pain), and *apavarga* (release from pain). By itself the *ātman* is unconscious and unintelligent. When *arthas* come into contact with the *indriyas* the information is related to the *ātman* via the *manas*. It is then that the *ātman* cognizes. Knowledge is merely an attribute of the *ātman* and not essential to it.

SOTERIOLOGY

The goal of the Nyāya school is to realize that the *ātman* is not identical with the *śarira*, the *buddhi*, and the *manas*. Rather, it is distinct from, and can be separated from, these three, from any cognition, and from knowledge, and can attain a state of unconsciousness. This is made possible through a complete understanding of Nyāya proposed logic, ontology, and epistemology. *Mithya-jñāna* (false knowledge) occurs when the *ātman* identifies with the *śarira*, the *buddhi*, and the *manas* and the arising cognitions, experiences pain, has desires, accumulates *karma*, and is reborn in the cycle of *karma-saṃsāra*. Liberation is first from the *śarira*, etc., then from consciousness, and subsequently from the cycle of birth and rebirth. They call this unconscious state *apavarga*.

THE TEXTS

There are several selections here from the *Nyāya Sūtras*. *Adhyāya* (book) 1, *āhnika* (chapter) 1 concerns the subject matter and purpose of the *Nyāya*

Sūtras, and the *pramāṇas*, the *prameyas*, and the nature of *nyāya* (argument). The next set is from *adhyāya* 2, *āhnika* 1 and concerns the validity of the *pramāṇas*, specifically, *pratyakṣa* (perception).

The second selection is from the *Nyāya-vārttika* of Uddyotakara (seventh century C.E.). The *Nyāya-vārttika* is a commentary on Vātsyāyana's *Nyāya-bhāṣya*, which is itself a commentary on the *Nyāya Sūtras*. This selection concerns arguments against the Yogācāra school of Buddhism, which puts forth an idealist position that all that is perceived is a projection of the mind and, moreover, that there are no objects external to the mind.

FROM GAUTAMA'S *NYĀYA SŪTRAS*

Book 1, Chapter 1

1. "Supreme felicity" is attained by the knowledge about the true nature of the sixteen categories: means of right knowledge (*pramāṇa*), object of right knowledge (*prameya*), doubt (*saṃśaya*), purpose (*prayojana*), familiar instance (*dṛṣṭānta*), established tenet (*siddhānta*), members (*avayava*), confutation (*tarka*), ascertainment (*nirṇaya*), discussion (*vāda*), wrangling (*jalpa*), cavil (*vitaṇḍa*), fallacy (*hetvābhāsa*), quibble (*chala*), futility (*jāti*), and occasion for rebuke (*nigrahasthāna*).

"Knowledge about the true nature of the sixteen categories" means true knowledge by the "enunciation," "definition," and "critical examination" of the categories. Book 1 (of the *Nyāya Sūtra*) treats of "enunciation" and "definition," while the remaining four books are reserved for "critical examination." The attainment of supreme felicity is preceded by the knowledge of four things: (1) that which is fit to be abandoned (viz. pain); (2) that which produces what is fit to be abandoned (viz. misapprehension, etc.); (3) complete destruction of what is fit to be abandoned; and (4) the means of destroying what is fit to be abandoned (viz. true knowledge).

2. Pain, birth, activity, faults, and misapprehension—on the successive annihilation of these in the reverse order, there follows *release*.

Misapprehension, faults, activity, birth, and pain—these in their uninterrupted course constitute the "world." Release, which consists in the soul's getting rid of the world, is the condition of supreme felicity marked by perfect tranquility and not tainted by any defilement. A person, by the true knowledge of the sixteen categories, is able to remove his misapprehension. When this is done, his faults (viz. affection, aversion, and stupidity) disappear. He is then no longer subject to any activity and is consequently freed from transmigration and pains. This is the way in which his release is effected and supreme felicity secured.

3. Perception, inference, comparison, and word (verbal testimony)—these are the *means of right knowledge.*

[The Cārvākas admit only one means of right knowledge, viz. perception (*pratyakṣa*); the Vaiśeṣikas and Buddhas admit two, viz. perception and inference (*anumāna*); the Sāṃkhyas admit three, viz. perception, inference, and verbal testimony (*āgama* or *śabda*); while the Naiyāyikas, whose fundamental work is the *Nyāya Sūtra*, admit four, viz. perception, inference, verbal testimony, and comparison (*upamāna*). The Prābhākaras admit a fifth means of right knowledge called presumption (*arthāpatti*), the Bhāṭṭas and Vedāntins admit a sixth, viz. nonexistence (*abhāva*), and the Purāṇikas recognize a seventh and eight means of right knowledge, named probability (*sambhava*) and rumor (*aitihya*).]

4. *Perception* is that knowledge which arises from the contact of a sense with its object, and which is determinate, unnameable, and nonerratic.

Determinate: This epithet distinguishes perception from indeterminate knowledge; as, for instance, a man looking from a distance cannot ascertain whether there is smoke or dust.

Unnameable: Signifies that the knowledge of a thing derived through perception has no connection with the name that the thing bears.

Nonerratic: In summer the sun's rays coming in contact with earthly heat quiver and appear to the eyes of men as water. The knowledge of water derived in this way is not perception. To eliminate such cases the epithet "nonerratic" has been used.

[This aphorism may also be translated as follows: *Perception* is knowledge and which arises from the contact of a sense with its object and which is nonerratic, being either indeterminate (*nirvikalpaka*, as "this is something") or determinate (*savikalpaka*, as "this is a Brāhmaṇa").]

5. *Inference* is knowledge that is preceded by perception, and is of three kinds, viz. a priori, a posteriori, and "commonly seen."

A priori is the knowledge of effect derived from the perception of its cause; e.g., one seeing clouds infers that there will be rain.

A posteriori is the knowledge of cause derived from the perception of its effects, e.g., one seeing a river swollen infers that there was rain.

"*Commonly seen*" is the knowledge of one thing derived from the perception of another thing with which it is commonly seen, e.g., one seeing a beast possessing horns, infers that it possesses also a tail, or one seeing smoke on a hill infers that there is fire on it.

6. *Comparison* is the knowledge of a thing through its similarity to another thing previously well known.

A man, hearing from a forester that a *bos gavaeus* is like a cow, resorts to a forest where he sees an animal like a cow. Having recollected what he heard he institutes a comparison, by which he arrives at the conviction that the animal he sees is *bos gavaeus*: This is knowledge derived through comparison. Some hold that comparison is not a separate means of knowledge, for when one notices the likeness of a cow in a strange animal one really performs an act of perception. In reply, it is urged that we cannot deny comparison as a separate means of knowledge, for how does otherwise the name *bos gavaeus* signify the general notion of the animal called *bos gavaeus*? That the name *bos gavaeus* signifies one and all members of the *bos gavaeus* class is not a result of perception, but the consequence of a distinct knowledge, called comparison.

7. *Word (verbal testimony)* is the instructive assertion of a reliable person.

A reliable person is one—maybe a *ṛṣi, ārya*, or *mleccha*—who was an expert in a certain matter and is willing to communicate his experiences of it.

[Suppose a young man coming to the side of a river cannot ascertain whether the river is fordable or not, and immediately an old experienced man of the locality, who has no enmity against him, comes and tells him that the river is easily fordable: the word of the old man is to be accepted as a means of right knowledge called "verbal testimony".]

8. It is of two kinds, viz. that which refers to *matter which is seen*, and that which refers to *matter which is not seen*.

The first kind involves matter that can be actually verified. Though we are incapable of verifying the matter involved in the second kind, we can somehow ascertain it by means of inference.

[*Matter which is seen*, e.g., a physician's assertion that physical strength is gained by taking butter. *Matter which is not seen*, e.g., a religious teacher's assertion that one conquers heaven by performing horse-sacrifices.]

9. Soul, body, senses, objects of sense, intellect, mind, activity, fault, transmigration, fruit, pain, and release—are the *objects of right knowledge*.

The objects of right knowledge are also enumerated as substance, quality, action, generality, particularity, intimate relation, [and nonexistence, which are the technicalities of the Vaiśeṣika philosophy.]

10. Desire, aversion, volition, pleasure, pain, and intelligence are the marks of the soul.

[These abide in the soul, or rather are the qualities of the substance called soul.]

11. *Body* is the site of gesture, senses, and sentiments.

Body is the site of *gesture*, inasmuch as it strives to reach what is desirable and to avoid what is hateful. It is also the site of *senses*, for the latter act well or ill, according as the former is in good or bad order. *Sentiments* that comprise pleasure and pain are also located in the body that experiences them.

12. Nose, tongue, eye, skin, and ear are the senses produced from elements.

None is of the same nature as earth, tongue as water, eye as light, skin as air, and ear as ether.

13. Earth, water, light, air, and ether—these are the *elements.*

14. Smell, taste, color, touch, and sound are *objects of the senses* and qualities of the earth, etc.

Smell is the object of nose and the prominent quality of earth, taste is the object of tongue and quality of water, color is the object of eye and quality of fire, touch is the object of skin and quality of air, and sound is the object of ear and quality of ether.

15. *Intellect,* apprehension, and knowledge—these are not different from one another.

16. The mark of the *mind* is that there do not arise (in the soul) more acts of knowledge than one at a time.

It is impossible to perceive two things simultaneously. Perception does not arise merely from the contact of a sense-organ with its object, but it requires also a conjunction of the mind. Now, the mind, which is an atomic substance, cannot be conjoined with more than one sense-organ at a time, hence there cannot occur more acts of perception than one at one time.

17. *Activity* is that which makes the voice, mind, and body begin their action.

There are three kinds of action, viz. *vocal, mental,* and *bodily*, each of which may be subdivided as good or bad.

Bodily actions that are *bad* are: (1) killing, (2) stealing, and (3) committing adultery.

Bodily actions that are *good* are: (1) giving, (2) protecting, and (3) serving.

Vocal actions that are *bad* are: (1) telling a lie, (2) using harsh language, (3) slandering, and (4) indulging in frivolous talk.

Vocal actions that are *good* are: (1) speaking the truth, (2) speaking what is useful, (3) speaking what is pleasant, and (4) reading sacred books.

Mental actions that are *bad* are: (1) malice, (2) covetousness, and (3) skepticism.

Mental actions that are *good* are: (1) compassion, (2) refraining from covetousness, and (3) devotion.

18. *Faults* have the characteristic of causing activity.

The faults are affection, aversion, and stupidity.

19. *Transmigration* means rebirths.

Transmigration is the series of births and deaths. Birth is the connection of soul with body, sense-organs, mind, intellect, and sentiments, while death is the soul's separation from them.

20. *Fruit* is the thing produced by activity and faults.

Fruit consists in the enjoyment of pleasure or suffering of pain. All activity and faults end in producing pleasure, which is acceptable, and pain, which is fit only to be avoided.

21. *Pain* has the characteristic of causing uneasiness.

Pain is affliction that everyone desires to avoid. The aphorism may also be translated as follows: "Pain is the mark of hindrance to the soul."

22. *Release* is the absolute deliverance from pain.

A soul that is no longer subject to transmigration is freed from all pains. Transmigration, which consists in the soul's leaving one body and taking another, is the cause of its ongoing pleasure and pain. The soul attains release as soon as there is an end of the body, and, consequently, of pleasure and pain. Those are mistaken who maintain that release enables the soul not only to get rid of all pains, but also to attain eternal pleasure, for pleasure is as impermanent as pain and the body.

23. *Doubt,* which is a conflicting judgment about the precise character of an object, arises from the recognition of properties common to many objects, or of properties not common to any of the objects, from conflicting testimony, and from irregularity of perception and nonperception.

Doubt is of five kinds, according as it arises from: (1) *recognition of common properties,* e.g., seeing in the twilight a tall object we cannot decide whether it is a man or a post, for the property of tallness belongs to both; (2) *recognition of properties not common,* e.g., hearing a sound, one questions whether it is eternal or not, for the property of soundness abides neither in man, beast, etc., which are noneternal, nor in atoms, which are eternal; (3) *conflicting testimony,* e.g., merely by study one cannot decide whether the soul exists, for one system of philosophy affirms that it does, while another system states that it does not; (4) *irregularity of perception,* e.g., we perceive water in the tank, where it really exists, but water appears also to exist in the mirage, where it really does not exist—a question arises whether water is perceived only when it actually exists, or even when it does not exist; (5) *irregularity of nonperception,* e.g., we do not perceive water in the radish where it really exists, and also on dry land where it does not exist—a question arises whether water is not perceived only when it does not exist, or also when it does exist.

24. *Purpose* is that with an eye to which one proceeds to act.

Purpose refers to the thing which one endeavors to attain or avoid.

[A man collects fuel for the purpose of cooking his food.]

25. *A familiar instance* is the thing about which an ordinary man and an expert entertain the same opinion.

[With regard to the general proposition "wherever there is smoke there is fire," the familiar instance is a kitchen in which fire and smoke abide together, to the satisfaction of an ordinary man as well as an acute investigator.]

26. *An established tenet* is a dogma resting on the authority of a certain school, hypothesis, or implication.

27. The tenet is of four kinds owing to the distinction between a dogma of all the schools, a dogma peculiar to some school, a hypothetical dogma, and an implied dogma.

28. *A dogma of all the schools* is a tenet that is not opposed by any school and is claimed by at least one school.

The five elements (viz. earth, water, light, air, and ether), the five objects of sense (viz. smell, taste, color, touch, and sound), etc., are tenets that are accepted by all the schools.

29. *A dogma peculiar to some schools* is a tenet that is accepted by similar schools, but rejected by opposite schools.

"A thing cannot come into existence out of nothing"—this is a peculiar dogma of the Sāṃkhyas. [The eternity of sound is a peculiar dogma of the Mīmāṃsakas.]

30. *An hypothetical dogma* is a tenet that, if accepted, leads to the acceptance of another tenet.

"There is a soul apart from the senses, because it can recognize one and the same object by seeing and touching." If you accept this tenet you must also have accepted the following: (1) that the senses are more than one, (2) that each of the senses has its particular object, (3) that the soul derives its knowledge through the channels of the senses, (4) that a substance that is distinct from its qualities is the abode of them, etc.

31. *An implied dogma* is a tenet that is not explicitly declared as such, but that follows from the examination of particulars concerning it.

The discussion of whether sound is eternal or noneternal presupposes that it is a substance. "That sound is a substance" is here an implied dogma. [The mind has nowhere been stated in the *Nyāya Sūtra* to be a sense-organ, but it follows from the particulars examined concerning it that it is so.]

32. *The members* (of a syllogism) are preposition, reason, example, application, and conclusion.

[1. *Proposition*: This hill is fiery,
2. *Reason*: Because it is smoky,
3. *Example*: Whatever is smoky is fiery, as a kitchen,
4. *Application*: So is this hill (smoky),
5. *Conclusion*: Therefore this hill is fiery.]

Some lay down *five more members* as follows:

1a. *Inquiry as to the proposition* (*jijñāsā*): Is this hill fiery in all its parts, or in a particular part?

2a. *Questioning the reason* (*saṃśaya*): That which you call smoke may be nothing but vapor.

3a. *Capacity of the example to warrant the conclusion* (*śakyaprāpti*): Is it true that smoke is always a concomitant of fire? In a kitchen there are of course both smoke and fire, but in a red-hot iron-ball there is no smoke.

4a. *Purpose for drawing the conclusion* (*prayojana*): Purpose consists in the determination of the true conditions of the hill, in order to ascertain whether it is such that one can approach it, or such that one should avoid it, or such that one should maintain an attitude of indifference towards it.

4b. *Dispelling all questions* (*saṃśayavyudāsa*): It is beyond all question that the hill is smoky, and that smoke is an invariable-concomitant of fire.

33. A *proposition* is the declaration of what is to be established.

Sound is noneternal—this is a proposition.

34. The *reason* is the means for establishing what is to be established through the *homogeneous* or affirmative character of the example.

Proposition: Sound is noneternal,

Reason: Because it is produced,

Example (*homogeneous*): Whatever is produced is noneternal, as a pot.

The example "pot" possesses the same character as is implied in the reason, viz. "being produced," inasmuch as both are noneternal.

35. Likewise through *heterogeneous* or *negative* character.

Proposition: Sound is noneternal,

Reason: Because it is produced,

Example (*heterogeneous*): Whatever is not noneternal is not produced, as the soul.

The example "soul" possesses a character heterogeneous to that which is implied in the reason, viz. "being produced," inasmuch as one is eternal and the other noneternal.

36. A *homogeneous* (or *affirmative*) *example* is a familiar instance that is known to possess the property to be established, and that implies that this property is invariably contained in the reason given.

Proposition: Sound is noneternal,

Reason: Because it is produced,

Homogeneous example: Whatever is produced is noneternal, as a pot.

Here "pot" is a familiar instance that possesses the property of noneternality and implies that whatever is "produced" is attended by the same property (noneternality).

37. A *heterogeneous* (or *negative*) *example* is a familiar instance that is known to be devoid of the property to be established and that implies that the absence of this property is invariably rejected in the reason given.

Proposition: Sound is noneternal,

Reason: Because it is produced,

Heterogeneous example: Whatever is not noneternal is not produced, as the soul.

Here the "soul" is a familiar instance that is known to be devoid of the property of noneternality and implies that if anything were produced, it would necessarily be deprived of the quality of eternality, i.e., "being produced" and "eternal" are incompatible epithets.

38. *Application* is a winding up, with reference to the example, of what is to be established as being so or not so.

Application is of two kinds: (1) *affirmative* and (2) *negative*. The affirmative application, which is expressed by the word "so," occurs when the example is of an affirmative character. The negative, which is expressed by the phrase "not so," occurs when the example is of a negative character.

Proposition: Sound is noneternal,

Reason: Because it is produced,

Example: Whatever is produced is noneternal, as a pot,

Affirmative application: So is sound (produced),

Conclusion: Therefore sound is noneternal.

Or:

Proposition: Sound is noneternal,

Reason: Because it is produced,

Example: Whatever is eternal is not produced, as the soul,

Negative application: Sound is not so (i.e., sound is not not-produced),

Conclusion: Therefore sound is not eternal.

39. *Conclusion* is the restating of the proposition, after the reason has been mentioned.

Conclusion is the confirmation of the proposition, after the reason and the example have been mentioned.

Proposition: Sound is noneternal,

Reason: Because it is produced,

Example: Whatever is produced is noneternal, as a pot,

Application: So is sound (produced).

Conclusion: Therefore sound is noneternal.

40. *Confutation*, which is carried on for ascertaining the real character of a thing of which the character is not known, is reasoning

that reveals the character by showing the absurdity of all contrary characters.

Is the soul eternal or noneternal? Here the real character of the soul, viz. whether it is eternal or non-eternal, is not known. In ascertaining the character, we reason as follows: if the soul were noneternal, it would be impossible for it to enjoy the fruits of its own actions, to undergo transmigration, and to attain final release. But such a conclusion is absurd: such possibilities are known to belong to the soul—therefore, we must admit that the soul is eternal.

41. *Ascertainment* is the removal of doubt, and the determination of a question, by hearing two opposite sides.

A person wavers and doubts if certain statements are advanced to him by one of two parties, but opposed by the other party. His doubt is not removed until by the application of reason he can vindicate either of the parties. The process by which the vindication is effected is called *ascertainment*. Ascertainment is not, however, in all cases preceded by doubt; for instance, in the case of perception things are ascertained directly. So also we ascertain things directly by the authority of scriptures or through discussion. But in the case of investigation, doubt must precede ascertainment.

Book 1, Chapter 2

42. *Discussion* is the adoption of one of two opposing sides. What is adopted is analyzed in the form of five members, and defended by the aid of any of the means of right knowledge, while its opposite is assailed by confutation, without deviation from the established tenets.

[*A dialogue* or *disputation* (*kathā*) is the adoption of a side by a disputant and its opposite by his opponent. It is of three kinds: *discussion,* which aims at ascertaining the truth, *wrangling,* which aims at gaining victory, and *cavil,* which aims at finding mere faults. A *discutient* is one who engages himself in a disputation as a means of seeking the truth.]

An instance of discussion is given below:

Discutient: There is soul.

Opponent: There is no soul.

Discutient: Soul is existent (*proposition*). Because it is an abode of consciousness (*reason*). Whatever is not existent, is not an abode of consciousness, as a hare's horn (*negative example*). Soul is not so, that is, soul is an abode of consciousness (*negative application*). Therefore soul is existent (*conclusion*).

Opponent: Soul is nonexistent (*proposition*). Because, etc., . . .

Discutient: The scripture that is a verbal testimony declares the existence of soul.

Opponent: . . .

Discutient: If there were no soul, it would not be possible to apprehend one and the same object, through sight and touch.

Opponent: . . .

Discutient: The doctrine of soul harmonizes well with the various tenets which we hold, viz. that there are eternal things, that everybody enjoys pleasure or suffers pain, according to his own actions, etc. Therefore, there is soul.

[The discussion will be considerably lengthened if the opponent happens to be a Buddhist, who does not admit the authority of scripture and holds that there are no eternal things, etc.]

43. *Wrangling*, which aims at gaining victory, is the defense or attack of a proposition in the manner aforesaid, by quibbles, futilities, and other processes that deserve rebuke.

A *wrangler* is one who, engaged in a disputation, aims only at victory, being indifferent whether the arguments he employs support his own contention or that of his opponent, provided that he can make out a pretext for bragging that he has taken an active part in the disputation.

44. *Cavil* is a kind of wrangling that consists in mere attacks on the opposite side.

A *caviller* does not endeavor to establish anything, but confines himself to mere carping at the arguments of his opponent.

45. *Fallacies of a reason* are the erratic, the contradictory, the equal to the question, the unproved, and the mistimed.

46. The *erratic* is a reason that leads to more conclusions than one.

An instance of the *erratic* reason is given below:

Proposition: Sound is eternal,

Erratic reason: Because it is intangible,

Example: Whatever is intangible is eternal, as atoms,

Application: So is sound (intangible),

Conclusion: Therefore sound is eternal.

Again:

Proposition: Sound is noneternal,

Erratic reason: Because it is intangible,

Example: Whatever is intangible is noneternal, as intellect,

Application: So is sound (intangible).

Conclusion: Therefore sound is noneternal.

Here from the reason there have been drawn two opposite conclusions: that sound is eternal, and that sound is noneternal. The reason or middle term is erratic when it is not pervaded by the major term, that is, when there is no universal connection between the major term and the middle term, as pervader and pervaded. "Intangible" is pervaded neither by "eternal" nor by "noneternal." In fact, there is no universal connection between "intangible" and "eternal" or "noneternal."

47. The *contradictory* is a reason that opposes what is to be established.

Proposition: A pot is produced,

Contradictory reason: Because it is eternal.

Here the reason is contradictory, because that which is eternal is never produced.

48. *Equal to the question* is the reason that provokes the very question for the solution of which it was employed.

Proposition: Sound is noneternal,

Reason that is equal to the question: Because it is not possessed of the attribute of eternality.

"Noneternal" is the same as "not possessed of the attribute of eternality." In determining the question, whether sound is noneternal, the reason given is that sound is noneternal, or, in other words, the reason begs the question.

49. The *unproved* is a reason that stands in need of proof, in the same way as the proposition does.

Proposition: Shadow is a substance,

Unproved reason: Because it possesses motion.

Here, unless it is actually proved that shadow possesses motion, we cannot accept it as the reason for the proposition that shadow is a substance. Just as the proposition stands in need of proof, so does the reason itself. It is possible that the motion belongs to the person who causes that obstruction of light which is called shadow.

50. The *mistimed* is a reason that is adduced when the time is passed in which it might hold good.

Proposition: Sound is durable.

Mistimed reason: Because it is manifested by union, as a color.

The color of a jar is manifested when the jar comes into union with a lamp, but the color existed before the union took place, and will continue to exist after the union has ceased. Similarly, the sound of a drum is manifested when the drum comes into union with a rod, and the sound must, after the analogy of the color, be presumed to have existed before the union took place, and to continue to exist after the union has ceased. Hence, sound is durable. The reason adduced here is mistimed, because the manifestation of sound does not take place at the time when the drum comes into union with the rod, but at a subsequent moment when the union has ceased. In the case of color, however, the manifestation takes place just at the time when the jar comes into union with the lamp. Because the time of their manifestation is different, the analogy between color and sound is not complete; therefore, the reason is mistimed.

Some interpret the aphorism as follows: The *mistimed* is the reason that is adduced in a wrong order among the five members, for instance, as, if the reason is stated before the proposition. But this interpretation, according to Vātsyāyana, is wrong; for a word bears its legitimate connection with another word (in a Sanskrit sentence) even if they are placed at a distance from each other, and, on the other hand, even the closest proximity is of no use if the words are disconnected in their sense. Moreover, the placing of members in a wrong order is noticed in the *Nyāya Sūtra* as a *nigrahasthāna* (occasion for rebuke), called *aprāpta-kāla* (inopportune).

51. *Quibble* is the opposition offered to a proposition by the assumption of an alternative meaning.

52. It is of *three* kinds: quibble in respect of a term, quibble in respect of a genus, and quibble in respect of a metaphor.

53. *Quibble in respect of a term* consists in willfully taking the term in a sense other than that intended by a speaker who has happened to use it ambiguously.

A speaker says: "This boy is *nava-kambala* (possessed of a new blanket)."

A quibbler replies: "This boy is not certainly *nava-kambala* (possessed of nine blankets), for he has only one blanket."

Here the word *nava*, which is ambiguous, was used by the speaker in the sense of "new," but has been willfully taken by the quibbler in the sense of "nine."

54. *Quibble in respect of a genus* consists in asserting the impossibility of a thing that is really possible, on the ground that it belongs to a certain genus that is very wide.

A speaker says: "This Brāhmaṇa is possessed of learning and conduct."

An objector replies: "It is impossible, for how can it be inferred that this person is possessed of learning and conduct because he is a Brāhmaṇa? There are little boys who are Brāhmaṇas, yet not possessed of learning and conduct."

Here the objector is a quibbler, for he knows well that possession of learning and conduct was not meant to be an attribute of the whole class of Brāhmaṇas, but it was ascribed to "this" particular Brāhmaṇa who lived long enough in the world to render it possible for him to pursue studies and acquire good morals.

55. *Quibble in respect of a metaphor* consists in denying the proper meaning of a word by taking it literally, while it was used metaphorically, and vice versa.

A speaker says: "The scaffolds cry out."

An objector replies: "It is impossible for scaffolds to cry out, for they are inanimate objects."

Here the objector is a quibbler, for he knew well that the word *scaffolds* was used to signify those standing on the scaffolds.

56. It may be said that quibble in respect of a metaphor is in reality quibble in respect of a term, for the first is not different from the second.

57. But it is not so, for there is a distinction between them.

Words are taken in their direct (literal) meanings in the case of "quibble in respect of a term," while they are taken in their direct (literal) as well as indirect (secondary) meanings in the case of "quibble in respect of a metaphor."

58. If you do not admit that one is different from another simply because there is some similarity between them, then we should have only one kind of quibble.

If "quibble in respect of a metaphor" were not different from "quibble in respect of a term," then these two also would not be different from "quibble in respect of a genus," because there is some similarity among all of them. This is absurd; hence the three kinds of quibble are different from one another.

59. *Futility* consists in offering objections founded on mere similarity or dissimilarity.

A disputant says: "The soul is inactive, because it is all-pervading as ether."

His opponent replies: "If the soul is inactive because it bears similarity to ether as being all-pervading, why is it not active because it bears similarity to a pot as being a seat of union?"

The reply is futile, because it overlooks the universal connection between the middle term and the major term that is existent in the arguments of the disputant, but wanting in the arguments of the opponent. Whatever is all-pervading is inactive, but whatever is a seat of union is not necessarily active.

Or again:

Disputant: Sound is noneternal, because unlike ether it is a product.

Opponent: If sound is noneternal because as a product it is dissimilar to ether, why is it not eternal because as an object of auditory perception it is dissimilar to a pot?

The reply is futile because it overlooks the universal disconnection between the middle term and the absence of the major term. There is a universal disconnection between "a product" and "not noneternal," but there is no such disconnection between "an object of auditory perception" and "not eternal."

60. *An occasion for rebuke* arises when one misunderstands, or does not understand at all.

If a person begins to argue in a way that betrays his utter ignorance, or willfully misunderstands and yet persists in showing that he understands well, it is of no avail to employ counterarguments. He is quite unfit to be argued with, and there is nothing left for his opponent but to turn him out or quit his company, rebuking him as a blockhead or a knave.

An instance of *occasion for rebuke*:

Whatever is not quality is substance,

Because there is nothing except color, etc. (*quality*).

A person who argues in the above way is to be rebuked as a fool, for his reason (which admits only quality) opposes his proposition (which admits both quality and substance)

Another instance:

Disputant: Fire is not hot.

Opponent: But the evidence of touch disproves such a statement.

Disputant, in order to gain the confidence of the assembled people, says: "O learned audience, listen, I do not say that fire is not hot," etc.

It is only meet that the opponent should quit the company of a man who argues in this way.

61. Owing to the variety of kinds, there is multiplicity of futilities and occasions for rebuke.

62. Some say that doubt cannot arise from the recognition of common and uncommon properties, whether conjointly or separately.

Conjointly: It is said that doubt about an object is never produced if *both* the common and the uncommon properties of the object are recognized. For instance, if we see in the twilight a tall object that moves, we do not doubt whether it is a man or a post. We at once decide that it is a man, for though tallness is a property possessed in common by man and post, locomotion is a property that distinguishes a man from a post.

Separately: Likewise, doubt about an object is said never to be produced if *only* the common or the uncommon properties are recognized. For instance, if we see a tall object in the twilight, we have no reason to doubt whether it is a man or a post. Tallness is certainly a property possessed in common by man and post, but the tallness of a man is not identical with that of a post: it merely resembles it. Now, the knowledge of similarity between the tallness of a man and that of a post presupposes a knowledge of the man and the post, of which two kinds of tallness are attributes. If there is already a knowledge of the man and the post, there cannot be any doubt about them, for knowledge is the vanquisher of doubt.

63. It is further said that doubt cannot arise either from conflicting testimony or from the irregularity of perception and nonperception.

64. In the case of conflicting testimony there is, according to them, a strong conviction (on each side).

Suppose a disputant (Naiyāyika) says: "There is soul." His opponent (Buddhist) replies: "There is no soul."

The disputant and his opponent are quite sure that their respective statements are correct. Hence there is no doubt, but on the contrary there is conviction, in the minds of both.

65. Doubt, they say, does not arise from the irregularity of perception and nonperception, because in the irregularity itself there is regularity.

An irregularity may be designated as such with reference to something else, but with reference to itself it is a settled fact. If the irregularity is settled in itself, it is regular and cannot cause doubt. On the other hand, if the irregularity is not settled in itself, it is devoid of its own character and cannot cause doubt.

66. Likewise, there is, they say, the chance of an endless doubt, owing to the continuity of its cause.

Recognition of properties common to many objects is, for instance, a cause of doubt. The common properties continue to exist, and hence there will, they say, be no cessation of doubt.

67. In reply, it is stated that the recognition of properties common to many objects, etc., are certainly causes of doubt, if there is no reference to the precise characters of the objects: there is no chance of *no*-doubt or of *endless*-doubt.

It is admitted that doubt does not arise from the recognition of common and uncommon properties conjointly. Aphorism no. 62 brings forth the objection that doubt is not produced even by the recognition of common or uncommon properties alone. It is said that while we see a tall object in the twilight, we at once think of a man and a post, both of which are tall. Thus there is knowledge rather than doubt about the man and post suggested by the tall object. The present aphorism dismisses the objection, by stating that there is certainly a common (nondistinctive) knowledge about a man and a post suggested by the tall object, but there is no precise (distinctive) knowledge about them. Precise knowledge (that is, knowledge of the precise character that distinguishes a man from a post) being absent, doubt must arise. Similar arguments will apply to doubt arising from the recognition of noncommon properties alone.

Aphorisms nos. 63 and 64 raise the objection that doubt does not arise from conflicting testimony, as the disputant and his opponent are both confident of their respective contentions. The present aphorism disposes of the objection by pointing out that, in the case of conflicting statements, one is led to believe that both statements are worth consideration, but is unable to penetrate into the precise characters of the statements. Hence, though the disputant and his opponent remain fixed, the umpire and the audience are thrown into doubt by their conflicting statements.

Aphorism no. 65 raises the objection that doubt cannot arise from the irregularity of perception and nonperception, as the irregularity is settled in itself. The present aphorism meets the objection by stating that the irregularity cannot be concealed by mere verbal tricks. The irregularity, though settled in itself, does not lose its own character until the objects that cause it are removed.

Aphorism no. 66 gives rise to the fear that there is the possibility of an endless doubt, inasmuch as the cause is continuous. The present aphorism removes the fear by stating that although materials of doubt, such as common properties, etc., continue to exist, we do not always recognize them. Unless there is recognition of the common properties, etc., there cannot be doubt.

68. *Examination* should be made in this way of each case where there is room for doubt.

It has been stated that knowledge about the true nature of the categories consists in the true knowledge of their enunciation, definition, and examination. In cases of well-known facts admitted by all, there should be no examination. We are to examine only those cases where there is room for doubt. The author explains, therefore, first the nature of doubt, and then proceeds to examine the other categories, lest there should be any room for doubt in them.

69. Perception and other means of knowledge, says an objector, are invalid, as they are impossible at all the three times.

According to the objector, perception is impossible at the present, past, and future times, or, in other words, perception can be neither prior to, nor posterior to, nor simultaneous with, the objects of sense.

70. If perception occurred anteriorly it could not, he says, have arisen from the contact of a sense with its object.

With reference to the perception of color, for instance, it is asked whether the color precedes perception or the perception precedes color. If you say that perception occurred anteriorly or preceded the color, you must give up your definition of perception, viz. that perception arises from the contact of a sense with its object.

71. If perception is supposed to occur posteriorly you cannot, he continues, maintain the conclusion that objects of sense are established by perception.

The objection stands thus: The means of right knowledge are stated by you to be perception, inference, comparison, and verbal testimony. All objects of right knowledge are said to be established by them. The objects of sense, for instance, are supposed to be established by perception: color is said to be established by visual perception. This conclusion will have to be abandoned if you say that perception occurs posteriorly to the objects.

72. If perception were simultaneous with its object there would not, says the objector, be any order of succession in our cognitions, as there is no such order in their corresponding objects.

Various objects of sense can exist at one time, e.g., color and smell exist in a flower at the same time. If we hold that perception is simultaneous with its object, we must admit that the color and the smell can be perceived at the same time, that is, our perception of color must be admitted to be simultaneous with our perception of smell. This is absurd, because two acts of perception, nay, two cognitions cannot take place at the same time. As there is an order of succession in our cognitions, perception cannot be simultaneous with its object.

The aphorism may also be explained as follows: In knowing a color we perform, we may say, two kinds of knowledge simultaneously, viz. perception and inference. As soon as our eye comes in contact with the color, perception results, which does not, however, enable us to be aware of the color. The color is brought home to us by inference, which, we may say, is performed simultaneously with the perception. Now, says the objector, perception and inference, being two different kinds of knowledge, cannot be simultaneous, as the mind, which is an atomic substance, cannot be instrumental in producing more than one kind of knowledge at a time.

73. In reply, it is stated that if perception and other means of right knowledge are impossible, the denial of them is also impossible.

Owing to absence of the matter to be denied, the denial is inoperative.

74. Moreover, the denial itself cannot be established, if you deny all means of right knowledge.

If you are to establish anything (e.g., denial), you can do so only by one or more of the means of right knowledge, viz. perception, inference, comparison, etc. If you deny them, there will be left nothing that will lead you to the establishment of the thing. Hence you will not be able to establish the denial itself.

75. If you say that your denial is based on a certain means of right knowledge, you do thereby acknowledge the validity of the means.

Suppose you deny a thing, because it is not perceived. You do thereby acknowledge that perception is a means of right knowledge. Similarly, inference, etc., are also to be acknowledged as means of right knowledge.

76. The means of right knowledge cannot, therefore, be denied. They are established in the manner that a drum is proved by its sound.

There is, says Vātsyāyana, no fixed rule that the means of right knowledge should precede objects of right knowledge or should succeed them or be simultaneous with them. The order of precedence is never uniform. Look at the analogous cases: a drum precedes its sound, and illumination succeeds the sun, while smoke is synchronous with fire.

77. The character of an object of right knowledge resembles that of a balance by which a thing is weighed.

Just as a balance is an instrument for measuring weight, but is a measured object when it is itself weighed in another balance, so the senses, etc., are said to be instruments of right knowledge from one point of view, and objects of right knowledge from another point of view. The eye, for instance, is an instrument of perception as well as an object of perception. So also the means of right knowledge may, if occasion arises, be also regarded as objects of right knowledge.

78. If an object of right knowledge, continues the objector, is to be established by a means of right knowledge, this latter needs also to be established by another means of right knowledge.

The objection stands thus: You say that an object of right knowledge is to be established by a means of right knowledge. I admit this, and ask how you establish the means of right knowledge itself. Since a means of right knowledge may also be regarded as an object of right knowledge, you are required to establish the so-called means of right knowledge by another means of right knowledge, and so on.

79. Or, he continues, if a means of right knowledge does not require another means of right knowledge for its establishment, let an object of right knowledge be also established without any means of right knowledge.

A means of right knowledge stands in the same category as an object of right knowledge, if you are to establish either of them. If the means of right knowledge is accepted as self-established, the object of right knowledge must also, according to the objector, be accepted as self-established. In such a contingency perception, inference, etc., will be superfluous.

80. It is not so: the means of right knowledge are established like the illumination of a lamp.

A lamp illumines a jar and our eye illumines the lamp. Though it is sometimes the lamp, and sometimes the eye, that illumines, you are bound to admit a general notion of illuminator. Similarly, you must admit a general notion of the means of right knowledge as distinguished from that of the objects of right knowledge. The means will not, of course, be regarded as such when included under the category of an object.

[The aphorism is also interpreted as follows: Just as a lamp illumines itself and the other objects, the means of right knowledge establish themselves and the objects of right knowledge. Hence perception establishes itself and the objects of sense.]

Note: Objections raised in the aphorisms in nos. 69, 70, 71, 72, 77, 78, and 79 emanated from the Buddhist philosophy. The replies given in the aphorisms in nos. 73, 74, 75, 76, and 80 represent the views of Brahmanic philosophers, who regard perception as a real act and objects as self-existent entities. According to the Buddhist philosophers, however, neither perception nor objects have any self-existence. They acquire an apparent or conditional existence, by virtue of a certain relation that exists between them. Cause and effect, long and short, prior and posterior, etc., are all relative terms. The whole world is a network of relations. The relations themselves are illusory, as the objects that are related have no self-existence. Hence the world is an illusion, or has a mere conditional existence. But where there is conditionality, there is no truth. Truth and conditionality are incompatible terms. That which neutralizes all relations is the void or absolute that lies beyond the conditional world. To speak the truth: the world is an absolute nothing, though it has a conditional existence.

81. Seeing that in some cases other proofs are not required and that in some cases there is need of other proofs, your argument is indecisive.

This is in reply to those who argue that just as a light does not require another light to illuminate it, even so the proofs—i.e., the means of right knowledge—also may not require anything else to prove them; in other words, that every means of right knowledge is also the means of its own right knowledge. The reply is that the example cannot be stretched so far, because there is nothing to distinguish the *hetu* (reason), viz. to be the illuminator, from the *udāharaṇa* (example), viz. the lamp, in this respect. The means of right knowledge and a lamp both illuminate objects; a lamp also illuminates itself; but it does not therefore follow that the means of right knowledge also illuminates itself. For a lamp, which illuminates objects, can also be illuminated by another lamp; and it would then follow on the same analogy that the means of right knowledge that illuminates objects may be also illuminated by other means. Thus your argument leads to opposite conclusions.

82. An objector may say that the definition of perception as given before is untenable, because incomplete.

Perception has been defined as knowledge that arises from the contact of a sense with its object. This definition is said to be defective because it does not notice the conjunction of soul with mind, and of mind with sense, which are also causes of perception.

83. Perception, it is said, cannot arise unless there is conjunction of soul with mind.

From the contact of a sense with its object so knowledge arises, unless, it is said, there is also conjunction of soul with mind. A sense coming in contact with its object produces knowledge in our soul, only if the sense is conjoined with the mind. Hence the conjunction of soul with mind should be mentioned as a necessary element in the definition of perception.

84. Were it so, observes one of the assembly, then direction, space, time, and ether should also be enumerated among the causes of perception.

Direction, space, time, and ether are also indispensable conditions in the production of knowledge. But even the objector does not feel the necessity of enumerating these among the causes of perception.

85. The soul, we point out, has not been excluded from our definition, inasmuch as knowledge is a mark of the soul.

Perception has been described as knowledge, and knowledge implies the soul, which is its abode. Consequently, in speaking of knowledge, the soul has, by implication, been mentioned as a condition in the production of perception.

86. The mind, too, has not been omitted from our definition, inasmuch as we have spoken of the nonsimultaneity of acts of knowledge.

Perception has been defined as knowledge. An essential characteristic of knowledge is that more than one act of knowing cannot take place at a time. This characteristic is due to the mind, an atomic substance, which is conjoined with the sense, when knowledge is produced. Hence, in speaking of knowledge, we have, by implication, mentioned the mind as a condition of perception.

87. The contact of a sense with its object is mentioned as the special cause of perception.

There are many kinds of knowledge, such as perception, recollection, etc. Conjunction of soul with mind is a cause that operates in the production of all kinds of knowledge, while the contact of a sense with its object is the cause that operates only in perception. In our definition of perception we have mentioned only the special cause, and have omitted the common causes that precede not only perception, but also other kinds of knowledge.

88. The contact of a sense with its object is certainly the main cause, as perception is produced even when one is asleep or inattentive.

Even a sleeping person hears the thundering of a cloud if his ear is open to it, and a careless person experiences heat if his skin is exposed to it.

89. By the senses and their objects are also distinguished the special kinds of knowledge.

The special kinds of knowledge are the five varieties of perception, viz. by sight, hearing, smell, taste, and touch. These are distinguished by the senses in whose spheres they lie, or by the objects they illumine. Thus the visual perception is called eye-knowledge or color-knowledge, the auditory perception is called ear-knowledge or sound-knowledge, the olfactory perception is called nose-knowledge or smell-knowledge, the gustatory perception is called tongue-knowledge or taste-knowledge, and the tactual perception is called skin-knowledge or touch-knowledge.

90. (The above, says the objector, is) no argument, because it is precluded.

The conclusion reached in the preceding three aphorisms is that the contact of the sense and the object, and not the contact of the sense and mind nor the contact of the soul and mind, should be stated to be the cause of perception. To this the objector puts in a rejoinder. The meaning is that if in certain circumstances, e.g., where the person is asleep or inattentive, perception takes place without the contact of the soul and mind, then there would be nothing to prevent several cognitions from being produced at one and the same time, and thus the tenet that the nonproduction of several cognitions simultaneously is the mark of the mind (*Nyāya Sūtra* no. 6 above) would be violated. Therefore the *sūtra* precludes, or is precluded by, the argument advanced in the preceding three aphorisms.

91. (We reply that there is) no (such preclusion or violation). (In the case of a person who is asleep or inattentive perception takes place) through the intensity of the sensible object.

The three aphorisms in question, nos. 87–89, do not imply that the contact of the soul and mind sometimes is, and sometimes is not, the cause of perception. They merely emphasize the fact that the contact of the sense and object is the principal cause of perceptual cognition. For the intensity of the object and the keenness of the sense directly establish contact of the object with the sense, and not of the sense with mind and the soul.

92. Perception, it may be urged, is inference, because it illumines only a part as a mark of the whole.

We are said to perceive a tree, while we really perceive only a part of it. This knowledge of the tree, as a whole, derived from the knowledge of a part of it is, according to the objectors, a case of inference.

93. But this is not so, for perception is admitted of at least that portion which it actually illumines.

The objectors themselves admit that a part is actually perceived. Hence, perception as a means of knowledge is not altogether denied, and it is accepted as different from inference.

94. There is, some say, doubt about the whole, because the whole has yet to be established.

The objectors say that parts alone are realities and that there is no whole behind them. A tree, for instance, is yellow in some parts and green in other parts. If the tree was one whole, then the contradictory qualities of yellowness and greenness could not have belonged to it simultaneously. Hence the parts alone must, according to them, be regarded as real.

95. If there were no whole, there would, it is replied, be nonperception of all.

All signifies substance, quality, action, generality, particularity, and intimate relation. None of these would be perceptible, if the whole were denied. Suppose that the parts alone are real. Then, since a part is not of fixed dimension, it may itself be divided into parts, these latter again into further parts, and so on, until we reach the atoms, which are the ultimate parts. Now the atoms, which possess no bulk, are not perceptible. Similarly, the quality, action, etc., that inhere in the atoms are also not perceptible. Consequently, if we deny that there is a "whole," neither the substance nor quality, etc., would be perceptible.

96. There is a *whole*, because we can hold, pull, etc.

If there were no whole, we could not have held or pulled an entire thing by holding or pulling a part of it. We say, "one jar," "one man," etc. This use of "one" would vanish, if there were no whole.

97. The illustration from an army or a forest does not hold good, for atoms cannot be detected by the sense.

If anyone were to say that just as a single soldier or a single tree may not be seen from a distance, but an army consisting of numerous soldiers or a forest consisting of numerous trees is seen, so a single atom may not be perceptible, but a jar consisting of numerous atoms will be perceptible, and these atoms being called "one jar," the use of "one" will not vanish, the analogy, we reply, does not hold good, because the soldiers and trees possess bulk and so are perceptible, whereas the atoms do not possess bulk and so are individually not perceptible. It is absurd to argue that, because soldiers and trees are perceptible in the mass, atoms are perceptible in the mass also: to avoid this conclusion, we must admit the existence of a whole beyond the parts.

98. *Inference*, some say, is not a means of right knowledge, as it errs in certain cases, e.g., when a river is banked, when something is damaged, and when similarity misleads, etc.

If we see a river swollen, we infer that there has been rain; if we see the ants carrying off their eggs, we infer that there will be rain; and if we hear a peacock scream, we infer that clouds are gathering. These inferences, says an objector, are not necessarily correct, for a river may be swollen because embanked, the ants may carry off their eggs because their nests have been damaged, and the so-called screaming of a peacock may be nothing but the voice of a man.

99. It is not so, because our inference is based on something else than the part, fear and likeness.

The swelling of a river caused by rain is different from that which results from the embankment of a part of it; the former is attended by a great rapidity of currents, an abundance of foam, a mass of floating fruits, leaves, wood, etc. The manner in which ants carry off their eggs just before rain is quite different from the manner in which they do so when their nests are damaged. The ants run away quickly in a steady line when rain is imminent, but fear makes them fly in disorder when their nests are damaged. The screaming of a peacock that suggests gathering clouds is quite different from a man's imitation of it, for the latter is not natural. If in such cases any wrong inference is drawn, the fault is in the person, not in the process.

100. There is, some say, no present time because when a thing falls, we can know only the time through which it has fallen and the time through which it will yet fall.

Inference has reference to three times. In the a priori inference we pass from the past to the present, in the a posteriori from the present to the past, and in the "*commonly seen*" from the present to the present. It is, therefore, proper that we should examine the three times. The reason that leads some people to deny the present time is that when a fruit, for instance, falls from a tree, we recognize only the past time taken up by the fruit in traversing a certain distance and the future time that will yet be taken up by the fruit in traversing the remaining distance. There is no intervening distance that the fruit can traverse at the so-called present time. Hence, they say, there is no present time.

101. If there is no present time, there will, it is replied, be no past and future times, because they are related to it.

The past is that which precedes the present, and the future is that which succeeds it. Hence, if there is no present time, there cannot be any past or future time.

102. The past and future cannot be established by a mere mutual reference.

If the past is defined as that which is not the future and the future is defined as that which is not the past, the definition would involve a fallacy of mutual dependency. Hence we must admit the present time, to which the past and future are related.

103. If there were no present time, sense perception would be impossible, knowledge would be impossible.

If you deny the present time, there cannot be any perception, which illumines only what is present in time; in the absence of perception, all kinds of knowledge would be impossible. Hence the present time is established by confutation or the principle of reductio ad absurdum.

104. We can know both the past and the future, for we can conceive of a thing as made and as about to be made.

The present time is indicated by what continues, the past by what has been finished, and the future by what has not yet begun.

105. *Comparison,* some say, is not a means of right knowledge, as it cannot be established either through complete or considerable or partial similarity.

On the ground of complete similarity we never say "a cow is like a cow"; on the ground of considerable similarity we do not say that "a buffalo is like a cow";

and on the ground of partial similarity we do not say that "a mustard seed is like Mount Meru." Hence comparison is regarded by some as not a means of right knowledge, for it has no precise standard.

106. This objection does not hold good, for comparison is established through similarity in a high degree.

The similarity in a high degree exists between such well-known objects as a cow and a *bos gavaeus*, etc.

107. Comparison, some say, is not different from inference, for both seek to establish the unperceived by means of the perceived.

We recognize a *bos gavaeus* at first sight through its special similarity to a cow, which we have often perceived. This knowledge of a previously unperceived object derived through its similarity to a perceived object is, it has been said, nothing but a case of inference.

108. It is not in a *bos gavaeus unperceived* that we find the real matter of comparison.

The matter of comparison is similarity, e.g., between a cow and a *bos gavaeus*. The *bos gavaeus* in which we notice the similarity is first perceived, that is, on perceiving a *bos gavaeus* we notice its similarity to a cow. Hence comparison supplies us with knowledge of a *perceived* thing, through its similarity to another thing also *perceived*. This characteristic distinguishes it from inference, which furnishes us with knowledge of an *unperceived* thing through that of a thing *perceived*.

109. There is nondifference, inasmuch as comparison is established through the compendious expression "so."

It is not true that comparison is identical with inference, because the former is established through the compendious expression "so." "As is a cow, *so* is a *bos gavaeus*"—this is an instance of comparison. This use of "so" makes it clear that comparison is a distinct means of right knowledge.

110. *Verbal testimony*, say some, is inference, because the object revealed by it is not perceived but inferred:

Inference gives us the knowledge of an unperceived object, through the knowledge of an object that is perceived. Similarly, verbal testimony enables us to acquire the knowledge of an unperceived object, through the knowledge of a word that is perceived. The verbal testimony is, therefore, supposed by some to be inference, as the object revealed by both is unperceived.

111. In respect of perceptibility the two cases are not, continues the objector, different.

In inference as well as in verbal testimony we pass to an unperceived object through an object that is perceived. In respect of perceptibility of the object through which we pass, the inference does not, continues the objector, differ from the verbal testimony.

112. There is, moreover, adds the objector, the same connection.

Just as in inference there is a certain connection between a sign (e.g., smoke) and the thing signified by it (e.g., fire), so in verbal testimony there is a connection between a word and the object signified by it. So inference, says the objector, is not different from verbal testimony.

113. In reply, we say that there is reliance on the matter signified by a word, because the word has been used by a reliable person:

In reference to the objections raised in the aphorisms in nos. 110 and 111, we say that we rely on unseen matter, not simply because it is signified by words, but because they are spoken by a reliable person. There are, some say, paradise, nymphs, Uttarakuras, seven islands, ocean human settlements, etc. We accept them as realities not because they are known through words, but because they are spoken of by persons who are reliable. Hence verbal testimony is not inference. The two agree in conveying knowledge of an object through its sign, but the sign in one is different from the sign in the other. In the case of verbal testimony, the special point is to decide whether the sign (word) comes from a reliable person.

The aphorism in no. 112 speaks of a certain connection between a word and the object signified by it. The present aphorism points out that the connection is not a natural one. We acknowledge that a word indicates a certain object, but we deny that the object is naturally or necessarily connected with the word. Hearing, for instance, the word "cow," we think of the animal signified by it, nevertheless the word and the animal are not connected with each other by nature or necessity. In the case of inference, however, the connection between a sign (e.g., smoke) and the thing signified (e.g., fire) is natural and natural and necessary. Therefore, the connection involved in inference is not of the same kind as that involved in verbal testimony.

114. There is no natural connection between a word and the object signified by it, as we do not find that the words food, fire, and hatchet are accompanied by the actions filling, burning, and splitting.

If a word were naturally connected with the object signified by it, then by uttering the words food, fire, and hatchet we should have found our mouth filled up (with food), burned (with fire), and split (by a hatchet). But such is never the case. Hence there is no natural connection between a word and the object signified by it, and consequently verbal testimony is not inference.

115. It cannot, says an objector, be denied that there is a fixed connection between words and their meanings.

A particular word denotes a particular meaning, e.g., the word "cow" denotes the animal of that name, but it does not denote a horse, a jar, or any other thing. There is, therefore, in the case of verbal testimony, a fixed connection between a word and its meaning, as there is in the case of inference a fixed connection between a sign and the thing signified. Hence verbal testimony is considered by the objector to be a case of inference.

116. We reply, it is through convention that the meaning of a word is understood.

The connection between a word and its meaning is conventional and not natural. The connection, though fixed by man, is not inseparable and cannot therefore be the basis of an inference.

117. There is no universal uniformity of connection between a word and its meaning.

The *ṛṣis, āryas,* and *mlecchas* use the same word in different senses, e.g., the word "*yava*" is used by the *āryas* to denote a long-awned grain, but by the *mlecchas* to denote a panic-seed. So the connection between a word and its meaning is not everywhere uniform, and consequently verbal testimony cannot be considered as inference.

118. The Veda, some say, is unreliable, as it involves the faults of untruth, contradiction, and tautology

The Veda, which is a kind of verbal testimony, is not, some say, a means of right knowledge. It is supposed by them to be tainted with the faults of untruth, contradiction, and tautology. For instance, the Veda affirms that a son is produced when the sacrifice for the sake of a son is performed. It often happens that the son is not produced, though the sacrifice has been performed.

There are many contradictory injunctions in the Veda, e.g., it declares "let one sacrifice when the sun has risen," also "let one sacrifice when the sun has not risen," etc. There is such tautology as "let the first hymn be recited thrice," "let the last hymn be recited thrice," etc.

119. The so-called untruth in the Veda comes from some *defect in the act, operator,* or *materials of sacrifice.*

Defect in the act consists in sacrificing not according to rules, *defect in the operator* (officiating priest) consists in his not being a learned man, and *defect in the materials* consists in the fuel being wet, butter being not fresh, remuneration (to the officiating priest) being small, etc. A son is sure to be produced as a result of performing the sacrifice, if these defects are avoided. Therefore, there is no untruth in the Veda.

120. Contradiction would occur if there were alteration of the time agreed upon.

Let a person perform sacrifice before sunrise or after sunrise if he has agreed upon doing it at either of the times. Two alternative courses being open to him, he can perform the sacrifice before sunrise or after sunrise, according to his agreement or desire. The Veda cannot be charged with the fault of contradiction, if it enjoins such alternative courses.

121. There is no tautology, because reinculcation is of advantage.

Tautology means a useless repetition, which never occurs in the Veda. If there is any repetition there, it is either for completing a certain number of syllables, or for explaining a matter briefly expressed, etc. "Let the first hymn be recited thrice," "let the last hymn be recited thrice"—such instances embody a useful repetition.

122. And because there is necessity for the classification of Vedic speech.

It is necessary to divide the Vedic speech into classes based on special characters.

123. The Vedic speech being divided on the principle of injunction, persuasion, and reinculcation.

The two main divisions of the Veda are (1) hymn and (2) ritual. The ritual portion admits of three subdivisions, viz. injunctive, persuasive, and reinculcative.

124. An injunction is that which exhorts us to adopt a certain course of action [as the means of attaining good].

The following is an injunction: "Let him who desires paradise perform the fire-sacrifice." This is a direct command.

125. Persuasion is effected through praise, blame, warning, and prescription.

Praise is speech that persuades us to a certain course of action by extolling its consequences, e.g., "By the Sarvajit sacrifice gods conquered all, there is nothing like Sarvajit sacrifice, it enables us to obtain everything and to vanquish every one, etc." Here there is no direct command, but the Sarvajit sacrifice is extolled in such a way that we are persuaded to perform it.

Blame is speech that persuades us to adopt a certain course of action by acquainting us with the undesirable consequences of neglecting it, e.g., "One who performs any other sacrifice, neglecting the Jyotiṣṭoma, falls into a pit and decays there." Here one is persuaded to perform the Jyotiṣṭoma sacrifice, the neglect of which brings about evil consequences.

Warning is the mentioning of a course of action, the obstruction of which by some particular person led to bad consequences, e.g., on presenting oblation one is to take the fat first and the sprinkled butter afterward, but alas as the Charaka priests first took the sprinkled butter which was, as it were, the life of fire, etc. Here the foolish course of action adopted by the Charaka priests should serve as a warning to other priests, who ought to avoid that course.

Prescription implies the mention of something as commendable on account of its antiquity, e.g., "By this the Brāhmaṇas recited the Sāma hymn, etc."

126. Reinculcation is the repetition of that which has been enjoined by an injunction.

Reinculcation may consist of (1) the repetition of an *injunction*, or (2) the repetition of that which has been *enjoined*. The first is called verbal reinculcation and the second objective reinculcation. In the Veda there is reinculcation, as in ordinary use there is repetition. "Noneternal, not eternal"—this is a verbal repetition. "Noneternal, possessing the character of extinction"—this is objective repetition.

127. There is, some say, no difference between reinculcation and tautology, as there is in either case a repetition of some expression already used.

Reinculcation is supposed by some to be a fault, inasmuch as it does not, according to them, differ from tautology.

128. There is a difference, because reinculcation serves some useful purpose, as, e.g., a command to go faster:

Tautology consists of a useless repetition, but the repetition in the case of reinculcation is useful, e.g., "go on, go on" signifies "go faster."

129. The Veda is reliable like the spell and the medical science, because of the reliability of their authors.

The spell counteracts poison, etc., and the medical science prescribes correct remedies. The authority belonging to them is derived from their authors, the sages, who were reliable persons. The sages themselves were reliable, because (1) they had an intuitive perception of truths, (2) they had great kindness for living beings, and (3) they had the desire of communicating their knowledge of the truths. The authors (lit. "the seers and speakers") of the Veda were also the authors of the spell and medical science. Hence, like the spell and medical science, the Veda must be accepted as authoritative. The view that the Veda is authoritative because eternal is untenable.

130. Some say that the means of right knowledge are more than four, because rumor, presumption, probability, and nonexistence are also valid,

In aphorism no. 3 above, the means of right knowledge have been stated to be four, viz. perception, inference, comparison, and verbal testimony. Some say that there are other means of right knowledge, such as rumor, presumption, probability, and nonexistence.

Rumor is an assertion that has come from one to another without any indication of the source from which it first originated, e.g., in this fig tree there live goblins.

Presumption is the deduction of one thing from the declaration of another thing: e.g., from the declaration that "unless there is cloud, there is no rain," we deduce that "there is rain, if there is cloud." A more familiar instance of presumption is this: the fat Devadatta does not eat during the day time. Here the presumption is that he eats in the night for it is impossible for a person to be fat if he does not eat at all.

Probability consists in cognizing the existence of a thing from that of another thing in which it is included, e.g., cognizing the measure of an *āḍhaka* from that of a *droṇa* of which it is a fourth part, and cognizing the measure of a *prastha* from that of an *āḍhaka* of which it is a quarter.

Of two opposite things, the *nonexistence* of one establishes the existence of the other, e.g., the nonexistence of rain establishes the combination of wind and cloud. When there is a combination of wind and cloud, drops of water cannot fall, in spite of their weight.

131. This, we reply, is no contradiction, since rumor is included in verbal testimony, and presumption, probability, and nonexistence are included in inference.

Those who maintain that rumor, presumption, probability, and nonexistence are valid do not really oppose our division of the means of right knowledge into four, viz. perception, inference, comparison, and verbal testimony.

Rumor partakes of the general characteristics of verbal testimony, and is a special kind of it.

Presumption is explained as the knowledge of a thing derived through the consideration of it from the opposite standpoint. For instance, the fat Devadatta does not eat during the day time: here the presumption is that he eats in the night. The fact of his eating in the night has not been expressly stated, but is ascertained from this consideration that a person who does not eat during the day cannot be strong unless he eats in the night. It is evident that presumption, like inference, passes from a perceived thing to an unperceived one, because they are in some way connected.

Probability is inference, because it is the cognizance of a part from knowledge of a whole with which it is inseparably connected.

Nonexistence is inference, inasmuch as it really infers the obstruction of a cause from the nonexistence of its effect through a certain connection, viz. if the obstruction occurs, the effect cannot occur.

Hence rumor, etc., are not independent means of right knowledge, but are included in the four, enumerated in aphorism no. 3.

132. Presumption, some say, is not valid, because it leads to uncertainty.

"If there is no cloud, there will be no rain": from this we are said to presume that if there is a cloud there will be rain. But it often happens that a cloud is not followed by rain. So presumption does not always lead to certainty.

133. We reply: if there is any uncertainty, it is due to your supposing that to be a presumption which is not really so.

"If there is no cloud, there will be no rain": from this we are entitled to presume that if there is rain there must have been a cloud. But if you pretend to presume that "if there is a cloud, there will be rain," your so-called presumption will be an invalid one.

134. The objection itself, we say, is invalid, because it leads to uncertainty.

"Presumption is not valid, because it leads to uncertainty": this is your objection. In it there are two points for consideration: (1) the validity of presumption and (2) the existence of presumption. Your objection refers to one of the points, viz. the validity of presumption. So you do not deny the existence of presumption. In some instances, however, your objection may refer to more points than one. In fact, the nature of your objection is not definite in itself, or, in other words, it leads to uncertainty. Hence your objection is invalid.

135. Or, if that be valid, then our presumption is not invalid.

Perhaps you will say that your objection is valid, because you can ascertain in each case whether one or more points are referred to by the objection. Similarly, we shall say that our presumption is not invalid, because we can ascertain in each case whether the presumption is capable of leading to more conclusions than one. Hence, if you say that your objection is valid, we shall say that our presumption is also valid.

136. Some say that *nonexistence* is not a means of right knowledge, because there is no object that is known by it.

137. Nonexistence, we reply, serves to mark out an object unmarked by the mark that characterizes other objects.

Suppose a person wants to bring a pot that is not blue. The absence of blueness is a mark that will enable him to mark out the particular pot he wants to bring, and to exclude the other pots that are blue. Thus an object may be known through the nonexistence (absence) of its mark.

138. If you say that the nonexistence (absence) of a mark is impossible where there was no mark at all, it is, we reply, not so, because the nonexistence (absence) is possible in reference to a mark elsewhere.

We can, says an objector, talk of a mark being nonexistent (absent), if it was previously existent (present). A pot is said to be not blue only in reference to its being blue previously. In reply, we say that it is not so. "Not-blue" is no doubt possible only in reference to "blue," but that blueness may exist elsewhere. For instance, we can talk of this pot being not-blue, in contrast to that pot which is blue.

139. Though a mark may distinguish the object that is marked, the nonexistence (absence) of the mark cannot, some say, distinguish the object that is not marked.

A blue pot is distinguished by the blueness that is its mark. But how can we, says the objector, distinguish an unmarked object by the nonexistence (absence) of a mark that it does not possess?

140. This is not so, because the nonexistence (absence) of a mark serves as a mark, in relation to the presence of the mark.

We can speak of a pot being not-blue, in relation to one which is blue. Hence, though not-blueness is not a positive mark, it serves as a (negative) mark, in relation to blueness.

141. Moreover, we perceive nonexistence as a mark antecedent to the production of a thing.

There are two kinds of nonexistence, viz. antecedent nonexistence and subsequent nonexistence. When we say that there will be a jar, we perceive the mark of nonexistence of the jar in the halves that are destined to compose it. This is antecedent nonexistence. Similarly, when we say that a jar has broken, we perceive the mark of nonexistence of the jar in the parts that composed it. This is subsequent nonexistence.

142. Sound is not eternal, because it has a beginning and is cognized by our sense and is spoken of as artificial.

Sound is noneternal, because it begins or arises from the concussion of two hard substances, e.g., an axe and a tree, etc. Another ground for the non-eternality of sound is that it is cognized by our sense. Moreover, we attribute to sound the properties of an artificial object, e.g., we speak of a sound being grave, acute, etc. This would be impossible if it had been eternal.

Some say that the so-called beginning of a sound is merely a manifestation of it, that is, sound does not really begin, but is merely manifested by the concussion of two hard substances. In reply, we say that the concussion does not manifest, but produces a sound. You cannot suppose the concussion to be the manifester and sound the manifested, unless you can prove that the concussion and sound are simultaneous. But the proof is impossible, as a sound is heard at a great distance even after the concussion of the substances has ceased. So sound is not manifested by the concussion. It is, however, legitimate to suppose that sound is produced by the concussion, and that one sound produces another sound, and so on, until the last sound is heard at a great distance.

143. Some will not accept this argument, because the nonexistence of a jar and the genus of it are eternal, and eternal things are also spoken of as if they were artificial.

Some say that it is not true that whatever has a beginning is noneternal. Look at the nonexistence (destruction) of a jar which began when the jar was broken. Whatever is cognized by our sense is noneternal: this is also said to be an unsound argument. When, for instance, we perceive a jar, we perceive also its genus (i.e., jarness), which is eternal. It is further said that we often attribute to eternal things the properties of an artificial object, e.g., we speak of the extension of ether as we speak of the extension of a blanket.

144. There is, we reply, no opposition because there is distinction between what is really eternal and what is partially eternal.

That which is really eternal belongs to the three times. But the nonexistence (destruction) of a jar does not belong to three times, as it was impossible before the jar was broken. Hence the nonexistence (destruction) of a jar that has a beginning is not really eternal.

145. It is only the things cognized by our sense as belonging to a certain genus that must, we say, be inferred to be noneternal.

The objectors have said that things cognized by our sense are not necessarily noneternal, e.g., as we perceive a jar, we also perceive its genus jarness, which is eternal. In reply, we say that not all things cognized by our sense are noneternal, but only those that belong to a certain genus. A jar, for instance, is noneternal, because we perceive it as belonging to the genus jarness. But jarness, which is cognized by our sense, is not noneternal, because it does not belong to a further genus, named jarness-ness. Similarly, sound is noneternal, because it is cognized by our sense as belonging to the genus called soundness.

The aphorism may also be interpreted as follows: Sound is noneternal, because it is inferred to advance in a series. We do not say that whatever is cognized by our sense is noneternal: our intention is to say that things cognized by our sense as advancing in a series are noneternal. Sound is cognized in that manner (i.e., sound advances like a wave), and hence sound is noneternal.

146. We further say that only artificial things are designated by the term *extension.*

When we speak of the extension of ether, we really mean that the extension belongs to an artificial thing, which has for its substratum the ether. Hence we do not in reality attribute to eternal things the properties of artificial objects.

147. Sound is noneternal, because neither do we perceive it before pronunciation, nor do we notice any veil that covers it.

If sound were eternal, it would be perceived before pronunciation. You cannot say that sound really existed before pronunciation but was covered by some veil, for we do not notice any such veil.

148. The veil, some say, really exists, because we do not perceive the nonperception thereof.

The objectors say: If you deny the veil because it is not perceived, we deny the nonperception of the veil because it is also not perceived. The denial of nonperception is the same as the acknowledgment of perception, or, in other words, the veil is acknowledged to be existent.

149. If you assert nonperception of the veil, though the nonperception is not perceived, we, continue the objectors, assert the existence of the veil, though it is not perceived.

You admit nonperception of the veil, though you do not perceive it (nonperception). Similarly, we, the objectors, admit the existence of the veil, though we do not perceive it.

150. This, we reply, is no reason, because nonperception consists of absence of perception.

A veil is a thing fit to be perceived. Our nonperception of it indicates its absence. On the other hand, the nonperception of a veil is not a thing fit to be perceived. Hence, nonperception of the nonperception leads us to nothing real,

151. Some say that sound is eternal, because it is intangible.

Ether, which is intangible, is eternal. Sound must, similarly, according to some, be eternal, because it is intangible.

152. This we deny, because action is noneternal.

Action is noneternal, though it is intangible. Hence, intangibility does not establish eternality.

153. An atom, on the other hand, is eternal though not intangible.

Tangibility is not incompatible with eternality, e.g., atoms are tangible, yet eternal

154. Sound, some say, is eternal, because of the traditional teaching.

A preceptor could not have imparted knowledge to his pupils by means of sounds, if these were perishable (noneternal). In fact, the traditional teaching would, according to the objectors, be impossible if the sounds were noneternal.

155. This is, we reply, no reason, because sound is not perceived in the interval.

Suppose a preceptor delivers certain sounds (in the form of a lecture) that are received by his pupil. The sounds are not audible in the interval between the preceptor giving them and the pupil receiving them. They would never be inaudible, if they were eternal.

156. This, say the objectors, is no argument, because there is the teaching.

The objectors say: If the sounds, as soon as they came out of the preceptor, were destroyed and did not reach the pupil, there could not be any teaching carried on. But there is the teaching, hence sound does not perish, or, in other, words, it is eternal.

157. In whichever of the two senses it is accepted, the teaching does not offer any opposition.

The word "teaching" may be interpreted either as (1) the pupil's receiving the sounds given by his preceptor, or as (2) the pupil's imitating the sounds of his preceptor, as one imitates dancing. Neither of these interpretations would support the eternality of sound. In consonance with the first interpretation we shall say that the sound coming out of the preceptor produces another sound, and so on, until the last sound reaches the pupil. This would make sound noneternal. It is obvious that the second interpretation similarly proves the non-eternality of sound.

158. Sound, continue the objectors, is eternal, because it is capable of repetition.

That which is capable of repetition is persistent or not perishable, e.g., one and the same color can be repeatedly looked at, because it is persistent. One and the same sound can similarly be repeatedly uttered; hence it is persistent or not perishable.

159. It is, we reply, not so, because even if sounds were "other" (different), repetition could take place.

Repetition does not prevent perishableness, because repetition is possible even if the things repeated are "other" or different, e.g., he sacrifices twice, he dances thrice, etc. Here the two sacrifices are different, and yet we use the repetitive word "twice"; similarly the three dancings are different, and yet we use the repetitive word "thrice."

160. Some say that there is no such thing as otherness, because what is called "other," in reference to some other, is not other in reference to itself.

We maintain that repetition is possible even if the things repeated are "other" or different. Our position is said to be untenable: the term "other" is described as unmeaning, as nothing is other than itself.

161. In the absence of otherness there would, we reply, be no sameness, because the two exist in reference to each other.

If there was no otherness, there would be no sameness. This would lead us to absurdity, as it would disprove both persistency and perishableness. Hence we must admit otherness, and if there is "other," there will be no flaw in our expression, viz. repetition is possible even if things were "other" or different.

162. Sound, some say, is eternal, because we perceive no cause why it should perish.

Whatever is noneternal is destroyed by some cause. Sound is said to have no cause of destruction, hence sound is held by some to be not noneternal (i.e., is regarded as eternal)

163. But by the same argument, we are afraid, nonperception of the cause of inaudition would mean constant audition.

If nonperception is to establish nonexistence, we should not cease to hear, because we do not perceive any cause of our not hearing. But such a conclusion is absurd.

164. Your position, we further say, is untenable, because there is no nonperception; on the contrary, there is perception of the cause of inaudition.

Suppose that a sound is produced by an axe striking against a tree. This sound will perish after producing another sound, which will again perish, giving rise to another, and so on, until the last sound is destroyed by some obstacle. In fact every sound that is produced is destined to perish. Hence there is no nonperception of the cause of inaudition; on the contrary, there is perception of such a cause. Consequently, sound is not eternal.

165. There is, we again say, no nonperception, because the sound [of a gong] ceases on the contact of our hand [with the gong].

You cannot say that there is nonperception of the cause of cessation of sounds because we actually perceive that by the contact of our hand we can stop the sound of a gong.

166. We call a thing eternal (persistent) if it continues to exist, and if we cannot perceive any cause why it should cease.

Sound does not continue to exist, and the cause of its cessation is also perceived. Hence sound is not eternal.

167. That the substratum of sound is intangible is no counterargument.

Sound has not for its substratum any of the tangible substances, viz. earth, water, fire, and air, for it is found to be produced even where these do not exist. For instance, sound is produced in a vacuum that is devoid of smell, taste, color, and touch, which are the qualities of tangible substances. The reason the sound produced in a vacuum does not reach our ears is that there is no air to carry it. Hence the substratum of sound is an intangible substance, viz. ether.

It is a peculiarity of sound that it cannot co-abide with color, etc. A tangible substance (e.g., earth) that is the abode of smell may also be the abode of color, taste, or touch. But the substance in which sound abides cannot be the abode of any other qualities. This distinguishes the substratum of sound from the substrata of other qualities. This peculiar substratum is called ether.

The fact of having an intangible substratum is no bar to the non-eternality of sound. Sound, though its substratum is the intangible ether, is produced by the contact of two hard substances. One sound produces another sound (or a certain vibration), which again causes another sound (or vibration), and so on, until the last sound (or vibration) ceases owing to some obstacle. Sound is therefore non-eternal.

168. Sound cannot be supposed to co-abide with other qualities, for there are also varieties of it.

In each tangible substance there is only one kind of smell, taste, touch, or color. If we suppose that sound abides with one or more of these qualities in a tangible substance, we must admit that sound is of one kind only. But sound is of various kinds, such as grave, acute, etc.; and even the same sound may vary in degrees, according to the nature of the obstruction it meets. This proves that sound does not abide with other qualities in a tangible substance. It further proves that sound is not unalterable or eternal.

Also signifies that this aphorism is to be considered along with the aphorism in no. 162, in which a reason for the non-eternality of sound is given.

169. From the injunction about modification and substitute there arises doubt.

The word "*dadhi*," conjoined with the word "*atra*," becomes "*dadhyatra*," by the rule of Sanskrit grammar. Looking at "*dadhi-atra*" and "*dadhyatra*," we notice that there is *i* in the former and *y* in the latter. Here some say that *i* undergoes modification as *y*, while others say that *y* comes as a substitute for *i*. Consequently we are thrown into doubt whether letters really undergo modifications or take up substitutes.

170. If letters underwent modification, an increase of bulk in the original material would be attended by an increase of bulk in the modification.

If we accept the theory of modification, the letter *y* that originated from the short *i* must be supposed to be less in bulk than the *y* that originated from the long *ī*. But in reality the *y* in both cases is of the same bulk. Hence it is concluded that letters do not undergo modification, but take up other letters as substitutes.

171. The foregoing argument, some say, is futile, because we find modification less than, equal to, and greater than, the original material.

The bulk of the modification does not, in all cases, correspond to the bulk of the original material, e.g., thread is of less bulk than cotton, which is its original material, a bracelet is equal in bulk to the gold of which it is made, and a banyan tree is greater in bulk than the seed from which it springs. Hence the argument against the theory of modification is, according to the objectors, baseless.

172. On account of the absence of both the positive and negative marks of inference, we say, the example does not establish the point.

The examples cited by the opponent are irrelevant. They are neither similar nor dissimilar to the case under consideration: they belong altogether to a different category. An example that can establish a point must contain the reason that is found present in the thing to be established. Not only are the examples not a means of proof here, but they are also not the examples required.

173. It is not so, because we spoke of those modifications that originated from different materials.

A modification may not correspond in bulk to its original material. But if the original materials are different, their modifications are expected to be different. Here *i* being different from *ī*, their modifications are expected to be different. But *y* issues from *i* as well as *ī*. Hence *y* is not a modification of *i* or *ī*.

174. There is, says an objector, difference between a letter and its modification, as there is between a substance and its modification.

According to the objector, there is difference between the letter *i* (or *ī*) and its modification *y*, as there is difference between the substance cotton and its modification thread.

175. In reply, we say that it is not so, because the character of a modification does not exist here.

A modification must be of the same nature as its original material, though the former may not correspond in bulk to the latter. A bracelet is no doubt a modification of gold or silver, but a horse is not a modification of a bull. Similarly, *y*, which is a semi-vowel, is not a modification of *i* (or *ī*), which is a full vowel.

176. A thing that has undergone modification does not again return to its original form.

Milk modified into curd does not again attain the state of milk. But *i* having reached the condition of *y* may again revert to its original form. Hence *y* is not a modification of *i*.

177. Some say that this is untenable, because golden ornaments may again be converted into their original forms.

A golden bracelet is converted into a mass of gross gold that may be again modified into a bracelet. The objector, relying on the analogy of golden ornaments, says that in the case of letters the theory of modification does not suffer by *i* reaching the condition of *y* and again returning to its original form.

178. The analogy, we say, is inapt, because the modifications of gold (called ornaments) do not relinquish the nature of gold.

A mass of gold when made into ornaments does not relinquish its own nature. But *i* when converted into *y* loses its own nature. Hence the analogy is unsuitable.

179. If the letter were eternal it could not be modified, and if it were impermanent it could not abide long enough to furnish the material for modification.

On the supposition of the letters being eternal, *i* cannot be modified into *y*; and on the supposition of their being impermanent, *i* must perish before it can be modified into *y*.

180. Though the letters be eternal, their modification, says an objector, cannot be denied, as some of the eternal things are beyond the grasp of the senses, while others possess a different character.

Just as some eternal things (as ether) are supersensuous while others (such as cowhood) are cognizable by the sense, so some eternal things, such as ether, may be unmodifiable while others, such as letters, may be susceptible to modification.

181. Even if the letters are impermanent, their modification, like their perception, is, according to the objector, possible.

Even if you say that letters are impermanent, you admit that they abide long enough to be capable of being perceived. Why then cannot they abide long enough to be capable of being modified?

182. In reply, we say that our position is unassailable, because there is no eternalness where there is the character of modification and because your so-called modification presents itself at a time subsequent to the destruction of the original material.

The letters cannot be modified if you say that they are eternal, because modification is the reverse of eternalness. When a thing is modified it assumes another nature, abandoning its own. Again, the letters cannot be modified if you say that they are impermanent, because there is no time for *i* (of *dadhi*) to be modified into *y* when *a* (of *atra*) follows. The sound "*dadhi*" is produced (pronounced) at the first moment, exists (continuously) during the second moment, and perishes at the third moment. The sound "*atra*" is produced (pronounced) at the second moment, exists (continues) during the third moment, and perishes at the fourth moment. Now, *i* (of *dadhi*) cannot be modified into *y* until *a* (of *atra*) has come into existence. But *a* comes into existence at the third moment, when *i* has already perished. So, on the supposition of impermanency of letters, modification is impossible.

183. Letters are not modified, because there is no fixity as to the original material of their modification.

In the case of real modifications there is a fixity as regards their original materials, e.g., milk is the original material of curd, but not vice versa. In the case of letters, however, there is no fixed rule, e.g., *i* is the original material of *y* in *dadhyatra* (*dadhi* + *atra*), but *y* is the original material of *i* in *vidhyati* (*vyadh* + *ya* + *ti*). Hence the operation of modification is not really applicable to letters.

184. Some say that there is no lack of fixity, because the absence of fixity itself is fixed.

I is sometimes modified into *y*, and *y* sometimes into *i*. So in respect of letters there is no fixity as to the original materials of their modification. This much, however, is fixed: that there is no fixity, or in other words, the absence of fixity is fixed. Hence the objector, who is a quibbler, contends that there is fixity at least as to the negative aspect of modification.

185. By saying that the absence of fixity is fixed, you cannot set aside our reason, because the fixity and its absence are contradictory terms.

Our reason is that in respect of letters there is no fixity as to their modification. You contend that, though there is no fixity, the absence of fixity is fixed. Our reply is that, though the absence of fixity is fixed, it does not establish fixity as a positive fact, because fixity is incompatible with the absence of fixity.

186. There is an apparent modification of letters in the case of their attaining a different quality, taking up substitutes, becoming short or long, and undergoing diminution or augmentation.

A letter is said to attain a different quality when, for instance, the grave accentuation is given to what was acutely accented. As an instance of a letter accepting a substitute, we may mention *gam* as becoming *gacch*. A long vowel is sometimes shortened, e.g., *nadī* (in the vocative case), becomes *nadi*. A short vowel is lengthened, e.g., "*muni*" (in the vocative case) becomes "*mune*." Diminution occurs in such cases as "*as+tas*" becoming "*stas*." In "*devānām*" (*deva+ām*) *na* is an augment.

187. The letters ended with an affix form a *word*.

Words are of two kinds: *nouns* and *verbs*. A noun ends in a *sup* affix, e.g., Rāmas (Rāma+*su*), while a verb ends in a *tiṅ* affix, e.g., *bhavati* (*bhū* + *ti*).

188. There is doubt what a *word* (noun) really means, as it invariably presents to us an *individual, form, and genus*.

The word "cow" reminds us of an individual (a four-footed animal), its form (limbs), and its genus (cowhood). Now, it is asked, what is the real signífication of a word (noun)—an individual, form, or genus?

189. Some say that the *word* (noun) denotes individual, because it is only in respect of individuals that we can use "that," "collection," "giving," "taking," "number," "waxing," "waning," "color," "compound," and "propagation."

"That cow is going"—here the term "that" can be used only in reference to an individual cow. Similarly, it is only in respect of individuals that we can use the expressions "collection of cows," "he gives the cow," "he takes the cow," "ten cows, "cow waxes," "cow wanes," "red cow," "cow-legs," and "cow gives birth to cow."

190. A *word* (noun) does not denote an individual, because there is no fixation of the latter.

Unless we take genus into consideration, the word "cow" will denote any individual of any kind. Individuals are infinite. They cannot be distinguished from one another, unless we refer some of them to a certain genus and others to another genus, and so on. In order to distinguish a cow-individual from a horse-individual, we must admit a genus called "cow" distinguished from a genus called "horse."

191. Though a word does not literally bear a certain meaning, it is used figuratively to convey the same, as in the case of "Brāhmana," "scaffold," "mat," "king," "flour," "sandalwood," "Ganges," "cart," "food,"

and "man," in consideration of association, place, design, function, measure, containing, vicinity, conjunction, sustenance, and supremacy.

If the word does not denote an individual, how is it that we refer to an individual cow by the expression "that cow is feeding"? The answer is that, though the word "cow" may not literally mean an individual, we may refer to the same figuratively. There are such instances, as "feed the staff" means "feed the Brāhmaṇa holding a staff," "the scaffolds shout" means "men on the scaffolds shout," "he makes a mat" means "he aims at making a mat," "Yama" (chastiser) means "a king," "a bushel of flour" means flour measured by a bushel, "a vessel of sandalwood" means "sandalwood placed in a vessel," "cows are grazing on the Ganges" means "cows are grazing in the vicinity of the Ganges," "a black cart" means a cart marked with blackness, "food" means "life," and "this person (Bharadvāja) is a clan" means "this person is the head of a clan."

192. Some say that the *word* (noun) denotes form by which an entity is recognized.

We use such expressions as "this is a cow" and "this is a horse" only with reference to the forms of the cow and the horse. Hence it is alleged by some that the word denotes form.

193. Others say that the *word* (noun) must denote genus, otherwise why in an earthenware cow, possessed of individuality and form, do we not find immolation, etc.?.

We can immolate a real cow, but not an earthenware cow, though the latter possesses individuality and form. The distinction between a real cow and an earthenware one is that the former comes under the genus cow, but the latter does not. Hence it is urged by some that a *word* (noun) denotes genus.

194. In reply, we say that it is not genus alone that is meant by a *word* (noun), because the manifestation of genus depends on the form and individuality.

The genus abides in the individual, and the individual cannot be recognized except by its form. Hence genus has reference both to the form and individual, or in other words, the genus alone is not the signification of a word.

195. The meaning of a *word* (noun) is, according to us, the *genus, form*, and *individual*.

The *word* (noun) signifies all the three, though prominence is given to one of them. For the purpose of distinction, the individual is prominent. In order to convey a general notion, preeminence is given to the genus. In practical concerns, much importance is attached to the form. As a fact, the word "noun" ordinarily presents to us the form, denotes the individual, and connotes the genus.

196. An *individual* is that which has a definite form and is the abode of particular qualities: 67.

An individual is any substance that is cognized by the senses, as a limited abode of color, taste, smell, touch, weight, solidity, tremulousness, velocity, or elasticity.

197. The *form* is that which is called the token of the genus.

The genus "cowhood," for instance, is recognized by a certain collocation of the dewlap, which is a form. We cannot recognize the genus of a formless substance.

198. *Genus* is that whose nature is to produce the same conception.

Cowhood is a genus that underlies all cows. Seeing a cow somewhere, we acquire a general notion of cows (i.e., derive knowledge of cowhood). This general notion enables us on all subsequent occasions to recognize individual cows.

FROM UDDYOTAKARA'S *NYĀYA-VĀRTTIKA*

It is not true that the means of knowledge and the objects of knowledge are supposed (to be existent) like (the objects in) a magic show, or the appearance of a castle in the cloud, or a mirage. For this (thesis) cannot be proved.

No reason is given when it is asserted that unreal objects are being supposed (to be existent) like dream-objects. What reason is there to maintain that the objects in a dream-experience are unreal?

Opponent: The reason is what is called *khyāti* (appearance of objects in experience). The reason for maintaining the thesis—viz. objects that are apprehended at the waking state of consciousness do not have a separate existence from consciousness—is the appearance of objects as in a dream.

Response: No. Your example (i.e., the dream-example) stands in need of a proof just as does your thesis.

What is the reason for believing that the objects that appear in a dream-experience are not distinct from the (dream-)consciousness?

Opponent: The objects do not exist since they are not apprehended by the waking person.

Response: If you think that these objects do not exist just because they are not apprehended by the waking person, then you are wrong. For you have added a qualification (unnecessarily).

It is implied that those objects that are apprehended by the waking person exist. And the qualification—those "that are not apprehended by the waking person"—is superfluous.

If you argue that the objects that are apprehended either in the waking experience or in a dream are unreal but the consciousness (of such objects) exists, (we ask:) what could be your reason?

The fact of being not apprehended by the waking person cannot be cited as a reason because it is incapable of establishing the "contrapositive" (*viparyaya*; viz. apprehension of objects by the waking person proves their existence).

If apprehension proves existence only then is it warranted that nonapprehension can prove nonexistence.

It is contended that the reason should be capable of establishing the "contrapositive" thesis (viz. apprehension proves existence).

Opponent: The objects are not distinct from the consciousness (of them) because they are subject to comprehension (by the consciousness) just as a particular feeling (of pain) is. Just as that which is apprehensible (*grāhya*), like a particular feeling, is not distinct from consciousness, so also the objects are not distinct from consciousness.

Response: A feeling is a feeling of either pleasure or pain. Consciousness is a cognitive state (of mind). A cognitive state is distinct from the feeling of pleasure or pain. Therefore, your supporting example is not correct. Pleasure and pain are what are apprehensible, and their apprehension is a cognitive state. Thus, the apprehensible must be distinct from its apprehension.

If you argue that consciousness is identical with the feeling (i.e., pleasure or pain), we still say that there is no supporting example where the apprehensible and the apprehension are (undoubtedly) identified with each other. For an act and the object to which that act is directed cannot be identical with each other.

If you wish to establish identity (between apprehension and the apprehensible) without caring for the evidence of the means of knowledge, you establish (only) four "personality" aggregates (instead of five, by equating feeling with consciousness); and this will contradict your doctrinal position (that there are five "personality" aggregates, viz. aggregates of matter, feeling, perceptions, mental forces, and consciousness).

If you do not accept even four aggregates but admit consciousness only that is (commonly) experienced, we then counter: since there are neither internal nor external objects to account for the distinctness of the states of consciousness, how can you explain the distinction of different states of consciousness?

Opponent: One state of consciousness is different from the other just as one dream is different from another.

Response: Even in that case, the distinction of consciousness-states should be explained as owing to the comprehension of (different) things that are observed and experienced. If, in the case of dreams also, the distinction of consciousness-states is asserted to be owing to the difference of comprehension, then we counter by pointing out the distinction of comprehension from the comprehensible. The comprehensible cannot be identical with comprehension.

All the dream-experiences that reveal cities, birds, gardens and chariots distinctly are erroneous cognitive states. And these erroneous cognitive states originate, sharing the generic features of the waking cognitive states.

Opponent: In my theory, all cognitive states will be held to be erroneous.

Response: If you say that, we ask you to point out the "principal" object *(pradhāna)* in such errors. There cannot be an erroneous cognition that is without any "principal" object.

Moreover, he who does not accept that the objects are distinct from consciousness should be countered with the refutation of this reason based upon the examination of its nature.

Is the nature of the object (in a dream) that of being external? If so, then the position becomes contradictory (viz. what is internal in consciousness is said to be external).

Is the nature of the dream-object that of being consciousness? If so, then the dream-object cannot be established because the states of consciousness cannot be communicated to others. For if the dream of one person is not expressed in words, the other person would not be able to know it.

Opponent: The states of consciousness taking the "forms" of words are conveyed to others.

Response: He who says this should explain the meaning of the word "form," *ākāra*. The "form" (in this context) is the apprehension by which something non-*x* appears as *x* depending upon the similarity of the "principal" object (e.g., "This is a snake"—this wrong apprehension has taken the "form" of a snake with regard to something that is not a snake but has similarity with the "principal" object, i.e., a snake).

Also, in your view, words are not real, and hence the sentence "The consciousness-state takes the 'form' of words" is a statement without a reference.

He who does not accept that objects are distinct from consciousness should also be asked to explain the distinction between a dream and a piece of waking experience. The objects are nonexistent as much in the waking experience as in the dream; hence, wherefrom could there be such a distinction as reflected in the statement "This is a dream and that is a waking experience?"

Even the discrimination of what begets merit and what begets demerit cannot be established (under your view). For just as one does not incur demerit by having illicit sexual relations in a dream, so also one would not incur demerit by doing so in the waking state.

Opponent: The (said) discrimination is maintained by the fact that in one case the person is overwhelmed with slumber, while he is not so overwhelmed in the other case.

Response: This is also wrong. How does one know that this odd behavior of the mind is caused by the influence of slumber?

Opponent: The clarity and unclarity of the states of consciousness distinguish the dream stage from the waking stage.

Response: You will have to explain the notion of clarity and unclarity without taking recourse to the objects (which are, according to you, nonexistent).

Opponent: It has been seen that states of consciousness can be distinct even when their objects are nonexistent. For example: The departed spirits originating from the maturation of similar "residual forces of action" (*karma*) see a river full of filth. No river is actually present there, nor any filth. And one thing cannot be many. But the states of consciousness are seen to be distinct, for some spirits see the same as a river full of water, and some others see it as a river full of blood. Thus it is ascertained that consciousness alone arises in different forms in the manner just described, depending upon its internal conditions, while the external objects as its conditioning antecedents do not exist.

Response: This is wrong because it runs into contradiction. If you say that consciousness appears in different forms in this manner while the external condition does not exist, we then ask: How is it so?

If consciousness takes the "form" of blood, you should explain the status of this blood. What is the status of this blood? In the same way, one should raise questions about the "form" of water or the "form" of the river. When each word in the sentence "They see a river of filth" is examined by analysis, the sentence becomes devoid of any objective reference if the aggregates of matter, etc., did not exist.

Regulation of place and time is also not possible. The departed spirits see the river full of filth in a particular place, not in just any place whatsoever. If objects did not exist, the reason for such regulation of place would have to be explained.

If, for a person, the existent object is determined by some "form" or other, then it is proper to hold that some of his cognitive states are erroneous. False cognitive states do not reject (the existence of) the "principal" object. Thus one should point out the "principal" objects in the cognition of the river of filth, etc. What applies to the cognition of the river of filth, etc., is also applicable to the cases of the magic show, appearance of the castle in the cloud, and mirage-water.

Opponent: "You imagine the 'perfuming' of action (*karma*) to be in one place and the result of it in another place" (Vasubandhu, *Viṃśikā*). The meaning of this (line) is that the (corresponding) result should be there where the action takes place. For him who takes objects to be different from their consciousness, the action will happen in one place while its result will be in another place, and thus the action and its result will have different substrata (but cause and effect are supposed to have the same substratum).

Response: This is not true, for I do not concede the point. I do not concede that the action and its result are occurring in different substrata. The action is located in the self *(ātman)* and the result is also in the same locus. Thus, the (supposed) fault (in my position) is rejected.

The objects (of my consciousness) are different from my consciousness because they possess generic features as well as specific features. They are distinct just as my consciousness-series is distinct from the consciousness belonging to another personality-series (i.e., another person).

The objects are different from consciousness because they can be established (as external) by means of knowledge. Also because they are "effects" (*kārya*, "causally conditioned"), they are temporal, and they are preceded by residual traces of action (*dharma*).

FURTHER READING

Chakrabarti, Kisor Kumar. *Classical Indian Philosophy of Mind: The Nyāya Dualist Tradition.* Albany: State University of New York Press, 1999.

Chatterjee, Satischandra, and Dhirendramohan Datta. *An Introduction to Indian Philosophy.* Calcutta: University of Calcutta, 1939.

Ganeri, Jonardon. *Indian Logic: A Reader.* Richmond, Surrey: Curzon, 2001.

Ingalls, Daniel H. H. *Materials for the Study of Navya-Nyāya Logic.* Delhi: Motilal Banarsidass, 1988.

King, Richard. *Indian Philosophy.* Edinburgh: Edinburgh University Press, 1999.

Matilal, Bimal Krishna. *Nyāya-Vaiśeṣika.* Wiesbaden: Harrassowitz, 1977.

Phillips, Stephen H. *Classical Indian Metaphysics: Refutations of Realism and the Emergence of "New Logic."* Delhi: Motilal Banarsidass, 1997.

Potter, Karl H. *Indian Metaphysics and Epistemology: The Tradition of Nyāya-Vaiśeṣika up to Gaṅgeśa.* Princeton: Princeton University Press, 1977.

Sharma, Chandradhar. *A Critical Survey of Indian Philosophy.* London: Rider, 1960.

7

VAIŚEṢIKA

HISTORY

The Vaiśeṣika system holds that liberation is brought about through a comprehensive analysis of nature. The natural world exists, is knowable, and is made up of a plurality of particular elements. Such knowledge is connected with the belief that *buddhi* (consciousness) is merely a *guṇa* (quality) of the *ātman* (self), which is itself a *dravya* (substance). Once one has gained this knowledge, the *ātman* will attain the desired state of existence without a consciousness.

Kāṇada (fl. ca. 200 B.C.E.–100 C.E.) is the author of the *Vaiśeṣika Sūtras*, the foundational text for the school. Kāṇada's *Sūtras* gave rise to Praśastapāda's *Padārtha-dharma-saṃgraha* (*Compendium of the Nature of the Fundamental Categories*) (ca. 550 C.E.), which, though categorized as a commentary, does not follow the format of the *Vaiśeṣika Sūtras*.

EPISTEMOLOGY

The Vaiśeṣika school accepts only two *pramāṇas* (sources of valid knowledge): *pratyakṣa* (perception) and *anumāna* (inference). It does not accept *śabda* (testimony) as a *pramāṇa*, despite upholding the authority of the Vedas. Unlike other schools of Indian philosophy that hold the Vedas to be a *pramāṇa*, the Vaiśeṣika thinkers hold that the Vedas are valid not because they have *svataḥ-prāmāṇya* (intrinsic validity), but because they are rooted in the *pratyakṣa* of *ṛṣis* (seers).

ONTOLOGY

According to the realist Vaiśeṣika school, the universe is composed of six *padārthas* (fundamental categories, lit. "what is predicated by the word"):

dravya (substance), *guṇa* (quality), *karman* (action), *sāmānya* (universal), *viśeṣa* (particularity), and *samavāya* (relation of inherence). Kāṇada posited a direct correlation between a word and the object to which it referred; hence the fundamental categories are predicated by the word.

Dravya possesses *guṇa* and *karman*; *pṛthivī* (earth), *jala* (water), *tejas* (light), and *vāyu* (air) are perceivable and material *dravya*. *Paramāṇus* (atoms) of these four *dravyas* comprise all material objects. *Paramāṇus*, which are six-sided, first combine to make dyads. Three dyads make a triad, which according to the Vaiśeṣika school is the smallest perceptible unit. *Ākāśa* (ether), *kālā* (time), *dik* (space), *ātman* (self), and *manas* (mind) are not material. *Buddhi* (consciousness) is produced through the contact of *manas* and the *ātman*. The *manas* is an inert instrument of knowing that acts to compile the data sent by the senses. By itself the *ātman* is unconscious.

According to Kāṇada there are seventeen *guṇas*; Praśastapāda states that there are twenty-four. Kāṇada's seventeen are: *paratva* (distance), *aparatva* (proximity), *saṃyoga* (conjunction), *vibhāga* (separation), *pṛthaktva* (distinctness), *parimāṇa* (size), *saṃkhyā* (number), *sparśa* (touch), *gandha* (smell), *rasa* (taste), *rūpa* (color), *iccha* (desire), *dveśa* (aversion), *prayatna* (effort), *buddhi* (consciousness), *sukha* (pleasure), and *duḥkha* (pain). To these Praśastapāda adds *saṃskāra* (tendency), *dravatva* (fluidity), *gurutva* (heaviness), *śabda* (sound), *dharma* (merit), *adharma* (demerit), and *sneha* (viscosity). Though dependent upon *dravyas*, *guṇas* are still conceived as distinct. *Dharma* and *adharma* are referred to together as *adṛṣṭa* (unseen), which is the power of causality in the mechanism of *karma*. Accumulating *adṛṣṭa* leads to rebirth.

There are five types of *karman* (action) that are found within *dravyas*. They are ephemeral and do not persist. These are upwards, downwards, expansion, contraction, and locomotion.

The Vaiśeṣika school posits that there are perceptible *sāmānyas* (universals). There is, for example, a bookness that is shared by all books, including this one. Though they are real, they do not exist (unlike the parallel concept described by Plato). An ontological status is thus given to class categories.

Viśeṣas (particularity) is the principle of individuality that is found on the atomic level. It is what distinguishes individual items that are otherwise alike, such as individual *paramāṇus* of *jala* (water).

Samavāya (relation of inherence) is an eternal relation between two entities, such as between *dravya* and *guṇa*. Take, for example, a purple shirt. The purple color has a *samavāya* relationship with the shirt. These inherent (and not contingent relations) are found between particulars and universals and wholes and parts.

Abhāva is a seventh *padārtha* that was added by later Vaiśeṣika thinkers. If all words have a perceptible referent, some Vaiśeṣika scholars argued, then the negation must also be accounted for. The cognition "The container is not there" is actually "The nonexistence of the container is there." Or, the cognition "This container has not water" is actually two cognitions: "This container is there" and "The absence of water is there." In this way *abhāva* explains the experience of negation.

SOTERIOLOGY

The goal of the Vaiśeṣika school is to realize that the *ātman* can be separated from *buddhi* and can attain a state of unconsciousness. Pain arises from the *saṃyoga* of the *ātman*, the *indriyas* (senses), the *manas*, and the objects of the senses. When the *ātman* is separated from the *indriyas* then neither *dharma* nor *adharma* is accumulated, rebirth cannot take place, and *mokṣa* is achieved. In *mokṣa* each *ātman* still has a *viśeṣa* and thus its individuality.

THE TEXTS

Included here is the entirety of Kāṇada's *Vaiśeṣika Sūtras*, which is composed of 373 *sūtras* (aphorisms) and is divided into ten chapters. Each chapter is subdivided into two *āhnikas* (lessons). The second selection is from Śrīdhara's *Nyāya-kandalī*, a commentary on Praśastapāda's *Padārtha-dharma-saṃgraha*, and concerns arguments for the existence of the atom and of aggregates.

KAṆĀDA'S *VAIŚEṢIKA SŪTRAS*

First Chapter, First *Āhnika*

1. Now we will explain *dharma*.

2. That is *dharma* (which leads to the) attainment of *abhyudaya* and *niḥśreyasa*.

3. That (teaching/tradition/collection) which explains this (*dharma*) is authoritative (*pramāṇa*).

4. The true knowledge of shared and differing properties of ontological categories, based in/generated by the particular attributes of those *padārthas*—*dravya, guṇa, karma, sāmānya, viśeṣa,* and *samavāya* —is productive of *niḥśreyasa*.

5. *Pṛthivī, āpa, teja, vāyu, ākāśa, kāla, dik, ātmā,* and *mana* are the *dravyas.*

6. Form or color, taste, odor, touch, number, measure, distinctiveness, conjunction, disjunction, *paratva, aparatva,* intellect, *sukha, duḥkha,* desire, aversion, effort, etc., are the *guṇas.*

7. Movement upward (rise), movement downward (fall), contraction, expansion, and movement (from one place to other) are the *karmas.*

8. *Sat, anitya,* substantive, effect, cause, *sāmānya, viśeṣa* are peculiar to *dravya, guṇa,* and *karma.*

9. *Dravya* and *guṇa* generate substances of their own class, (which is) a common property (shared by them).

10. *Dravya* generates *dravya* and *guṇa* too (generates) other *guṇas.*

11. *Karma* cannot be formed by *karma.*

12. And neither is *dravya* destroyed by its effect or its cause.

13. (But) *guṇas* (are destroyed) by both (effect and cause).

14. Effect (*karma*'s) is opposed by *karma.*

15. (Having) actions, *guṇas,* and (being) coinherent cause are the characteristics of *dravya.*

16. Residing in *dravya,* not possessing *guṇa,* and (when independent) not being a cause of contact or disjunction are the features of *guṇa.*

17. (Residing at a time) in one *dravya,* (being) devoid of *guṇa,* and (being) the unbiased independent cause of conjunction and disjunction are the features of *karma.*

18. *Dravya* is the common cause of *dravya, guṇa,* and *karma.*

19. So is *guṇa* (too the common cause of *dravya, guṇa,* and *karma*).

20. *Karma* is the common cause of conjunction, disjunction, and motion.

21. *Karma* is not (a cause) of *dravya.*

22. (Because) it is excluded (from them).

23. *Dravya* is the common effect of *dravyas.*

24. Because of its dissimilarity from *guṇa, karma* is not (an effect) of *karmas.*

25. (In *guṇas* like) numbers, (which are) duality, onwards, separateness, conjunction, and disjunction (are generated by more than one *dravya*).

26. (Due to its) *asamavāya* (in more than one *dravya*) *karma* is not the common effect (of several *dravyas*).

27. A *dravya* is (the effect) of conjunctions.

28. A color/form is (the effect) of colors/forms.

29. (The *guṇa*) upward movement (is the effect) of heaviness, effort, and contact.

30. Conjunction and disjunction are also (the effect) of *karma.*

31. In (the treatment of) cause in general, *karma* is not considered to be a cause of *dravya* and *karma.*

First Chapter, Second *Āhnika*

32. In the absence of cause is the absence of effect.

33. But in the absence of effect there is no absence of cause.

34. (Both) *sāmānya* and *viśeṣa* depend upon the intellect.

35. Being/existence, being the cause of continuity, is *sāmānya.*

36. *Dravya, guṇa,* and *karma* are both *sāmānya* and *viśeṣa.*

37. *Viśeṣa,* being (the constituent of) ultimate differences, exists independent (of any percipient).

38. By which *dravya, guṇa,* and *karma* appear to be existent, that is *sattā.*

39. *Sattā* is different from *dravya, guṇa,* and *karma.*

40. It is existent in *guṇa* and *karma,* so it is neither *guṇa* nor *karma.*

41. And also (because of the) nonpresence of *sāmānya* and *viśeṣa* (*sattā* is different from others).

42. *Dravyatva* is stated by its being in many *dravyas.*

43. And also (because of the) nonpresence of *sāmānya* and *viśeṣa.*

44. So is *guṇatva* stated by its being in *guṇas.*

45. And also (because of the) nonpresence of *sāmānya* and *viśeṣa.*

46. *Karmatva* is stated by its being in *karmas.*

47. And also (because of the) nonpresence of *sāmānya* and *viśeṣa.*

48. *Sattā* exists because of the nonparticular mark of the being and the nonexistence of the mark of *viśesa.*

Second Chapter, First *Āhnika*

49. (One which has) color, taste, odor, and touch is *pṛthivī.*

50. (Having) color, taste, and touch, *āpa* is fluid and smooth.

51. *Teja* has color and touch.

52. *Vāyu* is touchable.

53. These (*guṇas,* namely, color, taste, odor, and touch) are not present in *ākāśa.*

54. Butter, lac, beeswax in contact with fire become (fluid, a property) common to (them and) water.

55. Tin, lead, iron, silver, and gold in contact with fire become (fluid, a property) common to (them and) water.

56. Horns, hump, hair at the tip of its tail, and a dewlap are the visible signs of a cow.

57. (Similarly) touch (is the sign) of *vāyu* too.

58. And this touch is not of the visible (things), hence *vāyu* has an invisible mark.

59. (*Vāyu* is) a *dravya* for not being (inherent) in other *dravyas.*

60. And by possessing *kriyā* and *guṇas* (*vāyu* is a *dravya*).

61. (For) not being in other *dravyas* (*vāyu*) is stated to be *nitya.*

62. The mixing of *vāyu* with *vāyu* is also the mark of its multiplicity.

63. (Since) the contact with *vāyu* is not perceptible there is no visible mark.

64. In the inference by general perception too (*vāyu*) is considered to be nonparticular.

65. Thus (the being of *vāyu*) has been handed down in the tradition.

66. (Just as) name and *karma* are marks of the particular distinguished things (similarly *vāyu* is known).

67. (Because by) perception, name and *karma* are known to have been produced.

68. Exit and entry are the marks of *ākāśa.*

69. These (exit and entry) cannot be the mark (since) *karma* can inhere in (only) one *dravya.*

70. And also because of its (*ākāśa*'s) difference from the marks of other causes.

71. From conjunction (results) nonexistence of *karma.*

72. Before the *guṇas* of the cause, the *guṇas* of the effect are seen.

73. In the nonappearance of other effects too *śabda* is not the *guṇa* of the tangible (entities).

74. (Since it, *śabda,* is) inherent and perceived elsewhere (in other *dravyas*) it is the *guṇa* neither of *ātmā* nor of *mana.*

75. It remains that (sound) is a mark of *ākāśa.*

76. (Its) *dravyatva* and *nityatva* are explained by *vāyu.*

77. Like being (existence) it is one.

78. (Since) *śabda* as a mark is nonparticular and due to the nonexistence of other *viśeṣa* marks (of *ākāśa,* it is a unity).

79. Thus by this order (unity) it (*ākāśa*) is one and is also separate from others.

Second Chapter, Second *Āhnika*

80. (When) flower and cloth are brought close together, the nonappearance of the other *guṇa* in the cloth is the mark of nonpresence of the odor (in the cloth).

81. (It is) established that odor is (the mark) of *pṛthivī.*

82. By this energy is explained.

83. Energy is (the mark) of *teja.*

84. Coldness is (the mark) of *āpa.*

85. (The idea of) "posterior" (in relation to) that which is posterior, simultaneity, slowness, and quickness are the marks of *kāla.*

86. Its *dravyatva* and *nityatva* is explained (as in) by *vāyu.*

87. Like being (existence) it is one.

88. (By) not being in *nitya* entities and being in *anitya* entities, *kāla* is a (technical) term of the cause.

89. "This is in this side (direction)" such a (nature of) mark is of *diśā.*

90. (Its) *dravyatva* and *nityatva* is explained (as in) by *vāyu.*

91. Like being (existence) it is one.

92. By (nature of its) particular effects it (*diśā*) is many (diverse).

93. (*Diśā* is) regarded as (in the case of) East with its past, present, and future relation to the sun.

94. So too is South, West, and North (*diśās*).

95. By this the other divisions of *diśā* are explained.

96. Perception of *sāmānya*, nonperception of *viśeṣa*, and memory of *viśeṣa* raise doubt.

97. (That which is) seen and seen before (are causes of doubt).

98. (That which is) perceived in a way (in the past) but not perceived similarly (at present) too (is a cause of doubt).

99. Knowledge and want of knowledge too (give rise to) doubt.

100. That (entity) which is apprehended by hearing is *śabda.*

101. (Doubt arises because) a particular class of sound is perceived in both homogeneous and heterogeneous things.

102. (It) inheres in one *dravya* only, hence (*śabda* is) not a *dravya.*

103. (It is) also not a *karma* since (it is) invisible.

104. (Though) its (*śabda*'s) *guṇa* to end (transiency) is a common feature (that it shares) with *karma.*

105. The mark of *sat* is absent (hence *śabda* is noneternal).

106. (It has) different *dharma* than the *nitya* (hence *śabda* is *anitya*, noneternal).

107. It is also *anitya* for it has a cause.

108. This (i.e., that *śabda* has a cause) is not unproved by change.

109. In manifestation (lies the) fault (thus meaning is not proven; *śabda* is not manifested).

110. Conjunction, disjunction, and (other) *śabdas* give birth to *śabda.*

111. *Śabda* is *anitya* too (because of) its mark.

112. (If *śabda* is *anitya* then) activities of both would not exist.

113. From the word *prathamā.*

114. Also from the existence of recognition (and memory of what has been spoken in the past).

115. All these arguments (for *śabda nityatva*) are doubtful.

116. (As sounds) commonly exist (as) enumerable.

Third Chapter, First *Āhnika*

117. The objects of senses are well known.

118. Cognition of senses and their objects is the mark of the existence of something other than senses and their objects.

119. That (argument which says senses are of the body) is invalid.

120. (Because there is) no knowledge in cause.

121. (And there would be) knowledge in effects.

122. (And) also nonknowledge (of the presence of consciousness in matter).

123. Another entity is the proof (of some other argument than the one supposed), hence (this too) is invalid.

124. A different entity (or mark, as an argument) for yet another entity (which is wholly unconnected) is also not valid.

125. The conjunct, the inherent, the coinherence in one thing, and the contradictory (are the types of proof).

126. An effect is (the mark of the existence) of another effect.

127. A nonexistent contradiction is (the mark) of the existent.

128. (That) which is is (the mark of) that which is not.

129. (That) which is is (also the mark of) that which has been.

130. (These types of inferences are valid because) knowledge of the mark is preceded by existent knowledge.

131. The unsubstantial is called fallacious (arguments).

132. The unproven and the dubious are (the two types of) fallacious (arguments).

133. Because it has horns thus it is a horse (is an example of the former type of fallacious argument).

134. Because it has horns it is a cow is an example of fallacy of plurality of consequents.

135. That (knowledge) which is proven by the proximity of *ātmā* and the object of senses is different (from the fallacious).

136. Activity and inactivity are seen in one's own *ātmā*, the mark is the same in others.

Third Chapter, Second *Āhnika*

137. (In cases of) proximity of *ātmā* and the objects of the senses, the existence and nonexistence of knowledge is the mark of *mana*.

138. Its *dravyatva* and *nityatva* is explained (as in) by *vāyu*.

139. (Because of) nonsimultaneity of efforts and nonsimultaneity of cognitions (it follows that) it (*mana*) is one (in every one).

140. Ascent and descent (of vital airs), opening and closing (of eyes), motions of life and *mana*, effects of the organs of sense, *sukha* and *duḥkha*, desire, aversion, and effort are the marks of *ātmā*.

141. Its *dravyatva* and *nityatva* is explained (as in) by *vāyu*.

142. "This is Yajñadatta," (in this) there is absence of perception as there exists no visible marks (of his *ātmā*, even) in contact (of organs of sense and of cognition).

143. Based on *sāmānya* (generalized) perception (of observable signs) it cannot be inferred as *viśeṣa*.

144. Thus it (the being of the *ātmā*) is proved (to exist) by the *āgama*.

145. The word "I" is different (in everyone, hence) the *āgama* is not the only proof.

146. If the perception "I am Devadatta, I am Yajñadatta" is seen (what is the need of inference?).

147. If the mark of *ātmā* were seen, it would be an assurance (for it would be) then evident as a precept.

148. "Devadatta goes, Yajñadatta goes" this could mean reference to the body.

149. This application is doubtful.

150. The "I" is cognized as a reference to each *ātmā* and (is a distinctive entity) not to any other, this difference is clearly seen.

151. "Devatta goes," this application through the self-conscious expression shows that it ("I") is presentative of the body.

152. This application is doubtful.

153. But the knowledge of Yajñadatta and Viṣṇumitra does not, due to their particular bodies, become an object.

154. The knowledge of the "I," individually established by its predominant and sensible attributes, does not depend on proof of the *āgama* alone for it is affirmed like *śabda* (by inference too).

155. Due to the common origin of *sukha, duḥkha*, and knowledge (in all bodies) *ātmā* is one.

156. (Because of) circumstances it (perception) is many (by special limitations as individuals).

157. And (so too) on the authority of the *śāstras*.

Fourth Chapter, First *Āhnika*

158. That (which is) eternal and uncaused is *nitya*.

159. Its effect is its mark.

160. (From) existence of cause is existence of effect.

161. *Anitya* is the negation of existence of the *viśeṣa*.

162. (The supposition of *anityatā* only rises out of) ignorance.

163. Perception is possible only of objects of magnitude (provided) they have more than one *dravya* and have color/form.

164. Though a compound of many dravyas and being of substantial magnitude, *vāyu* is not perceptible because of the nonpresence of color.

165. Color is perceived only when there is a particular color or there is coinherence of more than one dravya.

166. By this the cognition of taste, odor, and touch is explained.

167. (In case of) its (taste, smell, and touch) nonexistence there will be no deviation.

168. (The *guṇas*) number, measure, separateness, conjunction, disjunction, otherness, non-otherness, and *karma* are visible to the eye (only if they) possess color.

169. In uncolored (things) they (the *guṇas* mentioned above) are not visible to the eye.

170. By this the existence of the *guṇas* and the cognition of all the senses is explained.

Fourth Chapter, Second *Āhnika*

171. That again *pṛthivī*, etc., *dravyas* exist in three forms—body, sense, and objects.

172. (If) the conjunction of perceptible and imperceptible (*dravyas*) is not visible then it (body) is not the compound of five elements.

173. (If) other *guṇas* are unmanifested, then too (*pṛthivī*, etc., other effective *dravyas* cannot be considered as the compound of five).

174. Not of three elements (*pṛthivī*, *āpa*, and *teja*—is body composed).

175. (Though a) conjunction of atoms is not denied.

176. Of these bodies are of two types—*yonija* and *ayonija*.

177. (Because early *ayonija* bodies) have antecedents in indeterminate time and space.

178. And (following) a particular *dharma*.

179. Also (because) linguistic evidence have existed.

180. Since naming (or language) is without a beginning.

181. (Thus) *ayonija* bodies exist.

182. Also Vedas are the marker (proof).

Fifth Chapter, First *Āhnika*

183. The conjunction with and the effort of the *ātmā* results in the *karma* of the hand.

184. Similarly, conjunction with the hand (and its being heavy) results in *karma* in the pestle.

185. But, the *karma* (produced) in the pestle is due to the impact and not because of its conjunction with hand but otherwise (is seen even without the conjunction).

186. Similarly, conjunction of the *ātmā* (is not the cause of) *karma* in the hand.

187. *Karma* in the hand is due to the impact and conjunction with the pestle.

188. *Karma* of *ātmā* is also due to conjunction with the hand and (motion).

189. In the nonpresence of contact (the pestle) falls due to its heaviness.

190. (In the) absence of a particular impulse the upward or sideward movement is not possible.

191. From particular effort results particular impulse.

192. From particular impulse results the particular jumping (upward).

193. By the *karma* of the hand the *karma* of a child is explained.

194. (And) so too, the bursting open of a burning object.

195. In the absence of effort sleep-walking results.

196. *Karma* in the grass is due to its contact with *vāyu.*

197. Movement of the gem (toward the thief), movement of the needle (toward the lodestone) are due to unseen causes.

198. In an arrow, many a time, particular conjunctions cause different *karma.*

199. From impulse (results) the arrow's first *karma,* the next from the inherent *saṁskāra* which the arrow gains (from the first), and so on.

200. The absence of *saṁskāra* and (the presence of) heaviness results in its (arrow's) fall (falling).

Fifth Chapter, Second *Āhnika*

201. From the impact of impulse and united contact (of entities) results the *karma* in *pṛthivī.*

202. These particulars are caused by unseen causes.

203. Water falls due to absence of contact and due to (the presence of) its heaviness.

204. Fluidity (being the nature of liquids) results in flow.

205. The rays of the sun in contact with *vāyu* (causes the) rise of water.

206. (Water rises up due to) the united contact, and the impulse of compression.

207. Circulation in trees is due to an unseen cause.

208. Freezing and melting of water, too is the result of its contact with *teja.*

209. The mark (of the presence of *teja*) is the lightning and thunder.

210. Also in Vedas (is it proved).

211. From the conjunction and disjunction of water (in the form of clouds) results lightning.

212. The *karma* of *teja* and *vāyu* are explained by the *karma* of *pṛthivī.*

213. The upward flaming of fire, the sideward movement of *vāyu,* the first *karma* of atoms and *mana* are due to unseen causes.

214. The *karma* of the hand explains the *karma* of *mana.*

215. From the conjunction of *ātmā,* senses, *mana,* and the object result *sukha* and *duḥkha.*

216. When *mana* gets situated in the *ātmā* there is absence of its beginning (of *sukha-duḥkha*), when there is nonexistence of *duḥkha* in the body, that is *yoga.*

217. The moving away and coming closer (of the *manas* to the *ātmā*), conjunctions of things eaten and drunk, and conjunctions with all other effects (all these) are done by unseen causes.

218. When there is nonexistence of this (*adṛṣṭa*), there is nonexistence of conjunction and nonexistence of manifestation that is *mokṣa.*

219. Darkness is a nonpresence, being dissimilar to the production of *dravya, guṇa,* and *karma.*

220. And because of the obscuring of *teja* (light) by other *dravya.*

221. *Diśā, kāla,* and *ākāśa* are also opposed to action; thus they are nondynamic.

222. By this are explained *karma* and *guṇa.*

223. The coinherence of nondynamic things is excluded from *karma.*

224. (But) *guṇas* as a cause (of *karma*) are noncoinherent.

225. By *guṇa diśā* is explained.

226. By cause time (is explained).

Sixth Chapter, First *Āhnika*

227. The statements of Vedas are created knowledgeably.

228. Names and *guṇas* in the Brāḥmaṇas are the mark of that.

229. Giving is wise.

230. And so is receiving.

231. (Because) the *guṇa* of one *ātmā* is not a cause with regard to another *ātmā.*

232. That (wisdom) is not present in impure food.
233. In impurity is *hiṁsā.*
234. Association with it results in *doṣa.*
235. That is not present in the nonimpure.
236. Again relation should be maintained with the superiors.
237. And with (those) similar and low (in stature).
238. By this the (nature of) reception among one another who are of the nature of superior, similar, and low is explained.
239. And apposed to this (receiving) is *tyāga.*
240. Give up the low.
241. For the similar give up the self or give them up.
242. To the superior give up the self.

Sixth Chapter, Second *Āhnika*

243. Actions of motives are seen or unseen, where it is unseen tends to *abhyudaya.*
244. Fasting, continence, residence in the *gurukula,* life in the forest, giving, oblation, knowing the *diśās* and the constellations, incantation of sacred texts, and following the seasons and observances of religion conduce to invisible result.
245. The duties of the four *āśramas* of life are rooted in *anupadhā* and *upadhā.*
246. Deficiency of faith is an *upadhā* and nondeficiency is an *anupadhā.*
247. That which is of the prescribed color, taste, odor and touch, which is oblated upon and sprinkled with water is pure.
248. Impurity is the negation of purity.
249. Different from the prescribed object (too is impure).
250. Even partaking pure food without following the prescriptions will result in absence of *abhyudaya.*
251. Or it occurs because restraint means something else.
252. There is nonexistence where it is not.
253. From pleasure arises desire.
254. Also through that being engrained.
255. Due to the unseen.
256. Also due to particularity of natures.
257. Due to desire or aversion man performs *dharma* or *adharma.*
258. By these are conjunction and disjunction (explained).
259. *Mokṣa* is explained as being dependent on the *karma* of the *ātmā.*

Seventh Chapter, First *Āhnika*

260. *Guṇas* have been stated.

261. The color, taste, odor, and touch of *pṛthivī*, etc., are *anitya* (since they are) *anitya dravyas.*

262. By this is said the *nityatva* in *nitya* things.

263. They (the *guṇas*) are nitya in *āp*, *teja*, and *vāyu* as they (the *dravyas*) are *nitya*.

264. In things *anitya* they (the *guṇas*) are *anitya* as the *dravyas* are *anitya*.

265. The change of *guṇas* produced by heat in *pṛthivī* has its beginning in the cause.

266. (Because there is) one *dravya* only.

267. The perception and nonperception of *aṇu* and *mahat* has been explained to be *nitya*.

268. In consequence of plurality too (*mahat* is produced).

269. Its opposite is an *aṇu*.

270. The notions of greater and smaller size are said to be relative on the existence or nonexistence of *viśeṣa*.

271. (Because there is) one time.

272. Examples too can be given.

273. The nonexistence of *aṇutva* and *mahattva* in *aṇutva* and *mahattva* is explained in *karma* and *guṇa*.

274. By *karmas karma* and by *guṇas guṇa* has been explained.

275. And also by *aṇutva* and *mahattva karma* and *guṇa* are explained.

276. By this the notions of length and shortness are explained.

277. In *anitya* (*dravyas*) these (four categories) are *anitya*.

278. In *anitya* (*dravyas*, these notions are) *nitya*.

279. The roundness (of atom) is *nitya*.

280. Ignorance is also the marker of knowledge.

281. *Ākāśa* and *ātmā* by merit of their size are called pervasive.

282. In (consequence of) nonpresence of that (pervasiveness) *mana* is small.

283. By *guṇas*, *diśā* is explained.

284. By cause (is explained) *kāla*.

Seventh Chapter, Second Āhnika

285. (By being) distinct from color, taste, odor, and touch, *ekatva* is a different entity.

286. Similarly *pṛthaktva.*

287. The nonexistence of *ekatva* and *pṛthaktva* in *ekatva* and *pṛthaktva* is explained by *aṇutva* and *mahattva.*

288. *Ekatva* does not exist in all things, for *karma* and *guṇa* are non-numbered.

289. That (notion) is wrong.

290. In nonexistence of *ekatva* secondariness does not exist.

291. Of cause and effect there is no *ekatva* and *pṛthaktva* in consequence of the nonexistence of *ekatva* and *pṛthaktva.*

292. This is explained in relation to the *anitya* (cause and effect).

293. A conjunct is produced by the *karma* of one of the two, by the *karma* of both, or by conjunction.

294. By this disjunction is explained.

295. The nonexistence of conjunction and disjunction in conjunction and disjunction is explained by *aṇutva* and *mahattva.*

296. *Karmas* in *karma* and *guṇas* in *guṇa* is explained (earlier) by *aṇutva* and *mahattva.*

297. There is neither conjunction or disjunction in cause and effect since they do not exist independently.

298. As it is a *guṇa.*

299. *Guṇa* is also implied.

300. As there is no action (thus no conjunction or disjunction).

301. Also the expression of "it is not" is used (in case of the nonexistent).

302. (Thus) the *śabda* and its meaning are without connection.

303. (Cognition of) that which is a conjunction (results from the knowledge of the conjunct, for example,) contact with a staff (and cognition of that) which possesses coinhesion from the particular.

304. Relation between the *śabda* and its meaning is significatory.

305. Otherness and non-otherness is (explained) by nearness and farness of objects residing in the same place at the same time.

306. From the closeness of cause otherness and from the farness of cause non-otherness (results).

307. The nonexistence of otherness and non-otherness in otherness and non-otherness is explained by *aṇutva* and *mahattva.*

308. (As) *karmas* is *karma* (is said earlier).

309. (As) *guṇas* in *guṇa* (has been explained in relation to *aṇutva* and *mahattva*).

310. *Samavāya* is that by the virtue of which cause and effect may be said to be in one another.

311. The negation of the essence of *dravyatva* and *guṇatva* is explained by (its) existence.

312. Its truth is (explained by) existence.

Eighth Chapter, First *Āhnika*

313. Cognition was explained in (chapter of) *dravyas.*

314. In them *ātmā* and *mana* are not visible.

315. The mode of origin of cognition has been stated in the enunciation of cognition.

316. Cognition of *guṇas* and *karmas* in close contact (with the sense-organs) should be considered as caused by *dravya.*

317. As *sāmānya* and *viśeṣa* do not exist in *sāmānya* and *viśeṣa* thus their cognition.

318. (Cognition of) *dravya, guṇa,* and *karma* presupposes the *sāmānya* and the *viśeṣa.*

319. In *dravya* (cognition) presupposes *dravya, guṇa,* and *karma.*

320. As *guṇa* and *karma* do not exist in *guṇa* and *karma* there is no (cognitive) presupposition of *guṇa* and *karma.*

321. If an entity is white that is in contact with *samavāya* and due to the knowledge of whiteness cognition arises in the white entity, the two (being and arising of cognition) stand in relation of cause and effect.

322. (Cognition arising in various) *dravyas* are not causes of one another.

323. The nonsimultaneous coming into being of cause and the causes being sequential in nature give rise to the sequence of cognition of pot, cloth, etc., not just as (direct) result of a cause.

Eighth Chapter, Second *Āhnika*

324. "This is," "that is," "you did it," "feed him"—such (cognition is resultant of) different intellects.

325. (Such expressions) exist in references to objects seen and not in objects unseen.

326. The term *artha* applies to *dravya, guṇa,* and *karma.*

327. In *dravya* identity with five elements was denied.

328. Being plural and having odor, *pṛthivī* is the (material cause for the) cognition of odor (by the nose).

329. Similarly, *āpa, teja,* and *vāyu* are the material causes of the organs of taste, sight, and touch.

Ninth Chapter, First *Āhnika*

330. In the absence of the interaction of *kriyā* and *guṇas*, before coming into being (an effect is said to be) nonexistent.

331. Existent (becomes) nonexistent.

332. In the absence of interaction of *kriyā* and *guṇa* it (existence) is distinct from nonexistence.

333. Existence also (is) nonexistent.

334. And that which is different (from both existence and nonexistence) is a nonexistence (which will never be in existence).

335. Perception of a nonexistent thing may also result from nonexistence of a past perception and a memory of the past, like the perception of an opposing object.

336. Likewise too from perception of existence is nonexistence.

337. Hereby the non-pot, non-cow, and *adharma* are explained.

338. There is no difference of meaning between that which has not been and that which is not.

339. There is no pot in the house in a negation of connection between an existent water-pot and the house.

340. Perceptual knowledge of *ātmā* is made possible by a particular conjunction between the *ātmā* and the *mana*.

341. Like perception of the different *dravyas*.

342. In those whose *mana* is not always meditative and in those whose *samādhi* is consummated there is the perception of *ātmā*.

343. (They also perceive) *karma* and *guṇa* from the coinherence of things.

344. *Ātmā* being in a form of coinherence there is also perception of the *guṇa* of *ātmā*.

Ninth Chapter, Second *Āhnika*

345. Anything connected with any other thing as effect, cause, in contact, as contrary, or as inseparably connected will serve as a mark.

346. That this is associated to this and the cause and effect are connected—such is known by examples.

347. By this is *śabda* explained.

348. There is no difference of meaning in argument, reason, mark, evidence, and instrument.

349. (Because) they are implicated in the notion of belonging to that (*śabda*).

350. *Smṛti* results from the particular conjunction of the *ātmā* with the *mana* and from *saṁskāra.*

351. So too, dreams (result from conjunction of *ātmā* and *mana*).

352. So too, consciousness in dreams.

353. And also from *dharma.*

354. Ignorance results from the *doṣa* of the organs of sense and from the *doṣa* of *saṁskāra.*

355. That (*avidyā*) is imperfect cognition.

356. Free from imperfection is knowledge.

357. Knowledge of seers and the perfect vision results from *dharma.*

Tenth Chapter, First *Āhnika*

358. Due to the difference between desirable and undesirable causes and by opposition, *sukha* and *duḥkha* are different in their being.

359. By their noninclusion of doubt and assurance they are different from cognition.

360. The production of them (doubt and assurance) is by means of perception and inference.

361. The notion of the past too (is a difference between the cognition of *sukha* and *duḥkha*).

362. And the effect (of such cognition) is not always observed.

363. (Because *sukha* and *duḥkha*) and observed to coinhere with the same object.

364. The head, the back, the stomach, and the vitals are in one (body) but their particularity results from the particularity (of their causes).

Tenth Chapter, Second *Āhnika*

365. That it is a cause, (this position) with regard to *dravya* (results) from the coinherence of effects.

366. Or from conjunction.

367. Coinherence in cause results in (noncoinherence in) *karma.*

368. Similarly color (results from) coinherence of the cause in the object.

369. Conjunction of cloth due to the coinherence of cause (is a non-coinherent cause).

370. Causation of contact also results from the coinherence of cause in cause.

371. (Because of) conjunct coinherence there is a special feature of fire (heat).

372. Observances (according to the injunction of the scriptures) and those (*karmas*) that are seen since they have no visible effects are the cause of prosperity.

373. Authoritativeness pertains to the teaching/tradition/collection since it is a declaration of that.

FROM ŚRĪDHARA'S *NYĀYA-KANDALĪ*

Exposition of the Atom-Theory

What trustworthy means of knowledge assures us of the existence of earth in its atomical form?

Siddhāntin:[1] The following syllogism (*anumāna*):

> At a certain point the continuant series of smaller and still smaller extensions comes to an end;
> because it is a continuant series of extensions;
> like the continuant series of greater and still greater extensions.

The point where [the series] stops, that [extension] than which there is no smaller, is the atom (or infinitesimal part).

For this reason too it is eternal:

> because it does not possess parts, whilst at the same time possessing substantiality;
> just like (physical) space).

Opponent: But the atom possesses parts; and thus it is not infinitesimal, because the notion will occur to simple people that the extension of the parts [of this, your supposed atom] is again smaller in comparison to the [atom, their] product.

Siddhāntin: Let then this part of that [which was at first considered to be an atom] be the atom.

Opponent: Neither will this be the case, because there will be again other parts.

Siddhāntin: So an endless regress would ensue; and consequently neither could the smaller and smaller [extensions] of aggregates exist insofar as the greatness or smallness of the number of the causes—[a greatness or smallness which is] the reason for the preeminence or inferiority of the extension—could not exist, since all things without exception would be produced from [an] endless [series of] causes. But this difference of extension [in the aggregates] *is*; ergo the atomical extension at a certain point does not allow a transgression. So the infinitesimal part is proved.

And this [atom] is one, and unproductive. For suppose this one eternal to be productive, then an uninterrupted arising of the effect [i.e., of the aggregates] would take place, insofar as it[, the atom,] would not be limited [in producing]. The indestructiveness [of everything] also would be a consequence; as neither an annihilation of the abode [i.e., of the atoms in which the aggregate "inheres"] nor a separation of the parts—[which annihilation or separation is] the cause of decay—would ever take place.

Neither can we attribute creative power to three atoms. For, with reference to the arising of "large" effect-substances, we learn by experience that only an effect-substance that [possesses in an absolute sense "largeness," *mahattva*, but] is of small extension compared with the extension of the thing in question [i.e., the product], is capable [of producing]. [To summarize this in a syllogistic form]:

> The threefold atom is only produced by effect-substance[s];
> because [this threefold atom] possesses "large" extension;
> like a pot.

Thus having rejected the productive power of three and one, we have proved: "that which is effected by two atoms is the double atom."

There is only effectuation by several [i.e., three or more] double atoms (also this restriction must be made); but not by two pairs of atoms. For if things that have infinitesimal size were effective, then this effectuation would be useless insofar as only infinitesimality would arise in accordance with the nature of the cause. There is, however, no restriction for higher numbers. Sometimes [an aggregate] is effected by three [double atoms], this is called a *tryaṇuka*, sometimes by four, sometimes by five; thus you may imagine as you wish [i.e., without limitation].—And there is no uselessness in effect; for we obtain [this result]: the greater the number of causes [i.e., constituent parts], the greater the degree of largeness. Neither, with matters standing thus, would the consequence be that a pot is effected by mere double atoms [without intermediate parts], for when a pot is broken, we see a separation of smaller and smallest parts and therefore we may conclude that the effectuation is correspondent to that.

The Existence of Aggregates

Opponent: Moreover, [those qualities as] color, etc., which are of an infinitesimal nature, transgress without exception the ken of the sense-organs; and an accumulation, independent of them, does not exist; therefore, what, according to your standpoint, is the object of sight and touch?

Siddhārtin: Though the atoms [i.e., the infinitesimal qualities of color, etc., which you uphold], taken separately, transgress the ken of the sense-organs, yet they become attainable to sense, whenever they come forth fitly and the internal organs of sense, etc., are present.

Opponent: No; for even on their fitly coming forth they do not abandon their innate nature of being ultimately subtle; moreover, when visibility is a mere consequence of the fitly coming forth, then both the internal and external organ of sense would be perceptible, since there is no difference [in this respect between the organs of sense and the external elements].

Siddhāntin: But if I should answer: my idea is this. Though the atoms, taken separately, are not gross (material, *sthūla*), yet heaped up together like a mass of hair, they get a gross appearance and become visible, and inasfar as there are no interspaces between then, they are [collectively] apprehended under [the idea of] oneness.

Opponent: Does then a one and gross form originate in these many [atoms], or is this [one and gross form] not really formed, but only perceived in them in consequence of our [own mental] projection, as it is in the case [of the oneness] of hairs?

Siddhāntin: If it really originates, then we have what we call an aggregate; but if it is experienced, when not being, then it is a false impression (*bhrānta*); and a false impression has a correct impression for its counterpart (*pratiyogin*); so then somewhere a one and gross [form] must be accepted as existing, and it is not true that its existence would only be in our cognition, because the idea "I am something material" does not arise and because the unwished-for consequence would be that the fact of [a thing] being a common object of several perceivers could not exist. Therefore this one and gross [form] is the object, since it always appears in a definite form and exhibits practical efficiency. This then is the proof for [the existence of] the aggregate.

Opponent: No doubt, a notion is proved when no (logical) impediment (*bādhaka*) exists; in that case we use the expression "so [it is]". But a refuting argumentation exists with reference to the existence of aggregates. To wit: when the hand trembles, then the body of which this hand is a part does not tremble, or if the foot trembles, then the body to which this foot belongs does not tremble. So then the consequence would be that one thing would possess contradicting qualities [scil. the body is at rest and at the same time in movement]. This is [logically] noncoherent; since no fixed rule exists for the body trembling necessarily whenever the hand trembles. But when a cause exists to make merely the hand move, then that only moves; and not the body, for [with reference to the latter] a cause is lacking; but when there is a cause for the movement of the body as well, then the body moves and has no rest. So where does contradiction come in, when the hand moves and not the body? Therefore there is *yutasiddhi* (relation of separability) between part and aggregate.

Siddhāntin: No; the relation of separability means an abiding in separate abodes. But movement and nonmovement are no [examples for that], because when a thing moves and its quality does not move [according to the general thesis that qualities do not possess action, i.e., do not move], then there is no relation of separability between this [thing and this quality]. The abiding in separate abodes is not seen in part and aggregate, even in the case when these two are separated from each other [for instance, when the hand is cut off from the body; in this case namely the former part begins to form an aggregate by itself]; so then there is no question of a relation of separability.

And the other point of refutation that is mentioned:

Refutation: When one part is hidden, then we do not perceive there the aggregate which inheres in that [part], but we perceive it so far as we perceive the parts uncovered; so then of one and the same thing a perception and nonperception at the same time ensue.

Answer: This is neither right. For when [only] one part is covered, then there is no concealment of the aggregate. For this, being one, abiding in many parts, is even perceived—though several parts are covered—by means of the perception of the many other, uncovered parts; because this [aggregate] is everywhere [i.e., over its whole extent] unremoted [i.e., present]. With reference to anything that is characterized by the perception of several parts [and not by the collective notion of oneness], the idea of grossness [gross = solid = *sthūla*] does not arise, because we do not perceive the accumulation of its several parts, whereas the perception would effect a notion [of ours] concerning an extensive dimension. But where a concealment of more parts and a perception of fewer parts take place, there the aggregate is not seized, for instance, when we see only the head of some one, submerged in water. When one part is painted, then the aggregate in that part is painted and in the other parts it is not painted; so then the consequence would be that the same thing is painted and not painted? With this we have no difficulty, because there is no inconsistency. The state of being painted means the conjunction with paint; and the state of not being painted is the nonexistence of that [conjunction]. And both [states] are found in one [thing], since conjunction does not cover [the whole object; i.e., need only take place in a part of it].

Opponent: This again is another point of refutation: Does an aggregate abide only partially or totally in each of its several parts?—a third way namely is not possible. The abiding then does not take place partially, since the [aggregate] without [all its] parts would not exist in that one place. On the other hand, if the [aggregate] abides [in any of the parts] totally, then it could not abide in the other parts, because should the nature of the thing be defined by its blending (*saṃsarga*) with one part, then the other parts would be excluded and another *svarūpa* (individual existence) [of the aggregate] could not be admitted in addition to the *svarūpa*, just now described.

Siddhāntin: We may give the following answer: Do you state the thesis "Whatever exists, exists (*vartate*) either partially or totally" as one upheld by yourself or as one defended by others? Certainly not as one upheld by your own [school]; no existence (abiding, *vṛtti*) of any thing in any place is upheld by the Buddhists [i.e., they believe in the existence neither of aggregates nor of atoms]; and the abiding of a thing in an either partial or total respect is not asserted by others, because the abiding is not of those two [of the whole and the parts] and because these two are neither causes of the abiding. Whatever exists (or abides) in reality, exists in a form that we may define as the relation of the abode and the abiding. And the blending (*saṃsarga*) of one thing with several is not contradictory. For the blending with the *ākāra* "yellow," etc., is experienced in the cognition of variegated color, which is [also] characterized by the *ākāra* "blue." And no differentiation of this [cognition] takes place according to [the manifoldness of] *ākāras*. If it were not possible for one [cognition] to arise from the seizing of several *ākāras*, then the absurd consequence would be that you could not possess the notion "variegated." Neither may the oneness of the *ākāras* be concluded from the unity of the cognition, since this is repugnant to [that which happens in the case of the] perception of variegated color. And in the same way as [one objective phenomenon, for instance, one color], enters [so to say], by our perception, into the other parts, *so that there arises* [lit. "with reference to"] the independent nature of one aggregate that is characterized by [or: in which dominates] one of the parts—similarly at the manifestation of one [thing] of a solid (*sthūla*) character, we become aware of a blending of several into one. And if [you refer to the case] where one abides in several, this does not make the slightest difference, inasfar as in both cases equally the blending of one is particularized by several. So then we have refuted both absurd consequences [which you, our opponents, try to deduce from our premises], namely, [the thesis] "Whatever is one, abides in only one place, so as one color or one aggregate" and [the other thesis] "Whatever abides in many [parts], is manifold, as, for instance, the *tāla*-fruits, which are divided into many portions, or an aggregate which abides in many, [in a manifoldness]." And the [two instances of] universal concomitance [expressed in these two propositions] are refuted both from our own and from another's [the opponent's] standpoint. From our own standpoint, namely, [as follows]: one cognition abides in several [factors]: object, external sense-organ, and internal sense-organ, inasfar as it abides in them by causal relation, while it possesses one undivided, individual nature. And also for the other, [the opponent], one thread abides equally in several jewels in a form [that is called] conjunction. So then the aggregate will abide in its parts by the relation of inherence and will yet not be many. Moreover, while this whole argumentation [of yours], based on *prasañga*, destroys [the notion of] abode, it annihilates too itself [i.e., makes all argumentation impossible]. For if no aggregate should exist and [consequently] the world [should consist] merely of atoms, then the notions [used in argumentations, such as] *dharma* (characteristic), *dharmin* (that which possesses the characteristic), *dṛṣṭānta* (example), etc., would become baseless; and [in accordance with this] no abiding (or existence) of a thing that has no abode could take place. Therefore, by that [argumentation of yours] the aggregate, which is proved by perception, cannot be annihilated; for it [scil. argumentation] is of less weight than that [i.e., perception], inasfar as [argumentation] is dependent on perception.

Opponent: If I should answer: perception is mistaken (illusionary, *bhrānta*)?

Siddhāntin: Why this?

Opponent: Because it is done away with by a refuting fact (*bādhaka*).

Siddhāntin: If perception is mistaken, then the refuting fact is proving; and if the refuting fact is proving, then perception is mistaken; so there arises [the logical fault of] mutual dependence [of propositions]. But no such rule exists in reference to perception, inasfar as it is independent [of other sources of knowledge]. And it is not right to say that such a thing [as perception], which is in agreement with the practical efficiency [of objective existence], which is trusted in by everybody, and which possesses an immediate evidence, should be mistaken. For [should it be so], then the unwished-for consequence would be that even the perception of [such elementary *ākāras* as] blue, etc., would be mistaken. So then your refuting fact has been put aside by us.

The Existence of the Atoms

Siddhāntin: The atoms, [the existence of] which can be deduced from the [existence of the] aggregates, must be called existent.

Opponent: The conjunction of the atom simultaneously with a sixfold [i.e., with six surrounding atoms] leads us to accept [the idea] that the atoms possess six parts (sides), and [consequently] excludes the existence of atoms.

Siddhāntin: How is this simultaneous conjunction to be taken? Is it either a simultaneous origination of the one atom with six other atoms? Or is it conjunction [that takes place] simultaneously? If it is a simultaneous origination—of a thing without parts [together with six other similar things]—in consequence of the simultaneity of the causes, what difficulty [could be raised]? But if it is a simultaneous conjunction, then neither is this inconceivable. For conjunction of objects does not concern their parts, for it also takes place with reference to (physical) space, which is without parts.

Opponent: If I should answer: You are wrong; for, supposing that one portion [of the atom] were [identical with] the other, then conjunction [would remain] within the limits of one atom and we should get the unwished-for consequence that it [scil. the object or aggregate] could not be perceived; however it is an object in reality.

Siddhāntin: The being subject to several conjunctions is possible, if simultaneous causes exist, just as well in reference to one undivisible atom, as in reference to a thing consisting of parts. Thus [you are] not [capable of] refuting [the existence of the atoms].

NOTE

1. "One who establishes a conclusion after noting and answering objections" (V. Shivaram Apte, *The Practical Sanskrit-English Dictionary* [Kyoto: Rinsen, 1986], 1681).

FURTHER READING

Chatterjee, Satischandra, and Dhirendramohan Datta. *An Introduction to Indian Philosophy*. Calcutta: University of Calcutta, 1939.

Faddegon, B. *The Vaiceṣika-System, Described with the Help of the Oldest Texts*. Wiesbaden: Dr. Martin Sandig, 1969.
Halbfass, Wilhelm. *On Being and What There Is: Classical Vaiśeṣika and the History of Indian Ontology*. Albany: State University of New York Press, 1992.
King, Richard. *Indian Philosophy*. Edinburgh: Edinburgh University Press, 1999.
Matilal, Bimal Krishna. *Nyāya-Vaiśeṣika*. Wiesbaden: Harrassowitz, 1977.
Potter, Karl H. *Indian Metaphysics and Epistemology: The Tradition of Nyāya-Vaiśeṣika up to Gaṅgeśa*. Princeton: Princeton University Press, 1977.
Sharma, Chandradhar. *A Critical Survey of Indian Philosophy*. London: Rider, 1960.

8

SĀṂKHYA

HISTORY

According to the Sāṃkhya school, suffering will end when the individual properly discerns the duality between *puruṣa* (consciousness) and *prakṛti* (materiality). They further believed that the material world emerged from *prakṛti*, given its association with *puruṣa*. The ultimate goal was thus for the *puruṣa* to see itself as distinct from the *prakṛti* and, consequently, for it to be no longer born in the cycle of birth and rebirth.

There are references to concepts that resemble Sāṃkhya ones in the *Upaniṣads*, and, most notably, within the *Mahābhārata*, in both the *mokṣadharma* section and the *Bhagavad Gītā*. In these texts, though, a systematic account is not presented. The school was made most well known by Īśvarakṛṣṇa (350–450 C.E.) in his *Sāṃkhya-kārikā*. Though Īśvarakṛṣṇa was not the founder of the tradition, the version of Sāṃkhya that he put forth became the reference point around which later scholars of Sāṃkhya oriented themselves.

The Sāṃkhya texts do not typically contain polemics or responses to attacks, as the texts of other schools of Indian thought do. Rather, they largely comprise concise lists of the various components of the system with the goal of directing the reader (or listener) toward a proper understanding of the relationship of duality between *puruṣa* and *prakṛti*.

EPISTEMOLOGY

As per the *Sāṃkhya-kārikā*, the Sāṃkhya school accepts three *pramāṇas* (sources of valid knowledge): *dṛṣṭa* (i.e., *pratyakṣa*) (perception); *anumāna* (inference); and *āptavacana* (i.e., *śabda*) (reliable verbal testimony). Given that the Sāṃkhya school is principally conceptual, both *anumāna* and *āptavacana* have more import than *dṛṣṭa*. *Puruṣa* (consciousness), the most important component of the system, for example, is inferred and held to be real by reason of Īśvarakṛṣṇa's *āptavacana.*

ONTOLOGY

According to the Sāṃkhya school, the universe is composed of only two elements, *puruṣa* and *prakṛti*, both real and eternally existent. No god who creates the universe is posited. *Puruṣa* is *cetanā* (pure consciousness), is a *sākṣitam* (witness), is *akartṛbhāva* (inactive), and is *kaivalya* (isolated). A multitude of *puruṣas* exist. In contrast, *prakṛti* is active and initially *avyakta* (unmanifest) (also known as *mūlaprakṛti* when *avyakta*). It is composed of three *guṇas* (constituent processes): *sattvas* (intelligibility process), *rajas* (activity process), and *tamas* (inertia process). These are in equilibrium until *prakṛti* comes into contact (*saṃyoga*) with *puruṣa*, after which their imbalance causes *prakṛti* to transform and to become *vyakta* (manifest). The *guṇas* are distributed unevenly in the emerging manifestations, known collectively as the twenty-five *tattvas* (entities). Although it may appear as if the *puruṣa* initiated the *guṇapariṇāma* (transformation of the constituent processes), it is merely its proximity to the *prakṛti* by which *prakṛti* begins manifesting.

Buddhi (intellect) (also known as *mahat*) is the first to emerge from *prakṛti*. It is followed by *ahaṃkāra* (ego), the *manas* (mind), the ten *indriyas* (capacities that enable sensing, motor functioning, and thinking), the *pañca-tanmātras* (five subtle elements), and the *pañca-bhūtas* (the five gross elements). The ten *indriyas* are separable into the five *buddhi-indriyas* (sense capacities) and the five *karma-indriyas* (action capacities). The *buddhi-indriyas* are *ghrāṇa* (smell), *rasana* (taste), *cakṣus* (sight), *śrotra* (hearing), and *tvac* (touch). The *karma-indriyas* are *vāc* (speaking), *pāṇī* (grasping), *pāda* (going), *pāyu* (excreting), and *upastha* (procreation). The *pañca-tanmātras* are the *mātras* (objects) of the *indriyas*, namely, *śabda* (sound), *sparśa* (feeling), *rūpa* (color), *rasa* (taste), and *gandha* (smell). The last set of emanations to derive from the *ahaṃkāra* is the *pañca-bhūtas* (the five elements) and they are the gross aspects of the *pañca-tanmātras*. They are *ākāśa* (ether), *vāyū* (air), *tejas* (fire), *ap* (water), *pṛthivī* (earth). These, then, comprise the subjective and objective modes of reality.[1]

The Sāṃkhya position is based on *satkārya-vāda*, the view that the effect exists in the natural cause, and would not be tenable without it. Nothing new is created. Rather, there is only a transformation of the *prakṛti*. The twenty-five *tattvas*, then, are manifestations of a previously unmanifested *prakṛti*. They are effects that were already existent in their cause, namely *mulaprakṛti*. The universe, then, is merely a *pariṇama* (transformation) of *prakṛti*. In fact, the existence of *prakṛti* can be inferred only from its effects.

SOTERIOLOGY

During the emergence of the *tattvas* from *prakṛti*, the *puruṣa*, which is initially a mere witness to the development, becomes associated with the *tattvas* and forgets that it is a witness rather than a participating actor. In so doing, the *puruṣa* seems to become part of *saṃsāra* (the neverending cycle of birth and rebirth) that is inherent to the processes of *prakṛti*. The goal of the classical Sāṃkhya is for each *puruṣa* to realize that it is free from *prakṛti* and not bound to the world and its suffering. The ultimate goal, then, is the *kaivalya* (isolation) of the *puruṣa*.

THE TEXT

The entirety of Īśvarakṛṣṇa's *Sāṃkhya-kārikā* is included here. This text is regarded as the first extant systematic presentation of Sāṃkhya. It is not a polemical text; rather, it is a simple outline of the Sāṃkhya position.

ĪŚVARAKṚṢṆA'S *SĀṂKHYA-KĀRIKĀ*

1. Because of the torment of the threefold suffering, (there arises) the desire to know the means of counteracting it. If (it is said that) this (desire; i.e., inquiry) is useless because perceptible (means of removal are available), (we say) no, since (perceptible means are not final or abiding).

2. The revealed (or scriptural, means of removing the torment) are like the perceptible (i.e., ultimately ineffective), for they are connected with impurity, destruction, and excess; a superior method, different from both, is the (discriminative) knowledge of the manifest (*vyakta*), the unmanifest (*avyakta*), and the knowing one (or knower; i.e., *puruṣa*).

3. Primordial nature (*mūlaprakṛti*) is uncreated. The seven—the great one (*mahat*), etc.—are both created and creative. The sixteen are created. *puruṣa* is neither created nor creative.

4. The attainment of reliable knowledge is based on determining the means of correct knowledge. The accepted means of correct knowledge are three because (these three) comprehend all means of correct

knowledge. These three means (are as follows:) (a) perception, (b) inference, (c) reliable authority.

5. Perception is the selective ascertainment of particular sense-objects. Inference, which is of three kinds, depends upon a characteristic mark (*liṅga*) and that which bears the mark (*liṅgi*). Reliable authority is trustworthy verbal testimony.

6. The understanding of things beyond the senses is by means of (or from) inference by analogy. That which is beyond even inference is established by means of reliable authority.

7. (Perception may be impossible due to the following:) (a) because something is too far away; (b) because something is too close; (c) because of an injured sense-organ; (d) because of inattention; (e) because of being exceedingly subtle; (f) because of intervention (of an object between an organ and the object to be perceived); (g) because of suppression (i.e., seeing the sun but no planets); (h) because of intermixture with what is similar.

8. The nonperception (of *prakṛti*) is because of its subtlety—not because of its nonexistence. Its apprehension is because of (or by means of) its effect. Its effect—the great one (*mahat*), etc.—is different from yet similar to *prakṛti*.

9. The effect exists (before the operation of cause) (*satkārya*) (a) because of the nonproductivity of nonbeing; (b) because of the need for an (appropriate) material cause; (c) because of the impossibility of all things coming from all things; (d) because something can only produce what it is capable of producing; (e) because of the nature of the cause (or, because the effect is nondifferent from the cause).

10. The manifest (*vyakta*) is (a) caused; (b) finite; (c) nonpervasive; (d) active; (e) plural; (f) supported; (g) mergent; (h) composite; (i) dependent. The unmanifest (*avyakta*) is the opposite.

11. (Both) the manifest and unmanifest are (a) (characterized by the) three *guṇas* ("constituents" or "strands"); (b) undiscriminated; (c) objective; (d) general; (e) nonconscious; (f) productive. The *puruṣa* is the opposite of them, although similar (to the *avyakta* as characterized in no. 10).

12. The *guṇas*, whose natures are pleasure, pain, and indifference, (serve to) manifest, activate, and limit. They successively dominate, support, activate, and interact with one another.

13. *sattva* is buoyant and shining; *rajas* is stimulating and moving; *tamas* is heavy and enveloping. They function for the sake of the *puruṣa* like a lamp.

14. Lack of discrimination, etc., is established because of (the manifest) having the three *guṇas* and because of the absence (of the *guṇas*) in the opposite of that (i.e., in the *puruṣa*). The unmanifest is likewise established because of the *guṇa*-nature in the cause of the effect (or because the effect has the same qualities as the cause).

15–16. (a) Because of the finiteness of specific things in the world, which require a cause; (b) because of homogeneity or sameness of the finite world; (c) because of the power or potency (of the cause) that the process of emergence or evolution implies; (d) because of separation or distinction between cause and its effect (with respect to modification or appearance); (e) because of the undividedness or uniformity of the entire world; the unmanifest (*avyakta*) is the cause; it functions because of or by the interaction of the three *guṇas*, modified like water, due to the specific nature abiding in the respective *guṇas*.

17. The *puruṣa* exists (a) because aggregations or combinations exist for another; (b) because (this other) must be apart or opposite from the three *guṇas*; (c) because (this other) (must be) a superintending power or control; (d) because of the existence or need of an enjoyer; (e) because there is functioning or activity for the sake of isolation or freedom.

18. The plurality of *puruṣas* is established (a) because of the diversity of births, deaths, and faculties; (b) because of actions or functions (that take place) at different times; (c) and because of differences in the proportions of the three *guṇas* (in different entities).

19. And, therefore, because (the *puruṣa*) (is) the opposite (of the unmanifest), it is established that *puruṣa* is (a) a witness; (b) possessed of isolation or freedom; (c) indifferent; (d) a spectator; and (e) inactive.

20. Because of the proximity (or association) of the two—i.e., *prakṛti* and *puruṣa* the unconscious one appears as if characterized by consciousness. Similarly, the indifferent one appears as if characterized by activity, because of the activities of the three *guṇas*.

21. The proximity (or association) of the two, which is like that of a blind man and a lame man, is for the purpose of seeing the *pradhāna* and for the purpose of the isolation of the *puruṣa*. From this (association) creation proceeds.

22. From *prakṛti* (emerges) the great one (*mahat*); from that (comes) self-awareness (*ahaṃkāra*); from that (comes) the group of sixteen. Moreover, from five of the sixteen (come) the five gross elements.

23. The *buddhi* ("will" or "intellect") is (characterized by) ascertainment or determination. Virtue, knowledge, nonattachment, and pos-

session of power are its *sāttvika* form. Its *tāmasa* form is the opposite (of these four).

24. Self-awareness (*ahaṃkāra*) is self-conceit (*abhimāna*). From it a twofold creation emerges: the group of eleven and the five subtle elements.

25. From self-awareness (known as) *vaikrta* ("modified") proceeds the group of eleven, characterized by *sattva* ("goodness" or "purity"); from self-awareness (known as) *bhūtādi* ("the origin of gross elements") proceed the five subtle elements (*tanmātras*), characterized by *tamas* ("darkness" or "delusion"); from self-awareness (known as) *taijasa* ("shining" or "passionate") both proceed.

26. The sense-organs (*buddhindriyas*) ("organs of the *buddhi*" or "organs of ascertainment") are called eye, ear, nose, tongue, and skin. The organs of action (*karmendriyas*) are called voice, hands, feet, and organs of excretion and generation.

27. The mind (*manas*) is of the nature of both; it is characterized by reflection (or synthesis or construction) and it is a sense because it is similar (to the senses). The variety of external things and the variety (of the organs) is because of the specific modifications (or transformations) of the *guṇas.*

28. The function of the five (sense-organs)—(hearing) sound, etc.—(is) mere awareness (*ālocanamātra*). The function of the five (organs of action) (is) speech, grasping, walking, excretion, and orgasm.

29. With respect to the specific characteristics of the three (i.e., of the *buddhi, ahaṃkāra,* and senses) each functions differently; the five vital breaths (or winds) (make up) their common function.

30. With respect to that which is presently in perception, the function of the four (i.e., *buddhi, ahaṃkāra, manas,* and any one of the senses) (is) simultaneous and successive. With respect to that which is not present in perception, the function of the three (i.e., *buddhi, ahamkāra,* and *manas* or the "internal organ") is based upon a prior perception.

31. (The external and internal organs) accomplish their own particular function in coordination with one another. The only motive is for the sake of the *puruṣa.* By nothing else is the instrument (i.e., the thirteenfold instrument) motivated.

32. The instrument (*karaṇa*) is thirteenfold (i.e., made up of *buddhi, ahaṃkāra, manas,* and the ten senses); (it is) characterized, by seizing, holding, and manifesting. (The instrument's) effect is tenfold (i.e., relating to the five senses and the five actions): the seized (or to be seized), the held (or to be held,) and the manifested (or to be manifested).

33. The internal organ (*antaḥkaraṇa*) is threefold (i.e., *buddhi, ahaṃkāra*, and *manas*); the external is tenfold and is known as the context (or range or sphere) of the threefold. The external (functions) in present time. The internal (functions) in the three times (i.e., in past, present, and future).

34. Of these, the five senses (*buddhīndriyas*) (function with) specific and nonspecific (i.e., gross and subtle) objects. Speech has sound only as its object, but the remaining (organs of action) have all five as objects.

35. Since the *buddhi* together with the other internal organs (i.e., *ahaṃkāra* and *manas*) comprehends every object; therefore, the threefold instrument is doorkeeper and the remaining (ten) are the doors.

36. These (organs—i.e., *ahaṃkāra, manas*, and the ten senses), which are different from one another and which are distinct specifications of the *guṇas*, present the whole (of being) to the *buddhi*, illuminating it for the sake of the *puruṣa* like a lamp.

37. (This is done) because the *buddhi* produces (or brings about) every enjoyment of the *puruṣa*; and, moreover, (because the *buddhi*) distinguishes (*viśinaṣṭi*) the subtle difference between the *pradhāna* and the *puruṣa*.

38. The subtle elements (*tanmātras*) are nonspecific. From these five (emerge) the five gross elements. These (gross elements) are considered (to be) specific, and are tranquil, turbulent, and delusive.

39. Subtle (bodies), (bodies) born of father and mother together with gross elements are the threefold kinds (of bodies). Of these the subtle (bodies) are constant; (bodies) born of father and mother are perishable.

40. The subtle body (*liṅga*), previously arisen, unconfined, constant, inclusive of the great one (*mahat*), etc., through the subtle elements (i.e., inclusive of *buddhi, ahaṃkāra, manas*, the ten senses, and the five subtle elements), not having enjoyment, transmigrates, (because of) being endowed with *bhāvas* ("conditions" or "dispositions").

41. As a picture (does) not (exist) without a support or as a shadow (does) not (exist) without a post, etc.; so, too, the instrument (*liṅga* or *karaṇa*) does not exist supportless without that which is specific (i.e., a subtle body).

42. This subtle entity, motivated for the sake of the *puruṣa*, appears like a player (who assumes many roles) by means of its association with efficient causes and effects (i.e., by means of its association with the *bhāvas*) and because of its association with the power of *prakṛti*.

43. The innate *bhāvas*, both natural and acquired—i.e., virtue (*dharma*), etc.—are seen to be dependent on the instrument (*karaṇa*) (i.e., thirteenfold instrument); whereas the embryo, etc., is dependent on the effected (i.e., the gross body).

44. By means of virtue (i.e., the *bhāva, dharma*) (there is) movement upward (in the scale of beings); by means of vice (*adharma*) (there is) movement downward; by means of salvation-knowledge (*jñāna*) (there is) final release or salvation (*apavarga*); from the opposite (of *jñāna*) bondage results.

45. From nonattachment (comes) dissolution in *prakrti*; from attachment that is passionate (*rājasa*) (comes) transmigration; from power (comes) nonobstruction; and the reverse of that from its opposite (i.e., from *anaiśvarya*).

46. This is the intellectual creation, and it is distinguished as ignorance, incapacity, complacency, and perfection. These are of fifty varieties because of the suppression of differing qualities.

47. There are five varieties of ignorance; twenty-eight varieties of incapacity, due to defects of the instrument; nine complacencies; and eight perfections.

48. There are eight varieties of obscurity and delusion; ten kinds of extreme delusion; both gloom and utter darkness are eighteenfold.

49. Injuries to the eleven organs together with injuries to the *buddhi* are said to make up incapacity; the injuries to the *buddhi* are seventeen due to the failure of the (ninefold) complacency and the (eightfold) perfection.

50. The nine complacencies are thought of (in two groups); four are internal, including nature, means, time, and destiny; and five are external due to the cessation or turning away from the objects of sense.

51.The eight perfections are proper reasoning, oral instruction, study, removal of the three kinds of suffering, friendly discussion, and generosity. The previous threefold division (i.e., ignorance, incapacity, and complacency) hinders the perfections.

52. The *liṅga* (or *karaṇa* or thirteenfold instrument together with the five subtle elements) cannot function without the *bhāvas* ("conditions," "dispositions," or "strivings"). The *bhāvas* cannot function without the *liṅga*. Therefore, a twofold creation operates (or functions) called *liṅga* and *bhāva*.

53. The divine or celestial (order) is eightfold; the subhuman (order) is fivefold; the human (order) is one variety; such, briefly, is the elemental or gross creation (*bhautika sarga*).

54. (In the) upper (world) (there is) a predominance of *sattva*. (In the) lower creation (there is) a predominance of *tamas*. In the middle, (there is) a predominance of *rajas*. (This is so) from Brahmā down to a blade of grass.

55. The *puruṣa*, which is consciousness, attains there the suffering made by decay and death, until deliverance of the subtle body; therefore, suffering is of the nature of things.

56. This creation, brought about by *prakṛti*—from the great one (*mahat*) down to the specific gross elements—(functions) for the sake of the release of each *puruṣa*; (this is done) for the sake of another, as if it were for her own (benefit).

57. As the unknowing (or unconscious) milk functions for the sake of the nourishment of the calf; so the *prakṛti* functions for the sake of the release of the *puruṣa*.

58. As (in) the world (a man) engages in actions for the sake of the cessation of a desire; so also does the *prakṛti* function for the sake of the release of the *puruṣa*.

59. As a dancer ceases from the dance after having been seen by the audience; so also *prakṛti* ceases after having manifested herself to the *puruṣa*.

60. (She) (*prakṛti*), possessed of the *guṇas* and helpful in various ways, behaves selflessly for the sake of him (*puruṣa*), who is without the *guṇas* and who plays no helpful part.

61. It is my thought that there is nothing more delicate than *prakṛti*, who (says to herself) "I have been seen," and never again comes into the sight of *puruṣa*.

62. No one, therefore, is bound; no one released; likewise no one transmigrates. (Only) *prakṛti* in its various forms transmigrates, is bound, and is released.

63. *prakṛti* binds herself by herself by means of seven forms (*rūpa* or *bhāva*); she releases herself by means of one form (*rūpa* or *bhāva*) for the sake of each *puruṣa*.

64. Thus, from the study (or analysis) of the principles (*tattvas*), the "knowledge" (or salvation-knowledge) arises, "I am not (conscious); (consciousness) does not belong to me"; the "I" is not (conscious) (and this "knowledge") is complete because free from error, pure, and solitary (*kevala*).

65. Then the *puruṣa*, comfortably situated like a spectator, sees *prakṛti*, whose activity has ceased due to the completion of her purpose, and who has turned back from the seven forms (*rūpa* or *bhāva*).

66. (Says the) indifferent one (or spectator), "I have seen (her)"; the other ceases (saying), "I have been seen." Though the two are still in proximity, no (further) creation (takes place).

67. Having arrived at the point at which virtue, etc., has no (further) cause, because of the attainment of direct knowledge (*samyagjñānādhig amād*), the endowed body (i.e., the body in association with *puruṣa*) yet continues because of the force of past impressions (*saṃskāras*), like a potter's wheel.

68. With the cessation of *prakṛti* due to its purpose having been accomplished, (*the puruṣa*) on attaining separation from the body, attains isolation (*kaivalya*), which is both certain and final.

69. This secret (or mysterious) "knowledge" for the sake of the *puruṣa*—wherein is analyzed the existence, origin, and termination of all beings—has been expounded or enumerated by the highest (or greatest) sage.

70. This excellent and pure (knowledge) the sage gave with compassion to Āsuri; Āsuri likewise to Pañcaśikha; and by him the doctrine (*tantra*) was expanded or modified.

71. Handed down by disciples in succession, it has been compendiously written in *āryā* meter by the noble-minded Īśvarakṛṣṇa, having fully learned the demonstrated truth.

72. The subjects of the complete *ṣaṣṭitantra* are indeed in the seventy (verses of Īśvarakṛṣṇa), although the illustrative tales together with the objections of opponents are not included.

73. Thus, this briefly expounded *śāstra* is not defective with respect to content, and is like a reflection in a mirror of the vast material of the *tantra*.

NOTE

1. Richard King, *Indian Philosophy* (Edinburgh: Edinburgh University Press, 1999), 175–176.

FURTHER READING

Burley, Mikel. *Classical Sāṃkhya and Yoga: An Indian Metaphysics of Experience*. London: Routledge, 2007.

Chatterjee, Satischandra, and Dhirendramohan Datta. *An Introduction to Indian Philosophy*. Calcutta: University of Calcutta, 1939.

King, Richard. *Indian Philosophy*. Edinburgh: Edinburgh University Press, 1999.

Larson, Gerald James. *Classical Sāṃkhya: An Interpretation of Its History and Meaning*. Delhi: Motilal Banarsidass, 1979.

Larson, Gerald James, and Ram Shankar Bhattacharya. *Sāṃkhya: A Dualist Tradition in Indian Philosophy*. Princeton: Princeton University Press, 1987.

Sen Gupta, Anima. *Classical Sāṃkhya: A Critical Study*. Delhi: Munshiram Manoharlal, 1981.

9

YOGA

yogaścittavṛttinirodhaḥ.

Disciplined meditation involves the cessation of the functioning of ordinary awareness.

—Patañjali, *Yoga Sūtras* 1.2

HISTORY

Like the Sāṃkhya school, the Yoga school holds that liberation is brought about by discerning the duality between *puruṣa* (consciousness) and *prakṛti* (materiality). They too believed that the material world emerged from *prakṛti*, given its proximity to *puruṣa*. The ultimate goal was thus for the *puruṣa* to see itself as distinct from the *prakṛti* and, consequently, for it to be no longer born in the cycle of birth and rebirth. Patañjali's school of Yoga offers a way to end the suffering of birth and rebirth that results in *citta-vṛtii-nirodha* (the cessation of ordinary awareness). Once one has ceased all mental functions, one will attain "concentration without content."[1] The *puruṣa*, then, reaches a *kaivalya* (isolated) consciousness and is liberated.

The Sāṃkhya and Yoga schools are very closely related and share some similar concepts. The two are often referred to together or even combined as "Sāṃkhyayoga." Despite these attempts to coalesce the two, they are still separate traditions with some significant differences.

Although the word *yoga* derives from the Sanskrit root √*yuj* ("to bind, yoke, join, or unite") and often refers to any sort of disciplined practice, the term is used in this context as "concentration" or "disciplined meditation." This characterization distinguishes the philosophical system described by Patañjali from earlier forms of disciplined practice. Little is known of Patañjali, purported author of the *Yoga Sūtras* (350–450 C.E.). Patañjali's *Yoga Sūtras* became the foundation of the Yoga school of Indian philosophy and is considered the foundation for the contemporary varieties of *yoga* that are practiced outside of India. It gave rise to two canonical commentaries: Vyāsa's *bhāṣya* (commentary), known as the *Vyāsa-bhāṣya* (350–450 C.E.), and Vācaspatimiśra's *bhāṣya*, known as the *Tattvavaiśāradī* (*Clarity Regarding the Truth* [*of Yoga as Set Forth in Vyāsa's Bhāṣya*]) (ca. 950 C.E.).

EPISTEMOLOGY

The Yoga school accepts three *pramāṇas* (sources of valid knowledge): *pratyakṣa* (perception); *anumāna* (inference); and *āgama* (valid testimony). *Pramāṇa*, moreover, is the first modification of the *citta* (awareness). The *citta* (awareness) is a cognitive faculty and is the first product of *prakṛti* (more on *prakṛti* below). When the *citta* comes into contact with objects it is modified.

ONTOLOGY

According to the Yoga school, the universe is composed of only two elements, *puruṣa* and *prakṛti*. Like the Sāṃkhya school, Patañjali proposed that the world is brought about through the interaction between the *puruṣa* and the *prakṛti*. The manifest world emerges from *prakṛti* in a series of transformations. Ultimately, *puruṣa* is *kaivalya* (isolated). God is mentioned in the *Yoga Sūtras* as a type of *puruṣa*. *Prakṛti* is composed of three *guṇas* (constituent processes).

The *citta* undergoes five kinds of *vṛttis* (transformations): *pramāṇa* (knowledge); *viparyaya* (error); *vikalpa* (conceptual construction); *nidrā* (sleep); and *smṛti* (memory). Through these modifications the *puruṣa* comes to know the world and, unfortunately and incorrectly, to identify with it. Since the *citta* is continuously modified, the goal is to end all of the mental functions through concentration. These modifications, moreover, are either *kliṣṭa* (afflicted) or *akliṣṭa* (unafflicted). When they are *kliṣṭa* they generate *karma* and lead to rebirth. When they are not *kliṣṭa* they do not give rise to *karma* and eventually lead to an awareness of the difference between *puruṣa* and *prakṛti*. Patañjali thus states that there are five *kleṣas* (afflictions) that result in birth and rebirth: *avidyā* (ignorance); *asmitā* (egoity); *raga* (attachment); *dveśa* (hatred); *abhiniveśa* (clinging to ordinary life).

SOTERIOLOGY

As already mentioned, the goal of the Yoga school is for adherents to realize that the *puruṣa* and the *prakṛti* are distinct. This is attainable by following the practices enjoined in the *aṣṭāṅga* (eight limbs) of Yoga, through which one can begin to control the *citta* and attain higher levels of awareness, eventually reaching *samādhi* (altered states of awareness) and the preeminent state of *kaivalya* (isolation). The *aṣṭāṅga* are: *yama* (restraint); *niyama* (observance); *asana* (posture); *prāṇāyāma* (breath control); *pratyahāra* (withdrawal of sense-organs); *dhāraṇa* (fixation); *dhyāna* (reflective meditation); and *samādhi* (cultivation of altered states of awareness).

THE TEXT

The entirety of Patañjali's *Yoga Sūtras* is included here. The *Yoga Sūtras* is composed of 195 *sūtras* (aphorisms) and is divided into four *pādas* (books). The first book, *Samādhi-pāda*, concerns the levels of awareness. Book 2, *Sādhana-pāda*, includes the means to attain these levels. Book 3, *Vibhūti-pāda*, is a characterization of the *siddhis* (powers) that one attains when one becomes more adept at Yoga. The fourth book, *Kaivalya-pāda*, concerns the nature of liberation. The *sūtras* are often enigmatic and consequently gave rise to a commentarial tradition. This translation has incorporated some of the commentary from Vyāsa's *Vyāsa-bhāṣya* (350–450 C.E.) and from Vācaspatimiśra's *Tattvavaiśāradī*.

PATAÑJALI'S *YOGA SŪTRAS*

Book 1. On Altered States of Concentration (*Samādhi-pāda*)

1. Herein begins an inquiry into disciplined meditation based upon past functioning of ordinary awareness (*citta*).

2. Disciplined meditation involves the cessation of the functioning of ordinary awareness.

3. Then, (that is, when the functioning of ordinary awareness has ceased) there is the condition of the seer (that is, *puruṣa*) as it is in itself

(*svarūpa*) (that is, without any content, or, in other words, pure contentless consciousness).

4. Otherwise, there is conformity with the functioning of ordinary awareness.

5. The functions of ordinary awareness are fivefold and are afflicted or unafflicted.

6. Correct awareness, error, verbal construction, sleep, and memory (are the five functions of ordinary awareness).

7. Correct awareness arise from perception, inference, and reliable testimony.

8. Error is false cognition based on the form of something appearing as what it is not.

9. Verbal (or conceptual) construction depends upon cognition arising from language alone without any substantive referent.

10. Sleep is a function of ordinary awareness based on the notion (or experience) of absence.

11. Memory is the retention of previously experienced cognitions (or contents).

12. The cessation (or restriction) of these functions of ordinary awareness is accomplished through practice and dispassion.

13. In regard to these two means, practice is restraint with respect to attaining cognitive stability.

14. Furthermore, it (practice) is a steady state brought about by uninterrupted effort over a long period of time.

15. Dispassion is a cognitive realization of complete control of (the *yogin*) who has turned away from all perceptible and scriptural objects.

16. That is supreme dispassion wherein there is a turning away from all the three *guṇas* due to the realization of the presence of *puruṣa*.

17. Concentration (*samādhi*) having content [relevant for disciplined meditation or yoga] is that derived from forms of empirical awareness, rational awareness, aesthetic awareness, and self-awareness.

18. The other (concentration, namely, *asaṃprajñaṭasamādhi*, or content-free concentration,) is a condition presupposing the practice of the contemplative realization of cessation wherein only predispositions that are outside of ordinary awareness remain operative.

19. The notion of becoming continues to be the case for the disembodied, and for *yogins* who attain only dissolution in primordial materiality.

20. Among others (that is, those *yogins* who follow the proper way of Yoga), (their path to concentration) presupposes the practice of faith, energy, mindfulness, the cultivation of concentration, and insight.

21. Concentration is close at hand for those *yogins* who practice with the greatest intensity.

22. Even within that group (of *yogins* practicing with the greatest intensity) a distinction can be made between mild, middling, and extreme (practice).

23. Or, content-filled concentration (*saṃprajñātasamādhi*) can also be attained through focusing on God (as the object of meditation).

24. God is a particular or unique consciousness (*puruṣa*) among consciousnesses, untouched by the afflictions, karmic tendencies, karmic fruits, and long-term karmic predispositions (that are characteristic of all other sentient beings associated with *puruṣas*).

25. In God the pinnacle of omniscience has been attained.

26. (God is) the teacher even of all preceding teachers inasmuch as God is not limited by time.

27. The verbal expression for God is the sacred syllable (*praṇava*) (or, in other words, the syllable *oṃ*).

28. Repetition of it (the sacred syllable) (and) meditation on the object of the expression (namely God) (should be practiced in order to achieve concentration).

29. Then, (when concentration has been properly cultivated) there is a going over into one's own pure consciousness and the disappearance of the obstacles as well.

30. The distractions of awareness, namely illness, dullness, doubt, heedlessness, laziness, worldliness, erroneous perception, failure to attain stability, and restlessness—these are the (principal) obstacles.

31. Frustration, depression, trembling of the body, and irregular breathing are the accompaniments of these.

32. The (meditative) practice (of focusing on) one principle or reality (*ekatattva*) is appropriate for the sake of negating these distractions (and their accompaniments).

33. Peace of mind (or stability of awareness) arises from the practice of friendliness toward those who are happy, compassion toward those who are in pain, joy toward those who are meritorious, and dispassion toward those who are behaving in a nonmeritorious manner.

34. Or, (stability of awareness, that is, the overcoming of the distractions) can be accomplished through retention and exhalation of breath.

35. Or, when there is the apprehension of certain kinds of contents, stability of the mind (can become possible).

36. Or, (stability of the mind can become possible) when the functioning of awareness is free from grief (and) brilliantly clear.

37. Or, (stability of the mind can become possible) when the contents of awareness are free from attachment.

38. Or, (stability of the mind can become possible) through focusing on the contents of knowledge that derive from sleep or dreaming.

39. Or, (stability of the mind can become possible) through reflective meditation on any pleasing object.

40. The complete control achieved by the *yogin* (who has attained stability of mind) extends from the smallest particle of reality to the largest entity.

41. (When the *citta* [of the *yogin*]) has been sufficiently cleansed of the dysfunctional functioning (*kṣīnavṛtti*) (and become) like a transparent jewel, there arises an engrossment with gross and subtle objects, the process of cognizing, and the subject of cognizing. (The *citta*) then shows forth or highlights the true nature of those contents.

42. The engrossment related to empirical awareness (*vitarka*) is mixed with verbal constructions (*vikalpa*) involving conventional sounds (words), objects (referents), and the resulting cognitions.

43. Engrossment with an empirical object becomes purified (*nirvitarkā*) when memory has been purified and only the object itself shines forth—as if even the act of cognizing is absent and there is only the object itself.

44. In the same way is to be explained the engrossment with subtle (intellectual or ideational) contents (*sūkṣmaviṣaya*), whether relating to specific intellectual notions (*savicārā*) or pure intellectual contemplation (*nirvicārā*).

45. And subtle objectivity encompasses all the nonempirical contents of awareness up through the unmanifest (*aliṅga*) (that is, primordial materiality or *mūlaprakṛti*).

46. All these engrossments represent content-filled concentration (or, in other words, all these are intentional awareness).

47. When the *yogin* has gained skill in cultivating the highest concentration (that is, the *nirvicārasamādhi*), there arises a tranquility pertaining to the presence of the real self.

48. Therein (that is, when there is tranquility in regard to the self as a result of skill in attaining the *nirvicārasamādhi*), (the *yogin* has attained) "truth-bearing insight."

49. This is a particular kind of awareness (direct perception) whose content is different from (the contents of) the cognitions arising from inference and reliable authority.

50. The trace (*saṃskāra*) born of that special cognition counteracts all other traces.

51. When there is cessation of even that special cognition, inasmuch as there is the cessation of everything (that is, all contents), there is a concentration without content (that is, a concentration that is "without seed" or content, *nirbīja*).

Book 2. On Practice (*Sādhana-pāda*)

1. The structured practice of disciplined meditation (*kriyāyoga*) involves ascetic exercises (for the body), sacred study/recitation (for speech and voice), and focusing on God (as a content of meditation) (for the mind).

2. (The structured practice of disciplined meditation) is for the sake of cultivating the various altered states of awareness and for the sake of decreasing the force of the afflictions.

3. The five afflictions are ignorance, egoity, attachment, hatred, and clinging to ordinary life.

4. The first of the five, namely ignorance, provides the basic context for the subsequent four (egoity, attachment, hatred, and clinging to life)—and these latter four may be quiescent, decreased, interrupted, or active.

5. Ignorance is the apprehension of what is permanent, pure, pleasant, and the self in what is impermanent, ugly, painful, and not the self.

6. Egoity is the appearance of the power of consciousness (*dṛś* or *puruṣa*) and of the power of ordinary awareness (*darśana* or *citta*) as if they were the same thing.

7. Attachment is closely related to what is pleasant.

8. Hatred is closely related to what is frustrating or painful.

9. Clinging to ordinary life in the sense of going with the flow of one's ordinary impulses is characteristic even of a learned person.

10. These subtle (afflictions) are to be overcome by reversing one's ordinary functioning.

11. The functioning of these (afflictions) are to be overcome by means of reflective meditation.

12. The storage place of *karma*, whose base content is the collocation of afflictions, will be experienced or reach fruition in the present or a future rebirth.

13. So long as this base content continues to exist, there is the ripening of that stored *karma* in terms of the form of life, the length of life, and the quality of life (that a sentient being will assume in its next rebirth).

14. Inasmuch as a person's stored *karma* has been meritorious or nonmeritorious, so those resulting experiences will have fruits that are pleasant or painful.

15. By reason of the frustrations brought about by fundamental change, pain (both mental and physical) and the resulting predispositions, and inasmuch as the three *guṇas* operate in contrary but inextricable ways, everything in ordinary experience is frustrating to the discriminating *yogin*.

16. Future frustration can be avoided.

17. The contact between the seer (*draṣṭṛ*, that is, *puruṣa*) and the seen (*dṛśya*, that is, *citta* or *prakṛti*) is the reason for the frustration that is to be.

18. The manifest world (*dṛśya*, or in other words *citta*) has for its purpose both ordinary experience and spiritual release, and encompasses all objects as well as all subjective apprehensions, and is constituted by the three constituent processes of intelligibility, activity, and objectification.

19. The components of the three *guṇas* include gross elements (*viśeṣa*), subtle elements (*aviśeṣa*), the internal organ (*liṅga* or *liṅgaśarīra*, made up of intellect, ego, mind, the five sense-organs, and the five action-organs), and the unmanifest primordial materiality (*aliṅga* or *mūlaprakṛti*).

20. The seer (*draṣṭṛ*, or pure consciousness), which is only sheer seeing, though inherently pure (or contentless), comes to reflect the intellectual creation (or the *pratyayasarga* of *buddhi* or *citta*).

21. The manifest world exists just for the sake of this pure seeing (that is, *tad-artha* = *puruṣa-artha*) [lit. "the nature or essence of the to-be-seen is just for the sake of that"].

22. (The manifest world), though ended in regard to any (*yogin*) whose purpose has been accomplished, is not ended totally inasmuch as the manifest world is common to all others.

23. Contact between the power of what is owned and the owner (or, in other words, between the power of *prakṛti* and that of *puruṣa*) is the occasion for the ascertainment of the inherent form of each (and the eventual dissolution of the contact).

24. The cause of that contact is ignorance.

25. When ignorance becomes absent, there is absence of contact, which means abandonment or, in other words, the realization of spiritual liberation (*kaivalya*) of the seer from the seen.

26. The means to abandonment is unshaking discriminative awareness.

27. The ultimate insight of that (*yogin*) is sevenfold.

28. When impurities have been destroyed as a result of the systematic practice of the limbs (or levels) of disciplined meditation (*yogāṅga*), knowledge comes to include the full illumination of discriminative awareness.

29. Restraint, observance, posture, breath control, withdrawal of sense-organs, fixation, reflective meditation, and cultivation of altered states of awareness are the eight limbs (or levels) (of disciplined meditation).

30. Restraints include nonviolence, truth-telling, nontheft, celibacy, and non-avarice.

31. (These restraints), which pertain to all conditions, regardless of form of life (species), place, time, or specific circumstance, are known as the Great Vow (*mahāvrata*).

32. Observances include purifications, contentments, ascetic exercises, study/recitation, and focusing on God (as a content of meditation).

33. When these (restraints and observances) get turned aside by this or that improper impulse, an appropriate counteracting meditation should be practiced.

34. Appropriate opposing meditative exercise (should be directed against) improper impulses such as violence and so forth accompanied by greed, anger, or delusion, either committed or caused to be committed or acquiesced in, that are mild, medium, or intense, and the fruits of which entail unending pain and ignorance.

35. When nonviolence has been established (by the *yogin*) there is abandonment of hostility (among all creatures) when drawing near to him.

36. When truth-telling has been established (by the *yogin*), there is a proper foundation for action and its fruits.

37. When nontheft (generosity) has been established (by the *yogin*), there is the coming forth of all kinds of wealth.

38. When celibacy has been established (by the *yogin*), there is the acquisition of virility.

39. When nonavarice has become steady (for the *yogin*), there arises understanding how rebirth occurs.

40. As a result of bodily purification, there is disgust with respect to one's own body and avoidance of contact with others.

41. (Also, as a result of purification), there is purification of the intelligibility constituent (*sattva*) (of the *buddhi* or *citta*), cheerfulness, one-

pointedness, control over the sense-organs, and ability with respect to apprehending the self.

42. As a result of contentment, there is the highest acquisition of happiness.

43. As a result of ascetic exercises, there is the perfection of the body and the sense-organs inasmuch as impurities have been destroyed.

44. As a result of study/recitation, there is contact with one's own chosen deity.

45. As a result of focusing on God (as a content of meditation), there arises the perfection of concentration.

46. Posture should be comfortably steady.

47. (Posture is perfected) through relaxed effort and engrossment with the infinite.

48. Then, (the *yogin*) is not tormented by dualities.

49. When (posture) has been perfected, there arises breath control, which involves stopping or control of the process of inhalation and exhalation.

50. (Breath control is) the operation of exhalation, inhalation, and suspension, observed with regard to place, time, and number, becoming long and subtle.

51. A fourth (level of breath control) pertains to going beyond external and internal operations.

52. Then the covering over the light (of knowledge) is destroyed.

53. And, the mind is then ready with respect to the meditative fixations.

54. The withdrawal of the sense-organs (occurs) when there is non-contact with their own objects—just as the inherent functioning of the mind (ceases when not being engaged).

55. Then, there is supreme control of the sense-organs.

Book 3. On Extraordinary Cognitive Capacities (*Vibhūti-pāda*)

1. Focus on a specific place (or object) is (known as) fixation of ordinary awareness.

2. (When fixation has been accomplished, the achievement of) an even flow of thought (in regard to the place or object) is (known as) reflective meditation (*dhyāna*).

3. That reflective state (that is, the *dhyāna* condition) in which only the object itself appears as if devoid of the presence of the meditator is (known as) concentration (*samādhi*).

4. This triad (that is, *dhāraṇā*, *dhyāna*, and *samādhi*), functioning together as one, is (known as) comprehensive reflection (*saṃyama*).

5. When comprehensive reflection is achieved, there arises authentic insight.

6. The application of this comprehensive reflection can be directed at all levels of awareness.

7. Of the eight limbs of disciplined meditation, this final triad (that is, the comprehensive meditation of *dhāraṇā*, *dhyāna*, and *samādhi*) may be considered to be the internal limbs or levels (while the first five may be considered to be external limbs or levels).

8. But even those internal limbs or levels are only to be considered as external limbs of the ultimate contentless state of awareness.

9. The coming into prominence of the predisposition toward cessation and the overcoming of the predisposition toward further ordinary awareness is (known as) the fundamental change tending toward cessation, which is characterized by (slowly increasing) moments of actual cessation.

10. On account of this trace (namely the tending toward cessation), there arises a tranquil flow within ordinary awareness.

11. When the many contents (in ordinary awareness) begin to subside and when one-pointedness becomes prominent, (this is known as) the fundamental change tending toward concentration.

12. Then, when the notion maintains continuity or remains the same, whether past or present, (this is known as) the fundamental change tending toward one-pointedness.

13. These three fundamental changes (tending toward cessation, toward concentration, and toward one-pointedness), which relate respectively to change in characteristic (*dharma*), change in temporal mode (*lakṣaṇa*), and change in overall condition (*avasthā*), have been described with respect (to understanding the various changes that occur) in the external, objective world (the *bhūta*-realm) and in internal, subjective awareness (the *indriya*-realm).

14. There is a substrate (*dharmin*, that is, a basic materiality) underlying these various characteristics of past, present, and future.

15. Variance in sequence (of characteristics) is the reason with respect to understanding the variance of fundamental changes.

16. Comprehensive reflection on these three kinds of fundamental change generates knowledge of the past and the future.

17. Inasmuch as word (*śabda*), object (*artha*), and notion (*pratyaya*) are mutually superimposed on one another, there is a basic confusion

(in understanding how communication occurs among sentient beings). To the extent that these components are distinguished through the practice of comprehensive reflection, knowledge of the various modes of symbolic communication through sound among all sentient creatures becomes possible.

18. Inasmuch as traces (come to be) intuitively perceived (by *yogins* through comprehensive reflection), knowledge of previous births becomes possible.

19. Inasmuch as a notion or idea (of someone else comes to be intuitively perceived through comprehensive reflection), knowledge of the cognitive contents of the minds of others becomes possible.

20. But such knowledge does not include knowing actual objects; it refers, rather, to the nonobjective cognition involved.

21. Inasmuch as the physical form of the body becomes the focus for comprehensive reflection, to the extent that the capacity of grasping that physical form can be stopped through breaking the connection between light, the eye, (and the physical body), invisibility becomes possible.

22. Inasmuch as action, whether undertaken or not undertaken, becomes the focus for comprehensive reflection relating to omens of one kind or another, knowledge of (impending) death becomes possible.

23. Inasmuch as universal friendliness and so forth (namely *maitrī, karuṇā, muditā,* and *upekṣā*, and cf. book 1, no. 33 above) become the focus for comprehensive reflection, various powers (*vibhūti*) become possible.

24. Inasmuch as these powers become the focus for comprehensive reflection, the strength of an elephant and other (comparable) extraordinary strengths become possible.

25. From practice (e.g., meditation on) seeing the higher functioning (of the mind), knowledge of what is subtle, concealed, or distant becomes possible.

26. When the sun [*sūryadvāra*, or "gate" in the region of the navel or heart] becomes the focus for comprehensive reflection, knowledge of (various) universes becomes possible.

27. When the moon [*candradvāra*, another "gate" in the body] becomes the focus for comprehensive reflection, knowledge of the orderly arrangement of the stars (or constellations) becomes possible.

28. When the pole star [yet another "gate" or region] becomes the focus for comprehensive reflection, knowledge of the motion of the stars or constellations becomes possible.

29. When the circle of the navel becomes the focus for comprehensive reflection, knowledge of the orderly arrangement of the body becomes possible.

30. When the base of the throat becomes the focus for comprehensive reflection, cessation of hunger and thirst becomes possible.

31. When the "tortoise-vein" (the *kūrmanāḍī*, or bronchial tube) becomes the focus for comprehensive reflection, steadiness becomes possible.

32. When the light at the top of the head becomes the focus for comprehensive reflection, a vision of the *siddhas* (the accomplished *yogins* of the past) becomes possible.

33. Or, (from comprehensive reflection on) higher intuition, (knowledge of) everything becomes possible.

34. When the heart region becomes the focus for comprehensive reflection, consciousness of ordinary awareness becomes possible.

35. The subject-object world (*parārtha*) of ordinary experience (*bhoga*) is a cognitive condition wherein there is no distinction between the intelligibility constituent (*sattva*) and consciousness (*puruṣa*), even though, in fact, the two are always separate; when one's own unique (and separate) consciousness becomes the focus of comprehensive reflection, cognition of the presence of *puruṣa* becomes possible.

36. Then, higher intuition, subtle hearing, subtle feeling, subtle seeing, subtle tasting, and subtle smelling become possible.

37. These extraordinary capacities can be hindrances when (the *yogin*) is in concentration, but they can be considered (valuable) psychic capacities in ordinary life.

38. Inasmuch as the causes of bondage are being loosened and inasmuch as there is a feeling of suppleness in awareness, there arises the sensation of being able to enter the body of another.

39. Inasmuch as the up-breath (the *udāna*, or speech-breath) has been controlled (there arises a sense of) dispassion in regard to earthly things like water, mud, thorns, and so forth, and a sense of moving upward.

40. Inasmuch as the middling breath (*samāna*, that is, the digestive breath) has been controlled, (there arises) burning energy.

41. When the relation between hearing and space becomes the focus of comprehensive reflection, celestial hearing (the "divine hearing") becomes possible.

42. When the relation between the body and space becomes the focus for comprehensive reflection, and there is a sense of becoming

very light like cotton, the sense of moving about in space or levitation becomes possible.

43. When it detaches itself from its intentional contents (that is, its outward involvements), ordinary experiencing becomes completely disembodied; then there is the elimination of the covers over the light (of pure consciousness).

44. When gross materiality, its inherent form, its subtle materiality, its relations, and its overall purposiveness become the focus for comprehensive reflection, control of the gross objective world becomes possible.

45. Then there occurs the manifestation of (the extraordinary cognitive capacities) becoming small like an atom and so forth, as well as perfection of the body and overcoming the noxious effects of gross embodiment.

46. Perfection of the body involves beauty, gracefulness, strength, virility, and muscularity.

47. When cognizing, its inherent form, its egoity, its relations, and its overall purposiveness become the focus for comprehensive reflection, control of the subtle subjective realm of cognition becomes possible.

48. Then there is quickness of mind, the power of acting beyond the sense-organs, and the control of *prakṛti.*

49. For (the *yogin*) given solely over to the discriminative realization of the difference between *sattva* and *puruṣa*, there arises a sense of supremacy over all beings and omniscience.

50. From renunciation even of these attainments, when there has been destruction of the seeds of all faults, (there arises) spiritual liberation.

51. Should there occur an invitation from high beings (*sthānins* or gods, and so forth), however, (there should arise in the *yogin*) neither pride nor attachment, since this would entail unwanted consequences.

52. When the (notion of) moment and sequence of moments become the focus for comprehensive reflection, discriminative knowledge becomes possible.

53. Then, there occurs the ascertainment of two always separate but similar entities (namely *prakṛti* and *puruṣa*, which are both unmanifest and existent ultimates), even though in ordinary awareness they cannot be distinguished in terms of species, temporal character, or spatial location.

54. Discriminative knowledge is universal (*tāraka*), all-encompassing, all-pervading, and immediate.

55. When the *sattva* and *puruṣa* have been clearly distinguished, (there arises) spiritual liberation.

Book 4. On Spiritual Liberation (*Kaivalya-pāda*)

1. (The experience of) extraordinary capacities may occur naturally (that is, as a result of inborn capacities at the time of rebirth), or from taking herbal medications (*oṣadhi*, including elixirs and hallucinogens), or from incantations (*mantra*), or from ascetic practices (*tapas*), or finally from concentrations (*samādhi*) (that occur as a result of practicing the comprehensive reflections just describe in the preceding section).

2. Dynamic transformation into another form of life (at the time of rebirth) is due to the potency or abundance of primordial materiality.

3. (There is) no need for an efficient cause among these potencies of materiality; but there is the assisting task of removing obstructions, like a farmer (who opens a water gate to allow water to flow into a field).

4. Individualized awarenesses (arise) solely from egoity.

5. With respect to difference in functioning (among the many different awarenesses), there is only one (pre-individualized) awareness providing the impetus for the many (individualized awarenesses).

6. Therein the awareness characterized by even-flowing reflective meditation does not become involved in perpetuating latent tendencies.

7. The *karma* of a *yogin* is neither black nor white; for others, it is threefold (that is, black, white, or some mixture of black and white).

8. Then (that is, on account of the karmic accumulation) there is the manifestation of subconscious impressions in keeping just with their appropriate karmic propensities.

9. Since memory and traces are uniform, there is a basic continuity (from rebirth to rebirth) even though there may be considerable separation in terms of form of life, location, or time.

10. Furthermore, these (latent tendencies) are beginningless, since the wish or desire to be is permanent.

11. Since subconscious impressions are triggered by cause, effect, mindset, and object, when these latter are absent, so they (that is, the impressions) also are absent.

12. The past and future actually exist, since their characteristic features have distinct existing modes.

13. These characteristics (of the existing modes of past, present, and future) are either manifest or subtle (that is, manifest in the case of

the present, and subtle in the case of the past and future) and have the *guṇas* as their essence.

14. There is such a thing as objective reality, since the fundamental changes (of material reality) remain uniform (rational) throughout.

15. Since there are separate awarenesses apprehending a uniform world, there must be two distinct dimensions (of realty, that is, subject and object).

16. The objective world is not dependent on a single awareness; (if such were the case) when there was nonapprehension of a thing by that single awareness, what (or where) would the thing be?

17. An objective thing is known or unknown to the extent that ordinary awareness is influenced by it.

18. The functionings of ordinary awareness are always being cognized, since *puruṣa* as the reflective power over ordinary awareness is not subject to fundamental change.

19. It (that is, ordinary awareness) is not self-reflective, since it is an object that can be apprehended.

20. And, again, it is not possible to ascertain both (that is, awareness and its object) at the same time.

21. In the event that one momentary awareness is to be perceived by another momentary awareness, this would entail a vicious infinite regress from intellect to intellect and would also lead to confusion of memories.

22. Although consciousness is not subject to change, the experience of one's intellect (*buddhi*) as if it were (itself) consciousness (*sva*) (occurs) when consciousness takes on or reflects the forms of awareness.

23. Ordinary awareness influenced by the seer (i.e., consciousness) and what is seen (what is not consciousness) is all-encompassing.

24. That (ordinary awareness), even though variegated by innumerable subconscious impressions, (nevertheless) works or functions for the sake of another (that is, for the sake of a *puruṣa*).

25. For the one who sees the distinction (between *citta* and *puruṣa*) there is a cessation of having to meditate upon the existence of the self.

26. Then at that time ordinary awareness is inclining toward discrimination and is headed for spiritual liberation.

27. In the interstices (or gaps) in this (awareness), there are other notions (leading in different directions) arising from (residual) traces.

28. Abandonment of those is said to be like abandonment of the afflictions.

29. Of the (*yogin*) taking no interest even in the highest elevation, the Cloud of Truth (*dharmamegha*) concentration (shows itself) all around on account of the realization of discrimination.

30. Then there is the cessation of afflictions and actions.

31. Then at that time, because of the vast extent of knowledge unencumbered by any obstructions or impurities, there is very little more to be known.

32. Then, (there is) completion of the sequence of fundamental changes of the *guṇas*, whose purposes have now been accomplished.

33. (The notion of) sequence, understood as the terminal point of a fundamental change, is a counterpart of (the notion of) moment.

34. The reversal or turning back of the *guṇas*, which now no longer have to function for the sake of consciousness, is spiritual liberation, or, put somewhat differently, there is now the presence of the power of pure consciousness (*citi-śakti*) in its own inherent form.

NOTE

1. Gerald Larson, *Yoga: India's Philosophy of Meditation* (Delhi: Motilal Banarsidass, 2008), 134.

FURTHER READING

Burley, Mikel. *Classical Sāṃkhya and Yoga: An Indian Metaphysics of Experience*. London: Routledge, 2007.

Chatterjee, Satischandra, and Dhirendramohan Datta. *An Introduction to Indian Philosophy*. Calcutta: University of Calcutta, 1939.

King, Richard. *Indian Philosophy*. Edinburgh: Edinburgh University Press, 1999.

Larson, Gerald James, and Ram Shankar Bhattacharya. *Sāṃkhya: A Dualist Tradition in Indian Philosophy*. Princeton: Princeton University Press, 1987.

——. *Yoga: India's Philosophy of Meditation*. Delhi: Motilal Banarsidass, 2008.

Sharma, Chandradhar. *A Critical Survey of Indian Philosophy*. London: Rider, 1960.

Whicher, Ian. *The Integrity of the Yoga Darśana: A Reconsideration of Classical Yoga*. Albany: State University of New York Press, 1998.

16

MĪMĀṂSĀ

HISTORY

yāgādir eva dharmaḥ.

Sacrifice and so on alone are *dharma.*

—Laugākṣi Bhāskara, *Arthasaṃgraha* 1.2

The Mīmāṃsā school was centered chiefly upon the proper interpretations of Vedic passages and the implementation of the injunctions found in them. Its proponents defended the authority, consistency, and integrity of the Vedas. In so doing, they sought to cement what they perceived to be the ultimate goal of the Vedas: to act according to one's *dharma* (duty/obligation) and to perform the *vidhis* (injunctions) found in the Vedas.

Reflections on the import of the Vedas can be traced to 1000 B.C.E., although they were not systematized until Jaimini composed the *Mīmāṃsā Sūtras* (ca. 25 C.E.).[1] The text was commented upon by Śabara (400 C.E.)[2] in his *Śabara-bhāṣya,* which was regarded as the standard point of reference in Mīmāṃsā. Subsequent commentaries by Mīmāṃsā thinkers were largely on the *Śabara-bhāṣya*. Two schools developed out of the tradition of commentary on the *Śabara-bhāṣya*, one founded by Kumārila Bhaṭṭa (the Bhāṭṭa school) and one by Prābhākara (the Prābhākara school), both of whom lived in the seventh century C.E. The systematic hermeneutic and theory of language that they developed was one of the most influential among the schools of Indian thought.

EPISTEMOLOGY

The Prābhākara school of Mīmāṃsā school accepts five *pramāṇas* (sources of valid knowledge): *pratyakṣa* (perception); *anumāna* (inference); *upamāna* (comparison); *śabda* (testimony); and *arthāpatti* (presumption). *Arthāpatti* refers to explanations that are given to make sense of something. For example, if Devadatta is never seen eating during the day, yet is growing increasingly corpulent, one can surmise that Devadatta is having (at the very least) a midnight snack. The Bhāṭṭa school adds *anupalabdhi* (noncognition) to this list of five. According to Kumārila, *anupalabdhi* makes the awareness of the absence of something possible. That is, the valid cognition "The monkey is not on my desk" is an apprehension of the nonexistence of the monkey upon one's desk.

Śabda (testimony), which includes the Vedas, is of the greatest importance, given its centrality to Mīmāṃsā. *Śabda* is of two varieties: *apauruṣeya* (impersonal) and *pauruṣeya* (personal). The Vedas are *apauruṣeya śabda*. The Mīmāṃsakas must argue that the Vedas are *svataḥ-prāmāṇya* (intrinsically valid), in addition to being eternal and infallible. Their argument relies on an epistemological theory by which all utterances are valid. The validity of a human utterance, however, is questionable. Since the Vedas are *apauruṣeya* (authorless, impersonal) they do not suffer this criticism. According to Śabara, a linguistic utterance gives rise to a cognition. If the cognition is clear and unambiguous, then one can act on it. Moreover, until the utterance has been falsified it cannot be judged as false.[3] This line of argument is at the core of the Mīmāṃsā position and its defense of the Vedas.

ONTOLOGY

According to the Mīmāṃsā school, the universe is real, as are the deities and places mentioned in the Vedas. Their *padārthas* (categories) are very similar to those put forth by the Nyāya-Vaiśeṣika school. Prabhākara holds that there are eight *padārthas*: *dravya* (substance); *guṇa* (quality); *karma* (action); *sāmānya* (generality); *paratantra* (inherence); *śakti* (power/potency); *sādrśya* (similarity); and *saṃkhyā* (number). To this list Kumārila adds *abhāva* (nonexistence). There are nine *dravyas* (substances): *pṛthivī* (earth); *ap* (water); *vāyu* (air); *agni* (fire); *ākāśa* (ether); *ātman* (self); *manas* (mind); *kāla* (time); and *dik* (space). To these Kumārila adds *tamas* (darkness) and *śabda* (sound).

There are three types of Vedic activities that give rise to *karma*: *nitya* (obligatory) acts; *kāmya* (optional) acts, which also give rise to *puṇya* (merit) that may lead to rebirth in *svarga* (heaven); and *pratisiddha* (forbidden) acts that give rise to *pāpa* (demerit).

Central to Mīmāṃsā ontology is *apūrva* (the invisible potency between cause and effect). *Apūrva* is an unseen potency that is generated when one engages in an action. It is because of the *apūrva* that the effect occurs, and it is thus the causal link that makes the *karma* mechanism possible.

SOTERIOLOGY

There are several goals for the Mīmāṃsaka: first, to follow the *dharma* of the Vedas, namely to fulfill Vedic *vidhis* (injunctions) to perform *yajñas* (sacrifices); second, to perform *kāmya-karma* (optional acts) that will result in rebirth in *svarga* (heaven).

THE TEXT

The Mīmāṃsā text here is a selection (1.1.2–1.1.4) from the *Tarkapāda* (*Section on Reasoning*) portion of the *Śabara-bhāṣya*. In it Śabara explains which *pramāṇas* give rise to knowledge of *dharma*. After defining *dharma* (1.1.2), he explains that the Vedas are the only means by which one learns about *dharma* (1.1.3, 1.1.4). Within this section can be found the beginnings of the arguments concerning *svataḥ-prāmāṇya*.

FROM ŚABARA'S *ŚABARA-BHĀṢYA*

1.1.2. *Dharma* is that which is indicated by [known by means of] the Veda as conducive to the highest good.

The term *chodanā* they use in the sense of the injunctive text; men are found saying "I am doing this act on being enjoined (*choditaḥ*) by the Teacher." *Lakṣaṇa* is that by which something is indicated (pointed out): for instance, when fire is indicated by smoke, they say that smoke is the *lakṣaṇa* (indicator) of fire. That which is indicated by the said injunctive text is *artha*, "something conducive to the highest good"; that is, it brings man into contact with his highest good. This is what we assert.

As a matter of fact, it is the Vedic injunction that is capable of making known (indicating) what is past, present, or future, also what is subtle or hidden or remote and such like; this cannot be done by any organ of sense. ["But what is indicated or made known by the Vedic text is only an act, something to be done, or things connected with that act, and not any accomplished thing," says Ṛjuvimalā].

Objection: "It is possible that the Veda may say what is wrong or false; just as it is possible for an ordinary assertion—such as 'There are fruits on the banks of the river'—to be true or false. [So that the proposition that 'the Veda brings happiness to man' would be doubtful; because the Veda is in the form of words, and words are found to be true as also false; hence there can be no certainty or confidence in what the Veda may assert; that is, there can be nothing of which the Veda could be regarded as the *lakṣaṇa* or *pramāṇa*, the means of right cognition]."

Our answer to the above is as follows: There is self-contradiction involved in the assertion that "the Veda asserts, and asserts what is false." When the Veda is said to "assert," what is meant is that it "makes known," i.e., becomes the means of something being known; when something becomes known on the presence of some means, this latter is said to make the former known. Such being the case, if on the presence of the Veda, it actually becomes known that "from the *Agnihotra* follows heaven," how can it be said that such is not the case [i.e., heaven does not follow from *Agnihotra*]? If such were not the case, how could it be spoken of as *becoming known*? To assert that a thing *does not exist* and yet *becomes known* involves a contradiction in terms. Then again, the idea brought about by the assertion "Desiring heaven, one should perform sacrifices" is not an uncertain one; i.e., it is not in the form "Heaven may or may not follow from the performance of sacrifices"; [in fact, the idea is a definitely certain one that *heaven does follow*], and when this is cognized for certain, it cannot be *false*. That cognition (or idea) alone is *false* which, having appeared, becomes sublated by the notion "Such is not the actual case"; the idea in question (that heaven follows from the performance of sacrifices) is never found to be so sublated at any time, or in regard to any person, or under any circumstances, or at any place. Hence it follows that it is not false or wrong.

As regards the assertion of ordinary men, if it emanates from a trustworthy person—or if it pertains to something that is directly perceived by the senses—it must be true; if, on the other hand, it emanates from an untrustworthy person—or if it pertains to something that cannot be perceived directly by the senses—then it is unreliable, proceeding as it does merely from the mind of a human being. Because such a thing (which is not perceptible by the senses) cannot be known by men except by means of words [and the words of an untrustworthy person cannot be reliable]. [*Dharma* being something not perceptible by the senses, it can be known only by means of words; and these words, to be entirely reliable, should not be such as proceed from a human source, which is not absolutely reliable, by reason of the inherent incapability of the human mind to comprehend things beyond the senses.] It might be argued that the man making the assertion had its source in the previous assertion of another man. But this previous assertion also would be as unreliable as the other one; and in regard to such things (as are beyond the senses) the words of men cannot be a reliable source of knowledge; just as the words of persons born blind cannot be a reliable source of knowledge regarding shades of color.

Objection: "It is not possible for persons not knowing a thing to impart instruction about it; and Manu and others have actually imparted instruction (about *dharma*); from this it follows that good men have possessed the knowledge (of *dharma*) [Read '*puruṣāḥ*' for '*puruṣāt*'; with '*puruṣāt*,' the meaning would be that 'good men have learned it from a human source'; this would not go with the next sentence]; just as the fact that color is apprehended by the eye is deduced only from the fact that the man sees it."

The answer to the above is as follows: As regards instructions, they might proceed from illusion or wrong knowledge also. [Hence the very fact of human beings having imparted instructions does not necessarily prove that these instructors possessed the *right knowledge* of *dharma*]; such instructions, in the absence of illusions, proceed also from the Veda [and in the case of the Veda there is no room for illusion or wrong knowledge, as there is no human agency involved, while in the case of human instructors there is always a chance of mistakes and illusions and ignorance]. But in the case of teachings emanating from human sources, the notion derived is in the form "This man, the speaker, knows this thing to be so and so," and not in the form "The thing *is* so and so"; and the reason for this lies in the fact that the notion derived from human assertions is not always compatible with the truth; in the case of the Vedic assertion on the other hand, there is nothing to indicate its falsity.—"There is the inference from analogy: Having found the human assertion to be false, we infer, from its analogy, that the Vedic assertion also, being an *assertion* (like the human assertion) must be false."—It is not so; because the two cases are not analogous; the falsity of one assertion cannot prove the falsity of another; simply because it is *another* (not the same, assertion); for instance, because Devadatta is dark, it does not follow that Yajñadatta also is dark. Then again your idea that "the Vedic assertion must be false because it is of the same kind as the human assertion (which is found to be false)" is of the nature of an indirect inference based upon a premiss, while the idea derived from the Vedic assertion is of the nature of direct cognition; and no indirect inferential cognition can have any validity when it is opposed to a direct cognition. From all this we conclude that "What is learned from the Veda is conducive to the highest good."

Objection: "If such is the case, then what should be enquired into is *something that is conducive to good* [which must be a well-established entity]; what could be the use of *enquiry into dharma* [which is not a well-established entity, but something that has itself got to be brought into existence]?"

The answer to this is that *what is conducive to good* is exactly what is expressed by the term *dharma*.

"How are we to know that this is so?"

If a man performs sacrifices, he is called a "performer of *dharma*" (*dhārmika*); when a man does an act, he is called after that act; e.g., the person who does the act of *purifying* [or *cooking*, if we accept the reading "*pāchakaḥ*" for "*pāvakaḥ*"] is called "the performer of purification" (*pāvaka*) and one who performs the act of cutting is called "the performer of cutting" (*lāvaka*). Thus it is that what brings to the man the highest good is what is spoken of by means of the word *dharma* ["sacrificing" brings the highest good to man, and it is the act of *sacrificing* that is denoted by the term *dharma*]. This is found to be so not only in common parlance; in the Veda also we find the passage "*yajñena yajñamayajanta devāḥ, tāni dharmāṇi prathamānyāsan*' [By sacrifice did the deities offer sacrifices, and these were the first *dharmas*]" (*Ṛg Veda* 10.9.16), where what is denoted by the term *yaji* (i.e., *yājña*, "sacrifice") is precisely what is spoken of as *dharma*.

As a matter of fact, the Veda indicates both what is moral and what is immoral. "What is moral?": that which is conducive to good, such as the *Jyotiṣtoma* and other acts. "What is immoral?": that which leads to evil (sin), such as the *Shyena*, the *Vajra*, the *Iṣu*, and other (malevolent) acts. Thus the *sūtra* has used the term *artha*, "what is conducive to good," in order to preclude the possibility of the immoral act (which is *not* conducive to good) being included under the term *dharma*.

Objection: "Why should the immoral act be so called?"

Reply: Because it involves inflicting of injury, and the inflicting of injury has been forbidden.

Objection: "How then is it that an immoral act (in the shape of the *Shyena* sacrifice, for instance) is enjoined as something that should be done?"

The answer to this is that the *Shyena* and other such (malevolent) sacrifices are nowhere found to be spoken of as what should be done; they are indicated only in the form that "if a man desires to inflict injury upon another, the performance (of the *Shyena*) would be the means for that purpose"; what the Vedic text says is only that "one desiring to inflict injury may perform the *Shyena*" (cf. *Saḍviṁsha-Brāhmaṇa* 8.1–2), not that "one should inflict injury." [The man is urged to undertake the performance of the *Shyena* entirely by his desire to inflict injury, not by any Vedic text enjoining that act as what ought to be done.]

Objection: "The *sūtra* as it stands is not capable of expressing all this: (a) that "*dharma* is that which is indicated by the Veda, and not what is indicated by the senses and other means of knowledge," (b) that "*dharma* is moral, not immoral." Because the *sūtra* contains a single sentence, and it would involve a syntactical split of the sentence, if it were taken as expressing the said two propositions."

The answer to this is that such a syntactical split is objectionable only in cases where the idea is meant to be expressed by a regularly formed sentence; and this is so only in the case of Vedic texts, not in *sūtras*; because a *sūtra* is understood to be merely indicative of what is gathered from other sources; so that it is only parts of propositions that are indicated (*sūtryatē*) in the *sūtra*; in fact that is why it is called a *sūtra* (aphorism). Thus it is that the present *sūtra* is to be taken as containing the parts of the two distinct propositions (mentioned above by the objector). Or, the *sūtra* may be construed as containing the single proposition that "*dharma* is that particular act conducive to the highest good that is indicated by the Veda"; so that there is a single proposition [and there is no syntactical split involved].

1.1.3. The examination of its means [follows].

It has been declared by us that "the knowledge of *dharma* is brought about by means of the Veda"; but that was a mere assertion; we shall now proceed to examine the means of that knowledge. Is the Veda alone the means, or is there something else also? Until this examination has been made, it cannot be known for certain that "*dharma* is that which is indicated by the Veda as conducive to the highest good" (no. 1.1.2).

1.1.4. That cognition by a person which appears when there is contact of the sense-organs is "sense-perception," and it is not a means (of knowing *dharma*), as it apprehends only things existing at the present time.

The examination (promised in the preceding *sūtra*) is as follows: Sense-perception is not the means (of knowing *dharma*). Why?: because the character of sense-perception is that it is "that cognition by a person, etc." (*sūtra*); that is, it is that cognition which a man has when his sense-organs are in contact with the object cognized. *Dharma*, however, is something that is yet to come, and it does not exist at the time that it is to be known, while sense-perception is the apprehending of an object that is actually present and not nonexistent at the time (of cognition)—hence sense-perception cannot be the means (of knowing *dharma*).

In the *sūtra*, no stress is meant to be laid upon either "cognition," or the "appearance," or upon mere "contact"; the only factor meant to be emphasized is the fact of its being such as is possible only when there is contact between the sense-organ and the object, and not when there is no such contact between them. If stress were laid upon several factors, then there would be syntactical split.

As for (the other means of cognition,) inference, analogy, and apparent inconsistency, these also presuppose (are based upon) sense-perception; hence these also cannot be the means (of knowing *dharma*).

Nor can *dharma* be amenable to "negation" [i.e., it cannot be regarded as nonexistent].

NOTES

1. Dan Arnold, *Buddhists, Brahmins, and Belief: Epistemology in South Asian Philosophy of Religion* (New York: Columbia University Press, 2005), 63.
2. Arnold, *Buddhists, Brahmins, and Belief*, 63 n. 13.
3. I am reliant on Arnold for the partial analysis here of *svataḥ-prāmāṇya*.

FURTHER READING

Arnold, Dan. *Buddhists, Brahmins, and Belief: Epistemology in South Asian Philosophy of Religion*. New York: Columbia University Press, 2005.

——. "Of Intrinsic Validity: A Study of the Relevance of Pūrva Mīmāṃsā." *Philosophy East and West* 51.1 (2001): 26–53.

Bhatt, Govardhan P. *Epistemology of the Bhāṭṭa School of Pūrva Mīmānsā*. Chowkhamba Sanskrit Studies 17. Varanasi: Vidya Vilas Press, 1962.

Bilimoria, Puroshottama. *Śabdapramāṇa: Word and Knowledge*. Dordrecht: Kluwer Academic, 1988.

Chatterjee, Satischandra, and Dhirendramohan Datta. *An Introduction to Indian Philosophy*. Calcutta: University of Calcutta, 1939.

Clooney, Francis X. *Thinking Ritually: Rediscovering the Pūrva Mīmāṃsā of Jaimini*. De Nobili Research Library 17. Vienna: Brill, 1990.

Dasgupta, Surendranath. *A History of Indian Philosophy*, vol. 1. Cambridge: Cambridge University Press, 1922.

D'Sa, Francis X., S.J. *Śabdaprāmāṇyam in Śabara and Kumārila: Towards a Study of the Mīmāṃsā Experience of Language*. De Nobili Research Library 7. Vienna: Brill, 1980.

Jha, Ganganatha. *Pūrva-Mīmāṃsā in Its Sources*. Benares: Benares Hindu University, 1942.

King, Richard. *Indian Philosophy*. Edinburgh: Edinburgh University Press, 1999.

Sharma, Chandradhar. *A Critical Survey of Indian Philosophy*. London: Rider, 1960.

Part III. SCHOOLS OF VEDĀNTA

athāto brahmajijñāsa.

Then, afterward, let there be a study of Brahman.

—Bādarāyaṇa, *Brahma Sūtras* 1.1.1

HISTORY

Vedānta was and is a commentarial tradition that holds the Vedas, specifically the *Upaniṣads*, to be its root texts. In fact, the term *vedānta* is a *tatpuruṣa* (a determinative compound) comprising two terms, *veda* and *anta*, and it means "the culminating sections of the Vedas." That Vedānta was named after this body of texts marks their importance and the centrality given to commentary. There are four Vedas, namely, the *Ṛg*, *Yajur*, *Sāma*, and *Atharva Vedas*. Each Veda can be further subdivided into the *Saṃhitās*, the *Brāḥmanas*, the *Āraṇyakas*, and the *Upaniṣads*. The Vedas are believed to be *śruti* (revealed root texts), *apauruṣeya* (without human origin), and *svataḥ-prāmāṇa* (intrinsically, or self-, valid). For this reason they are held to be *nitya* (eternal) and *nirdoṣa* (free from defects). The *Upaniṣads* were central to Vedānta commentary.

Vedānta's immediate predecessor is the Mīmāṃsā school (Jaimini composed the *Mīmāṃsā Sūtras* in ca. 25 C.E.), which devoted the entirety of its intellectual efforts to interpreting the ritual injunctions prescribed in the Vedas. Much of the hermeneutic foundations of Vedānta can be found in Mīmāṃsā texts. For these reasons, Vedānta is sometimes known as Uttara Mīmāṃsā (later investigation). Vedānta is distinguished from Mīmāṃsā by the importance that it gives to the *jñāna-kāṇḍa* (portions of the Vedas concerning metaphysical knowledge), and the diminished value it places on *karma-kāṇḍa* (portions of the Vedas concerning ritual).

Although the schools of Vedānta include the Vedas in their canon, each expanded its boundaries to include additional texts. Leaving aside these supplements to the canon, the *Upaniṣads*, the *Bhagavad Gītā*, and the *Brahma Sūtras* are the primary root texts for all the schools of Vedānta and are the critical objects of commentary. These three are known collectively as the *prasthāna-traya* (triple foundations) and were commented upon by nearly every school of Vedānta.

The *Brahma Sūtras* (also called the *Vedānta Sūtras*), composed by Bādarāyaṇa (also known as Vyāsa) in the fifth century C.E., is regarded as a systematization of the teachings of the *Upaniṣads*. The text is four chapters long and is comprised of 564 *sūtras* (pithy aphorisms). Its brevity makes it difficult to read without the commentaries produced by the founders of each of the schools of Vedānta and the multiple subcommentaries produced by subsequent thinkers. Above all, the *Brahma Sūtras* characterized the nature of the relationship between *Brahman* (the divine principle) and the *ātman* (individual self). Knowledge of this relationship would lead to *mokṣa* (liberation) from *saṃsāra* (the cycle of birth and rebirth).

SCHOOLS

The *Upaniṣads*, the *Bhagavad Gītā*, and the *Brahma Sūtras* were interpreted in conflicting ways by each school of Vedānta, and each has its own theory about the nature of *mokṣa* and how it can be achieved. There are three major schools of Vedānta. These are the Advaita school, founded by Śaṃkarācārya in the eighth century C.E.; the Viśiṣṭādvaita school, founded by Rāmānujācārya between the eleventh and twelfth centuries C.E.; and the Mādhva school (also known as the Dvaita school), founded by Madhvācārya between the thirteenth and fourteenth centuries C.E. The idealist Advaita school posits that the relationship between *Brahman* and the individual *ātman* is *advaita* (nondual). The Viśiṣṭādvaita school posits that the relationship between *Brahman* and the individual *ātman* is *viśiṣṭādvaita* (a nonduality of that which is qualified). The realist Mādhva (Dvaita) school posits that the relationship between *Brahman* and the individual *ātman* is *dvaita* (dual).

FURTHER READING

Clooney, Francis X. *Theology After Vedānta: An Experiment in Comparative Theology*. Albany: State University of New York Press, 1993.

King, Richard. *Indian Philosophy*. Edinburgh: Edinburgh University Press, 1999.

Nakamura, Hajme. *A History of Early Vedanta Philosophy, Part One*. Delhi: Motilal Banarsidass, 1983.

——. *A History of Early Vedanta Philosophy, Part Two*. Delhi: Motilal Banarsidass, 2004.

ADVAITA VEDĀNTA

HISTORY

The Advaita school posits that the relationship between *Brahman* (the impersonal absolute) and the *ātman* (individual self) is *advaita* (nondual). Furthermore, the universe is not composed of differences and different entities, as it seems. Knowing this, adherents can eventually obtain *mokṣa* (liberation) from *saṃsāra* (the cycle of birth and rebirth).

The first references to the idealist Advaita position are found in the *Gauḍapādīya-kārika* of Gauḍapāda (eighth century C.E.),[1] which is a commentary on the *Maṇḍūkya Upaniṣad*. The most important expounder of Advaita, though, is Śaṃkarācārya (788–820 C.E.),[2] and he traced his lineage to Gauḍapāda. Śaṃkarācārya studied with Govindapāda, who may have been a student of Gauḍapāda.[3] A large number of texts are attributed to Śaṃkarācārya and of these the majority are *bhāṣyas* (commentaries) on the canonical texts of Vedānta. His *Upadeśāhasrī* (*A Thousand Teachings*) is an independent treatise and is widely held to be authentic. His most famous text is his *Brahma Sūtra-bhāṣya,* a commentary on the *Brahma Sūtras* of Bādarāyaṇa.

Several branches of the Advaita school have developed since its inception. These are Vācaspati Miśra's Bhāmati school (tenth century C.E.) and Prakāśātman's Vivaraṇa school (thirteenth century C.E.), and they were named after subcommentaries on Śaṃkarācārya's *Brahma Sūtra-bhāṣya.*

EPISTEMOLOGY

The Advaita school accepts five *pramāṇas* (sources of valid knowledge): *pratyakṣa* (perception); *anumāna* (inference); *upamāna* (comparison); *arthāpatti* (presumption); and *śabda* (testimony). *Śabda* is central to all schools of Vedānta, given that they are exegetical ones whose sole objects of commentary are the *śruti* (revealed root texts). According to the Advaita school, all *śabda* is *śruti*. While *anumāna* is held to be a *pramāṇa*, it must not contradict *śruti*. Rather, it is in service to *śruti*. On the other hand, the scope of *śruti* is only that which is outside of direct perception. In this way, valid knowledge gained by *pratyakṣa* cannot be contradicted by *śruti*.

ONTOLOGY

The only entity in the universe is *Brahman* (the impersonal absolute). *Brahman* is outside of language and it is beyond duality. *Brahman* is *sat* (being), *cit* (consciousness), and *ānanda* (bliss). Difference that one normally perceives is only apparent and is a result of *adhyāsa* (superimposition) of something remembered onto another. *Brahman* is incorrectly superimposed upon. Thus it appears as if there is a multiplicity of *ātman* (individual selves). This too is only apparent, as the *ātman* are mistakenly understood to be different from *Brahman*. The error, Śaṃkarācārya explains, is a result of *māya* (illusion) and *avidyā* (ignorance), terms that he uses interchangeably.

There are two standard examples for illustrating the mechanism of *adhyāsa*. One is incorrectly seeing a rope as a snake at dusk. The other is seeing nacre (i.e., mother-of-pearl) and mistakenly thinking that it is silver. In both cases there is a false cognition of something previously known, as the previously known snake is superimposed on the rope and the previously known silver is superimposed on the nacre. Similarly, there is an *adhyāsa* of a thing onto *Brahman* that leads to a false belief that there is difference, when in fact there is nonduality.

Śaṃkarācārya also refers to *upādhi* (limiting adjunct) in his works. The *upādhi* creates apparent differences that did not exist before. It is applied to *Brahman* and the result is that what is unity is incorrectly perceived as multiplicity. All that is perceived, for example, is an *upādhi* of *Brahman*. The Advaita school contends that *bheda* (difference) that is perceived is not real, that it is an *upādhi* of *Brahman*, and that the only real entity is *Brahman*. They are, of course, a product of *avidyā*.

Like his Madhyamaka counterparts, Śaṃkarācārya proposes that there are two levels of truth, *paramārthasatya* (higher truth) and *vyavahārasatya* (normal truth). Though things are certainly *advaita* in *paramārthasatya*, they nonetheless function in *vyavahārasatya* and exhibit subject-object duality. The words on this page (and, for that matter, this book) only appear to exist in *vyāvahara-avasthā* (the normal way of seeing). Ultimately, in *paramārtha-avasthā* (the higher way of seeing), they can be seen as products of *adhyāsa*, mere *upādhis*.

SOTERIOLOGY

Mokṣa (liberation), the goal of the Advaita school, is the realization that the *ātman* has a nondual relationship with *Brahman*. The incorrect equation, moreover, of the *jīva* with the body is a result of *adhyāsa* and must be understood to obtain *mokṣa* (liberation). Just as one incorrectly sees a rope as a snake, one sees the *jīva* as the body. The *avidyā* that gives rise to *adhyāsa* must be eliminated.

Advaita Vedānta permits *mokṣa* to occur for those who appear to be living. These *jīvanmuktas* (ones living while liberated) persist as long as one has *prārabdha* (latent) *karma*. That is, the accumulated *karma* manifested itself until it was depleted. *Mokṣa* is only nominally "attained." After all, there is ultimately no ontological change in the aspirant since there merely is a loss of *avidyā*.

THE TEXT

The selection included here is from the *Brahma Sūtra-bhāṣya* of Śaṃkarācārya. In the preamble to the first *sūtra* (decree) of the *Brahma Sūtras* Śaṃkarācārya outlines his basic position regarding *adhyāsa* and *avidyā*.

FROM ŚAṂKARĀCĀRYA'S *BRAHMA SŪTRA-BHĀṢYA*

Preamble: It being an established fact that the object and the subject, that are fit to be the contents of the concepts "you" and "we" (respectively), and are by nature as contradictory as light and darkness, cannot logically have any identity, it follows that their attributes can have it still less. Accordingly, the superimposition of the object, referable through the concept "you," and its attributes on the subject that is conscious by nature and is referable through the concept "we" (should be impossible), and contrariwise the superimposition of the subject and its attributes on the object should be impossible. Nevertheless, owing to an absence of discrimination between these attributes, as also between substances, which are absolutely disparate, there continues a natural human behavior based on self-identification in the form of "I am this" or "This is mine." This behavior has for its material cause an unreal nescience and man resorts to it by mixing up reality with unreality as a result of superimposing the things themselves or their attributes on each other.

If it be asked, "What is it that is called superimposition?," the answer is: It is an awareness, similar in nature to memory, that arises on a different (foreign) basis as a result of some past experience. With regard to this, some say that it consists in the superimposition of the attributes of one thing on another. But others assert that wherever a superimposition on anything occurs, there is in evidence only a confusion arising from the absence of discrimination between them. Others say that the superimposition of anything on any other substratum consists in fancying some opposite attributes on that very basis. From every point of view, however, there is no difference as regards the appearance of one thing as something else. And in accord with this, we find in common experience that the nacre appears as silver, and a single moon appears as two.

Opponent: How, again, can there be any superimposition of any object or its attributes on the (inmost) Self that is opposed to the non-Self and is never an object (of the senses and mind)? For everybody superimposes something else on what is perceived by him in front; and you assert that the Self is opposed to the non-Self and is not referable (objectively) by the concept "you."

The answer (of the Vedāntin) is: The Self is not absolutely beyond apprehension, because it is apprehended as the content of the concept "I"; and because the Self, opposed to the non-Self, is well known in the world as an immediately perceived (i.e., self-revealing) entity. Nor is there any rule that something has to be superimposed on something else that is directly perceived through the senses; for boys superimpose the ideas of surface (i.e., concavity) and dirt on space (i.e., sky) that is not an object of sense-perception. Hence there is nothing impossible in superimposing the non-Self on the Self that is opposed to it.

This superimposition, that is of this nature, is considered by the learned to be *avidyā* (nescience). And the ascertainment of the nature of the real entity by separating the superimposed thing from it is called *vidyā* (illumination). This being so, whenever there is a superimposition of one thing on another, the locus is not affected in any way either by the merits or demerits of the thing superimposed. All forms of worldly and Vedic behavior that are connected with valid means of knowledge and objects of knowledge start by taking for granted this mutual superimposition of the

Self and non-Self, known as nescience; and so do all the scriptures dealing with injunction, prohibition, or emancipation.

Opponent: How, again, can the means of valid knowledge, such as direct perception as well as the scriptures, have as their locus a cognizer who is subject to nescience?

The (Vedāntin's) answer is: Since a man without self-identification with the body, mind, senses, etc., cannot become a cognizer, and as such, the means of knowledge cannot function for him; since perception and other activities (of a man) are not possible without accepting the senses, etc., (as his own); since the senses cannot function without (the body as) a basis; since nobody engages in any activity with a body that has not the idea of the Self superimposed on it; since the unrelated Self cannot become a cognizer unless there are all these (mutual superimposition of the Self and the body and their attributes on each other); and since the means of knowledge cannot function unless there is a cognizership; therefore it follows that the means of knowledge, such as direct perception as well as the scriptures, must have a man as their locus who is subject to nescience.

Moreover, there is no difference (of the learned) from the animals (in regard to empirical behavior). Just as animals and others turn away from sound, etc., when these appear to be unfavorable after their ears, etc., come in contact with them, and they move toward these when they are favorable; and just as by noticing a man approaching them with a raised stick, they begin to run away, thinking, "This one wants to hurt me," and they approach another carrying green grass in his hands, similarly even the wise are repelled by the presence of strong, uproarious people with evil looks and upraised swords, and are attracted by men of opposite nature. Therefore the behavior of men with regard to the means and objects of knowledge is similar to that of animals. And it is a familiar fact that the animals use their means of perception, etc., without discrimination (between the body and the Self). From this fact of similarity, the conclusion can be drawn that so far as empirical behavior is concerned, the use of the means of perception by the wise is similar to that of lower animals(, it being a result of superimposition). Of course, it is a fact that a man acting intelligently does not acquire the competence for scriptural duties unless he has a knowledge of the relationship of his soul with the next world. Still (a knowledge of) the absolute Reality, that is the Self, is not a prerequisite for such a competence; for it (i.e., Reality) has no relevance here, and it is opposed to such competence, inasmuch as it is beyond hunger and thirst, free from such differentiation as *brāhmaṇa*, *kṣtriya*, etc., and is not subject to birth and death. And the scriptures, which are operative before the dawn of the real knowledge of the Self, cannot transgress the limits of their dependence on people groping in ignorance. To illustrate the point: Such scriptural injunction as "A *brāhmaṇa* shall perform a sacrifice" can become effective only by taking for granted various kinds of superimposition of caste, stage of life, age, condition, etc. And we said that superimposition means the cognition of something as some other thing. Thus in accordance as one's wife, children, or other relatives are hale and hearty with all their limbs intact, or as they suffer from the loss of those limbs, one thinks, "I myself am hale and hearty" or "I myself am injured"; thus one superimposes external characteristics on the Self. Similarly one superimposes the characteristics of the body when one has such ideas as "I am fat," "I am thin," "I am fair," "I stay," "I go," or "I scale." So also one superimposes the attributes of the senses and organs when one thinks, "I am dumb," "I have lost one eye," "I am a eunuch," "I am deaf," or "I am blind." Similarly one superimposes the attributes of the internal organ, such as desire, will, doubt, perseverance, etc. In the same way, one first superimposes the internal organ, possessed of the idea of ego, on the Self, the witness of all the manifestations of that organ; then by an opposite process, one superimposes on the internal organ, etc., that Self which is opposed to the non-Self and which is the witness of everything. Thus occurs this superimposition that has neither beginning nor end but flows on eternally, that appears as the manifested universe and its apprehension, that conjures up agentship and enjoyership, and that is perceived by all persons. In order to eradicate this source of evil and in order to acquire the knowledge of the unity of the Self, is begun a discussion (after the study) of all the *Upaniṣads*. We shall show in this discussion about the nature of the embodied soul, that this is the purport of all the *Upaniṣads*.

NOTES

1. See Richard King, *Early Advaita Vedānta and Buddhism: The Māhāyana Context of the Gauḍapādīya-kārikā* (Albany: State University of New York Press, 1995), 15–50, for more on Gauḍapāda's dates.
2. See Bradley Malkovsky, *The Role of Divine Grace in the Soteriology of Śaṃkarācārya* (Leiden: Brill, 2001), 1–8, for more on Śaṃkarācārya's dates. I am reliant upon Malkovsky's lucid characterization of Advaita Vedānta for much of this summary.
3. Malkovsky, *Role of Divine Grace*, 6–7.

FURTHER READING

Clooney, Francis X. *Theology After Vedānta: An Experiment in Comparative Theology*. Albany: State University of New York Press, 1993.

Deutsch, Eliot. *Advaita Vedānta: A Philosophical Reconstruction*. Honolulu: East–West Center Press, 1969.

Fort, Andrew O. *Jīvanmukti in Transformation: Embodied Liberation in Advaita and Neo-Vedānta*. Albany: State University of New York Press, 1998.

Hirst, J. G. Suthren. *Śaṃkara's Advaita Vedānta: A Way of Teaching*. London: Routledge-Curzon, 2005.

Ingalls, Daniel H. H. "Saṃkara on the Question: Whose Avidya?" *Philosophy East and West* 3.1 (1953): 69–72.

King, Richard. *Early Advaita Vedānta and Buddhism: The Māhāyana Context of the Gauḍapādīya-kārikā*. Albany: State University of New York Press, 1995.

——. *Indian Philosophy*. Edinburgh: Edinburgh University Press, 1999.

Mahadevan, T. M. P. *The Philosophy of Advaita*. New Delhi: Arnold-Henemann, 1976.

Malkovsky, Bradley. *The Role of Divine Grace in the Soteriology of Śaṃkarācārya*. Leiden: Brill, 2001.

Potter, Karl, ed. *Advaita Vedānta up to Śamkara and His Pupils*. Delhi: Motilal Banarsidass, 1981.

Ram-Prasad, Chakravarthi. *Advaita Epistemology and Metaphysics: An Outline of Indian Non-Realism*. London: RoutledgeCurzon, 2002.

12

VIŚIṢṬĀDVAITA VEDĀNTA

HISTORY

The Viśiṣṭādvaita school posits that the relationship between *Brahman* (the impersonal absolute) and the *ātman* (individual self) is a nondualism (*advaita*) qualified by difference (*viśiṣṭa*). *Brahman* is thus a qualified unity and all parts of reality, including the *ātman*, are *prakāra* (attributes) of *Brahman. Brahman*, moreover, is the only independent entity. By knowing this, exhibiting the appropriate *bhakti* (devotion), and following the path of *prapatti* (self-surrender), adherents can eventually obtain the grace of God and be granted *mokṣa* (liberation) from *saṃsāra* (the cycle of birth and rebirth).

The first references to the Viśiṣṭādvaita position are found among the Āḷvār saints and Tamil Ācāryas who propounded Śrī Vaiṣṇava devotionalism. The founder of the Viśiṣṭādvaita school of Vedānta is Rāmānujācārya (1017–1137 C.E.).[1] His most famous text is his *Brahma Sūtra-bhāṣya,* commentary on the *Brahma Sūtras* of Bādarāyaṇa. Several branches of the Viśiṣṭādvaita school have developed since its inception. These are the Vaḍagalais of Piḷḷai Lokācārya and the Tangalais of Vedānta Deśika, also known as Veṇkaṭanātha. The chief difference between the two subschools concerns the importance they place on the degree of effort required of the adherent to obtain God's grace.

EPISTEMOLOGY

The Viśiṣṭādvaita school accepts three *pramāṇas* (sources of valid knowledge): *pratyakṣa* (perception); *anumāna* (inference); and *śabda* (testimony). *Śabda* is central to all schools of Vedānta, given that they are exegetical ones whose sole objects of commentary are the *śruti* (revealed root texts). In addition to the *śruti,* Rāmānujācārya adds the *Pañcarātra Āgamas* (Vaiṣṇava sectarian texts), the *Vaiṣṇava Purāṇas*, the Tamil *Prabhandam*, and some traditional texts such as *Mānava-dharma-śastra* (*Treatise on Proper Duty According to Manu*).

ONTOLOGY

According to the Viśiṣṭādvaita school, the universe is composed of six *dravyas* (substances). These are *prakṛti* (materiality), *kāla* (time), *cit* (consciousness), Īśvara (*Brahman*/Viṣṇu), *dharma-bhūta-jñāna* (attributive knowledge), and *śuddhasattva* (pure *sattva*). *Dharma-bhūta-jñāna* is both a substance and an attribute and is only an attribute of the individual *cit*. *Śuddhasattva* is the substance that comprises liberated *cits* and forms the body of God as well as Viakuṇtha (Viṣṇu's abode).

There are ten *adravyas* (nonsubstances). These are the three *guṇas* (*sattva, rajas,* and *tamas*), *śabda* (sound), *sparśa* (touch), *gandha* (smell), *rasa* (taste), *rūpa* (color), *śakti* (potency of a substance that produces an effect), and *saṃyoga* (conjunction).

The only *svatantra* (independent) entity in the universe is *Brahman*, also known as Viṣṇu. The universe is comprised of *tattva-traya* (three reals): *cit* (sentients); *jaḍa* (nonsentients); and Iśvara (i.e., Viṣṇu). *Cit* and *jaḍa* are dependent upon, and attributes of, Viṣṇu. *Cit* and *jaḍa* have a relationship of *apṛthaksidhi* (inseparability) with Viṣṇu. They are *viśeṣaṇa* (attributes) of a *viśeṣya* (substance). Viṣṇu is thus *viśiṣṭa* (qualified). Hence there is a nondualism of *Brahman* and the universe, qualified by difference. The individual *jīvas* (which comprise the *cit*) are thus the *śarīra* (body) of God, who is the *śarīrin*, the vital force, that rules and controls them.

SOTERIOLOGY

Mokṣa (liberation), the goal of the Viśiṣṭādvaita school, is the realization that the *ātman*/*cit* is dependent upon, and is an attribute of, *Brahman*. It is the correction of the false belief that the individual *cit* is identical with the body and different from *Brahman*. The individual *ātman* should surrender (*prapatti*) to God and, by God's grace, will be granted *mokṣa*.

THE TEXT

The selections included here are from the *Vedārthasaṃgraha* of Rāmānujācārya. In sections 3–8 Rāmānujācārya offers a basic account of his position as a short summary of the Advaita position. In sections 75–76 he explains that *Brahman* is the *śarīrin* (vital force) of the universe, which is characterized as the *śarīra* (body). In the last section, 141–145, Rāmānujācārya offers a description of *bhakti* (devotion).

FROM RĀMĀNUJĀCĀRYA'S *VEDĀRTHASAMGRAHA*

Basic Positions

§3. The only meaning that is to be found in the most important part of the whole body of *śrutis*, which set forth what is blissful for the entire universe, is as follows: True knowledge of the individual soul and of the Supreme Spirit, applied to the obligations imposed by the various *dharmas* pertaining to each stage and station of life, are to precede pious and humble acts of devotion for and meditation on the Supreme Spirit—acts held extremely dear by the devotee—that ultimately result in the attainment of the Supreme Spirit.

§4. In truth, all declarations of the Vedānta are meant to set forth the knowledge of the proper form and nature of the individual soul, which are different from the body; the proper form and nature of the Supreme Spirit, who is the inner ruler of the soul; the worship of the Supreme Spirit; and the apprehension of *Brahman* as perfect boundless bliss, which presupposes the revelation of the proper form of the soul that results from the worship of the Supreme Spirit. By setting forth all this the declarations of the Vedānta serve to remove the danger of rebirth, which is inevitable since it results from the misconception of the individual soul that it is identical itself with that one of the four types of bodies—sc. gods (from Brahmā onward), men, animals, inanimate beings—into which it has entered by the impulsion of the continuous flow of good or evil *karma* amassed during ageless ignorance.

Such declarations are met with in *śrutis* like "Thou art That, this soul is *Brahman*, He who, although residing in the soul, is different from that soul, whom the soul does not know, whose body is the soul, and who directs the soul from within, He is the immortal inner ruler of thy soul, He is the inner soul of all beings, free from all evil, the divine and sole God Nārāyaṇa, 'tis He whom the *brahmans* aspire to know by repeating the Vedas, by sacrifice, charity, mortification, and fasting, he that knows *Brahman* attains the Most-High, he that knows this is immortal: there is no other way to tread," and so on and so forth.

§5. The proper form of the soul is free from all various differentiations consisting in the distinctions that are brought about by the natural evolution of *prakṛti* into the bodies of gods, men, etc. In essence it is only characterized by knowledge and beatitude. When these differentiations of god, man, etc.—which have been brought about by the *karma* of the soul—have vanished there persists a differentiation in its proper form; it is beyond the power of expression and can only be known by the soul itself. So the soul can only be defined as essentially knowledge; and this essential nature is common to all souls.

§6. The proper form of the inner Ruler is as follows: He is the sole cause of the cessation of *saṃsāra*, which itself consists in the origination, subsistence, and dissolution of the phenomenal world constituted by the above spiritual and nonspiritual entities. His proper form is therefore distinct from all entities other than Himself, since He is absolutely opposed to all evil and comprises solely infinite perfection. His beautiful qualities are immeasurable, perfect, and innumerable. He is known in the entire Veda under the various designations of "Soul of all," "the Supreme Brahman," "Supreme Glory," "Supreme Principle," "Supreme Spirit," "Real Being," etc.—all of which denote the Venerable Lord Nārāyaṇa, the Supreme Person. The *śrutis* are meant to set forth his manifestation, so they expound the universal dominion of the Supreme Spirit as the inner Soul of the totality of spiritual and nonspiritual entities by expressions like "His power," "His portion," "His manifestation," "His form," "His body," "His shape," etc., and by *sāmānādhikaraṇya* constructions.

§7. While attempting to explain these *sāmānādhikaraṇya* constructions, etc., which in fact only propound *Brahman*'s manifestation, some philosophers contend that *Brahman* is nothing but nondifferentiated knowledge. Although it is eternally released and by its very nature self-illuminating, it is identical with the individual soul; this identity is concluded from *sāmānādhikaraṇya* constructions such as "Thou art That." Accordingly, *Brahman* itself is nescient and as such may be in bondage as well as released. The entire universe, with its infinite variety of sovereign lord, submissive souls, etc., is false, for it is different from pure nondifferentiated spirituality. The distinction that one soul is in bondage and the other soul is released cannot be made at all. It is false that some souls have attained release before: only one single body has an in-dwelling soul and all other bodies have no souls at all; but which body that is cannot be positively determined. The preceptor who imparts knowledge is false, the person who has correct knowledge of the *śāstra* is also false. All this is to be gathered from the *śāstra*, which is false itself.

§8. Others occupy a different position and hold that *Brahman*, though having all perfections like freedom from evil, etc., is—because of the conception of identity—afflicted with some sort of adjunct, so that he may be alternatively in bondage or in released state and is consequently the abode of evolution, which takes the form of various imperfections.

Brahman as the *Śarīrin*

§75. This is the reason all terms that denote *prakṛti* and *puruṣa*—modes of the Lord—whether in their subtle or in their gross phase, denote in their primary sense the Supreme Spirit as being differentiated by the modes they constitute: in the very same manner as the terms "god," "man," etc., denote the individual souls incorporated by the bodies god, man, etc. To put it differently: in the same manner as the terms "god," "man," etc., in their primary sense denote the embodied soul that is their modified substratum, since the diverse evolved products of *prakṛti*—such as god, man, etc.—are *padārthas* only insofar as they are modifications of the embodied soul: thus all terms denoting any spiritual and nonspiritual entity denote in their primary senses the Supreme Spirit, since that entity denoted modifies the Supreme Spirit by constituting his body.

§76. The relation between soul and body means the relation between substratum and dependent entity incapable of functioning separately, between transcendent controller and thing controlled, between principal and accessory. In this relation the one term is called *ātman,* or "soul," because this is the one who obtains an object since he is in all respects the substratum, the controller, and the principal; the other term is called body, i.e., "form," because it is a modification that is inseparably connected since it is in all respects dependent entity, thing controlled, and accessory. For such is the relation between the individual soul and its body. Consequently, inasmuch as all constitute the body of the Supreme Spirit, he can be denoted by all terms.

Bhakti

§141. We have already declared that the means of attaining *Brahman* is a superior *bhakti* in the form of rememorization staggered to a state of extremely lucid perception, which is immeasurably and overwhelmingly dear to the devotee. It is achieved by complete devotion of *bhakti,* which is furthered by the performance of one's proper acts preceded by knowledge of the orders of reality as learned from the *śāstra*. The word *bhakti* has the sense of a kind of love, and this love again that of a certain kind of knowledge.

However, according to people in the world love has no other sense than that of pleasure, and pleasure that is to be realized by a certain kind of knowledge is a different thing altogether.

No, for whatever kind of knowledge is said to lead to pleasure is pleasure itself.

§142. In other words: cognitions with a content fall either under pleasure or suffering, or the state of neither pleasure nor suffering, and they become one or the other of these three according to their content or object. If knowledge particularized by a particular object excites pleasure, it is held dear accordingly. The cognition that has that pleasurable object is pleasure itself, and we do not notice any different thing: particularly because this cognition leads to the practical behavior of being happy. The capacity of particularizing such a pleasurable cognition is but relative and impermanent in any object different from *Brahman*, but in *Brahman* itself it is absolute and permanent: it is said that "*Brahman* is bliss." Since knowledge is pleasurable if its object is pleasurable, *Brahman* is pleasurable as such. This is declared in: "He is pleasure: He that obtains this pleasure becomes happy," i.e., *Brahman* being pleasure, one is happy when one has attained *Brahman*." The Supreme Person, being in His own right and of His own accord boundless and absolute bliss, becomes bliss to another too, because there is no differentiation in that he is beatitudinous. So the meaning of our text is: He that has *Brahman* as the object of his knowledge becomes happy. When it is realized that the soul stands in a relation of subservience to the Supreme *Brahman* because this Supreme *Brahman*—treasury of hosts of innumerable absolute and immeasurable beautiful qualities, irreproachable, possessing an infinite supernal manifestation, ocean of immeasurable and absolute goodness, beauty, and love—is the Principal to which the soul is accessory or subservient, then the Supreme *Brahman* who is thus an object of absolute love leads the soul to Himself.

§143. However, this would mean in other words that the soul's absolute subservience itself is immeasurable and absolute happiness: but this is contradicted by all experience, for we see that literally all spiritual beings have one great wish: to be completely independent; compared with that, dependence means suffering. And there is the *smṛti* "All dependence means suffering," and in the same line: "Service is called a dog's way, so try to avoid it."

This attitude reveals the misconceived identification of body and soul by those who have not learned that the soul is essentially different from the body. For the body, which, as a matter of fact, is a mass in which qualities, such as the generic structure of man, etc., subsist, is held to be independent and they who are bound to *saṃsāra* think that the body is the "I." Whatever misconception one has of one's own soul, one holds the end of life to agree with that. What is pleasure is differently determined according to the body for which the soul is mistaken—lion, tiger, boar, man, *yakṣa*, *rakṣas*, *piśāca*, god, *dānava*, male, female, etc.—and these different pleasures are mutually incompatible. So everything is judged by whatever aim of life corresponds to the mistaken identity of the soul. The proper form of the soul has, however, knowledge for its one and only form, and is essentially different from the body, god, etc., and the soul's essence is that it is subservient to another. When this conception of the soul as it really is has been formed the end of life is held to be that which is in accordance with that. The *smṛti* "The soul is pure knowledge" declares that the soul's only form is knowledge. From numerous *śrutis* of the kind of "the Master of all" we know that the soul's sole form is to be subservient to the Supreme Spirit. Therefore the wishful misconception of independence must be regarded as an erroneous cognition due to *karma*, just as the wishful misconception that the soul is identical with the body of a lion, tiger, etc. Consequently it is also due to *karma* that objects other than the Supreme Person are pleasurable. Therefore they are slight and impermanent, while the Supreme Person is happiness in Himself, so that this happiness is permanent, immeasurable, and absolute, on the authority of the *śruti* "*Brahman* is joy, *Brahman* is space; *Brahman* is bliss, *Brahman* is real, knowledge, infinite." No entity other than *Brahman* is essentially happiness, and if it happens to be pleasurable, it is impermanent because it is due to *karma*: this has been declared by the venerable Parāśara[2]: "Sinful *karma* and auspicious *karma* are called hell or heaven, one and the same thing may lead to suffering, pleasure, and jealousy and wrath: so for what reason has that thing that character?" i.e., what makes an entity that is completely or enduringly pleasure, pain, etc., just that entity? This exclusive character is due to good and evil *karma*. After showing the want of consistency when we consider a number of persons, in that the pleasure of one is the suffering of another, he says that that same inconsistency holds also in one and the same person: "That which led to joy now leads again to pain, and what led to wrath now leads to peace," i.e., that any thing is markedly pleasure or pain is due to the effects of *karma*, not to the proper form of that thing itself; hence it disappears when an end is put to *karma*.

§144. The *smṛti* that you just quoted, "All dependence means suffering," declares as a matter of fact that since there is no mutual relationship of principal and subservient terms with entities that are different from the Supreme Person, any subservience to something different from Him is suffering. In "Service is called a dog's way" it is stated that obedience to one who is not worth it is a dog's way. According to the text "For He alone should be worshiped by all always in all stages of life," only the Supreme Person is worthy of the obedience of all those who know what the true nature of the soul is. As the Venerable Lord put it: "When a man serves Me through unerring devotion to *bhakti,* he will pass beyond the *guṇas* and become *Brahman.*" This service in the form of *bhakti* is denoted by the word for "knowing" in the *śrutis*: "He that knows *Brahman* attains the Most-High," "He that knows this, becomes immortal," "Knowing *Brahman*, he becomes *Brahman*," etc. From the specifying text "He whom He chooses may attain Him," we understand from the clause "whom He chooses" that one must be elected and that the most beloved one is elected. The most beloved of the Lord is he in whom boundless and absolute love for the Lord has been inspired: this is stated by the Lord in: "For I am exceedingly beloved of the knower and he is beloved by Me." Therefore it is knowledge which has risen to superior *bhakti* that is really the means of attaining the Lord, as the lord Dvaipāyaṇa declares in the *Mokṣadharma* by way of comment upon all the *Upaniṣads*: "His form is not to be beheld and no one perceives Him with the eye, only he who has concentrated on his soul espies—by *bhakti* and discrimination—the proper form of knowledge in this life," i.e., after having realized one's own soul by *discrimination*, one sees the Supreme Spirit by *bhakti*, sc. one has immediate presentation of Him, attains Him: this follows because the meaning is the same as in the text: "but by exclusive *bhakti* can I . . . ." Since *bhakti* is taken as a form of cognition, everything is established.

§145. Considering that there must be people who are at once profound enough and without professional jealousy and who know how to discriminate between what is of the essence and what not, I have written for them this summary of the meaning of the Veda.

NOTES

1. See John B. Carman, *The Theology of Rāmānuja* (New Haven: Yale University Press, 1974) for more on Rāmānujācārya's dates.
2. Parāśara is the speaker of the *Viṣṇu Purāṇa.*

FURTHER READING

Bartley, C. J. *The Theology of Rāmānuja.* London: RoutledgeCurzon, 2002.

Carman, John B. *The Theology of Rāmānuja.* New Haven: Yale University Press, 1974.

Chakravarti, V. R. Srisaila. *The Philosophy of Sri Rāmānuja.* Chennai: V. S. R. Chakravarti, 1974.

Lipner, Julius. *The Face of Truth.* Albany: State University of New York Press, 1986.

Sharma, Chandradhar. *A Critical Survey of Indian Philosophy*. London: Rider, 1960.

Srinivasachari, P. N. *The Philosophy of Viśiṣṭādvaita*. Chennai: Adyar Library and Research Centre, 1978.

Van Buitenen, J. A. B. *Rāmānuja's Vedārthasaṃgraha*. Poona: Deccan College Postgraduate and Research Institute, 1956.

13

MĀDHVA VEDĀNTA

jīveśvarabhidā caiva jaḍeśvarabhidā tathā | jīvabhedo mithaś caiva jaḍajīvabhidā tathā | mithaś ca jaḍabhedo 'yaṃ prapañco bhedapañcakaḥ | so 'yaṃ satyo.

The universe has five [intrinsic] differences: There is a difference between [each] *jīva* (enduring self), and Lord [Viṣṇu]. There is a difference between Lord [Viṣṇu] and *jaḍa* (nonsentient material entities). There is difference between the individual *jīvas*. There is a difference between *jīvas* and *jaḍas*. There is a difference between one *jaḍa* and another. The [difference between these five] is real.

—Madhvācārya, *Viṣṇutattva(vi)nirṇaya*

HISTORY

The Mādhva school (also known as the Dvaita school) posits that the relationship between *Brahman* (the impersonal absolute) and the *ātman* (individual self) is *dvaita* (dual). Furthermore, Madhvācārya, a realist, claims that the universe is governed by *pañcabheda*, five types of differences that are real and not illusory, as seen above.

Madhvācārya (1238–1317 C.E.), the founder of the tradition, was born of Shivalli Brahmin parents in the village of Pājakakṣetra near modern-day Udupi in the Tulunadu area of southern Karnataka.[1] According to Madhvācārya himself, he traveled to Mahābadarikāśrama, the home of Vyāsa, who was the author of the *Brahma Sūtras*, to study with the founder of the Vedānta tradition. Vyāsa was believed to be an *avatāra* (incarnation) of Lord Viṣṇu, the deity around which Mādhva Vedānta is centered.[2] Madhvācārya himself had an unusual background as he proclaimed himself to be the third *avatāra* of Vāyu, the wind god, who is also the son of Viṣṇu.[3]

The *Brahma Sūtra-bhāṣya* is Madhvācārya's most important work and is, indirectly, a summary of the essence of the Mādhva position. In addition, he wrote several independent treatises that contain summaries of his own position and arguments against his Advaita opponents. Although a large number of followers of Mādhva Vedānta composed commentaries on texts in Madhvācārya's entire corpus and independent treatises on Mādhva doctrine, two scholars are especially noteworthy, Jayatīrtha and Vyāsatīrtha. They, along with Madhvācārya, are known as the *munitrayam* (the three major thinkers) of Mādhva Vedānta. The two commentators, Jayatīrtha and Vyāsatīrtha, composed works that changed the trajectory of Mādhva Vedānta, both in terms of Mādhva ratiocinative method and as a result of the sustained damage their arguments effected against competing schools.

EPISTEMOLOGY

The Mādhva school accepts three *pramāṇas* (sources of valid knowledge): *pratyakṣa* (perception); *anumāna* (inference); and *śabda* (testimony). *Śabda* is central to all schools of Vedānta, given that they are exegetical ones whose sole objects of commentary are the *śruti* (revealed root texts). In addition to the *śruti*, Madhvācārya adds the *Pañcarātra Āgamas* (Vaiṣṇava sectarian texts), the *Vaiṣṇava Purāṇas*, *Mahābhārata*, the *Rāmāyaṇa*, the *Tantras*, and some traditional texts such as *Mānava-dharma-śastra* (*Treatise on Proper Duty According to Manu*).

ONTOLOGY

Madhvācārya separates all of reality into *svatantra* (independent) and *asvatantra* (dependent) entities. The only independent entity is Viṣṇu. All other entities are *asvatantra*. Among the *svatantra* existent entities, there are those that are *cetana* (sentient) and those that are *acetana* (not sentient). The *acetana* are comprised of the Vedas, the Purāṇas, *kālā* (time), and *prakṛti* (materiality). According to Madhvācārya, *prakṛti* has twenty-four emanations. The *buddhi* (intellect) (also known as *mahat*) is the first to emerge from *prakṛti*. It is followed by *ahaṃkāra* (ego), the *manas* (mind), the ten *indriyas* (capacities that enable sensing, motor functioning, and thinking), the *pañca-tanmātras* (five subtle elements), and the *pañca-bhūtas* (the five gross elements).

All creatures are located in a *tāratamya* (hierarchy/gradation) wherein Viṣṇu holds the highest position. He should be worshiped always. In fact, one achieves release (*mokṣa*) from the seemingly neverending cycle of birth and rebirth only by means of His grace obtained via enlightened *bhakti* (devotion). The emphasis that Madhvācārya places on *bhakti* distinguishes his system from Advaita Vedānta, which upholds *jñāna* (knowledge) as the primary means to *mokṣa*. According to Madhvācārya, Viṣṇu is to be worshiped, is the object of meditation, and can be known, in part, after in-depth study. Proper knowledge of the nature of God and one's dependence upon Him eventually leads to *aparokṣa-jñāna* (unmediated knowledge) of Viṣṇu granted by Viṣṇu himself.

Madhvācārya explains that *bheda* (difference) is real and perceivable. He holds that a *viśeṣa* (distinguishing property) resides between any object and its attribute. The difference between two atoms lies in the *viśeṣa* that resides in each of the two. Madhvācārya explains that *viśeṣa* is *sva-nirvāhaka* (possessing self-sufficiency) and thereby does not require another *viśeṣa* to differentiate each *viśeṣa* from its substrate. By positing this capacity possessed by all substances, Madhvācārya is able to solve the problems of relating substances with their attributes as well as relating entities that are different from one another. In the light of *viśeṣa*, it is possible for Viṣṇu to be related to his attributes via the *viśeṣa*. In fact, all objects are related to their attributes by means of the *viśeṣa*. This capability is intrinsic to all objects and is not itself an attribute.

Madhvācārya believes that *bheda* (difference) constitutes the *svarūpa* (essence) of all objects. Difference is apprehended when the *svarūpa* of any object is apprehended. An immediate awareness of the difference of an object is an awareness of its uniqueness. Madhvācārya explains that, in general, the *svarūpa* of an object distinguishes it from all other objects. If the *svarūpa* were not constituted by difference, then the immediate comprehension of the general uniqueness of an object would not occur. If this basic understanding that "this object is different" did not occur, then, Madhvācārya jokes in his *Viṣṇutattva(vi)nirṇaya*, it would be possible to doubt whether oneself was a pot! One would not be able to see oneself as being unique and different from all other things! The difference is apprehended in the same way as the *viśeṣa* is apprehended: instantaneously.

SOTERIOLOGY

Mokṣa (liberation), the goal of the Mādhva school, is the realization that the *ātman* is dependent upon *Brahman*. Madhvācārya holds that *bhakti-yoga* (the path via devotion) is the only way to achieve *aparokṣa-jñāna* (unmediated knowledge) of *Brahman* and, subsequently, *mokṣa*. According to

Madhvācārya, this vision is the climax of intellectual life of all *bhaktas* in *saṃsāra* (worldly experience).

THE TEXTS

Three selections are included here. These are Madhvācārya's *Māyāvādakhaṇḍana* (*Refutation of the Māyā Position*) (in its entirety), *Upādhikhaṇḍana* (*Refutation of the Upādhi Position*) (in its entirety), and selections from the *Viṣṇutattva(vi)nirṇaya* (*The Complete Ascertainment of the Nature of Viṣṇu*). These three texts are pointed criticisms of positions that are essential to Advaita epistemology.

The *Māyāvādakhaṇḍana* (hereafter *MVK*) is partly a reaction to arguments found in the twelfth-century C.E. Advaita scholar Śrīharṣa's *Khaṇḍanakhaṇḍakhādya*. Not surprisingly, the arguments in the *MVK* cannot be removed from the fundamental component of the schools of Vedānta, namely the *śruti* (revealed texts), also known here as the *śāstra*. Not only do arguments in Vedānta center around the interpretation of these texts, but they are often attempts to show that the opponent is not acknowledging their centrality. To address this issues of centrality, the schools of Vedānta hold that *śāstra* has four elements, each of which must exist and be satisfied. If one can show that the position of the opponent does not include, or excludes, one of these four, then victory is guaranteed. If a school of Vedānta does not uphold the importance of the *śāstra*, then it is no longer a commentarial tradition! For each school, then, it follows that there must be:

1. *adhikāri* (an eligible student): devotees who are eligible to study the *śāstra* and have a desire to study them.
2. *viṣaya* (scope): a defined subject matter of *śāstra*. Does *śāstra* teach that there is difference or identity? It cannot teach both and must be consistent.
3. *prayojana* (purpose): an aim or purpose for *śāstra*. It cannot stand apart from the practical concern of being granted *mokṣa*.
4. *saṃbandha* (connection): a relationship between the *adhikāri*, *viṣaya*, and *prayojana*. If one were to make either of the others irrelevant, then there would be no *saṃbandha*.

In his *MVK* Madhvācārya shows that each of these prerequisites cannot be satisfied if one adheres to the Advaita position. To do so he attacks their position that there is an *aikyam* (identity) between the *Brahman* and the *ātman*, using it as the starting point. Madhvācārya's contentions are in service of a proper understanding of the *śāstras* and do not stand independently of that goal. For these reasons, the *MVK* is a superb example of Mādhva polemics.

Madhvācārya's *Upādhikhaṇḍana*, like the *MVK*, is an attack against the heart of the Advaita position. Here Madhvācārya shows that there are problems with the concept of *upādhi* (limiting adjunct). The *upādhi* creates apparent differences that did not exist before. It is applied to *Brahman* and the result is that what is unity is incorrectly perceived as multiplicity. All that is perceived, for example, is an *upādhi* of *Brahman*. The Advaita school contends that *bheda* (difference) that is perceived is not real, that it is an *upādhi* of *Brahman*, and that the only real entity is *Brahman*. Madhvācārya questions the ontology of the *upādhi* and then the locus of *ajñāna* (ignorance). Toward the end of the *Upādhikhaṇḍana* he employs a strategy similar to what he used in the *MVK* and argues that if one were to accept the Advaita position, there would be problems with the *adhikāri*, *viṣaya*, *prayojana*, and *saṃbandha*. He again shows that one can neither uphold *śāstra* nor read it properly if one follows the Advaita position.

The *Viṣṇutattva(vi)nirṇaya* contains a variety of refutations of Advaita positions. The passages included here are from the first section and are refutations of *ekajīvavāda* (the Advaita position that all of reality is the product of one *jīva* [i.e., *ātman*], namely, *Brahman*). Madhvācārya correlates *ekajīvavāda* with the belief that the universe is the product of one person's dream. The argument is focused on the practical implications of the Advaita position for the teacher, for the students, and for the goal of Vedānta, namely to obtain *mokṣa*.

MADHVĀCĀRYA'S *MĀYĀVĀDAKHAṆḌANA*

1. Narasiṃha ("Man-lion", i.e., Viṣṇu in his fourth incarnation), who, [as] the sun [destroys] darkness, [destroys] the opinions [deriving from ignorance], who is the boundless ocean, unsurpassed bliss and [his] immeasurable power, [he] is preeminent.

2. That dubious [*śāstra*] need not be studied for it imparts false [knowledge about the universe]. Whatever [gives false knowledge] in this manner, is [like] that [and should not be studied]. Similarly, [the *śāstra*] assented to [by the Advaita school that proclaims the identity of the *Brahman* and the *jīva* imparts false knowledge and should not be studied].

3. [According to the Advaita school,] the *aikyam* (identity) [between] *Brahman* [and the *jīva*] is definitely not real. [If it were real, then there

would be a] difference [of the *aikyam* (identity) from *Brahman*'s] own nature [and there would be more than one entity that was real. Both *aikyam* and *Brahman* would be real]. [This would lead to] the abandoning of the *advaita* (nondualism) [position since there would be two real entities, namely *Brahman* and *aikyam* (identity)].

4. [If *aikyam* (identity)] is not different [from *Brahman* but is its very] nature, then [since *Brahman*] is self-luminous[, *aikyam* would also be self-luminous]. [Therefore *aikyam* would already] possess the means for establishing itself [and would not require *śāstra* to be known. Therefore, the *śāstras* would be superfluous].

5. [Being without difference,] the *ātman*[, that is, *Brahman*] has no characteristics. [Since] the characteristics are [already] known [then there is no need to study the *śāstras* to learn more about *Brahman*].

6. [If] the nature [of *Brahman*] is [already] known and there are no characteristics [of *Brahman* to be known, then] ignorance conceals [nothing and studying *śāstra*, which is known to destroy ignorance, would have no *viṣaya* and would be superfluous].

7. It is known [that the Advaita school and the Bhāṭṭa school of Mīmāṃsā hold that] *pramāṇa* (the means of valid knowledge) is that which leads to a meaning that was not already known. [From this, it follows that, for the Advaita school, *śāstra* would not be a *pramāṇa* since *Brahman* would already be known.]

8. Given that [*Brahman* and the *jīva*] are identical and that *Brahman* has no ignorance it is impossible [that the *jīva* is] ignorant and it follows that the entirety of their [i.e., the Advaita school's] theories are malicious.

9. If the *aikyam* (identity) [between *Brahman* and the *jīva*] is false, then the *āgamas* [i.e., the *śāstras* that the Advaita school believes to prove this purported identity] would be proclaiming fallacies [and would not buttress the Advaita position].

10. And [if the Advaita position of *aikyam* (identity) between *Brahman* and the *jīva* is false, then] the difference [between the two] is true.

11. [If *aikyam* were true] then *mokṣa* would already be established [for the *jīva*, given its] nature [as identical with *Brahman*]. There would [then] be a destruction of the utility [of the *śāstras,* which, according to the Advaita school, is a prerequisite for *mokṣa*].

12. As ignorance is impossible [and the Advaita position untenable, then], the fourth category [neither *sat* (real) or *asat* (unreal)] is [also] absent. [If there is no fourth category, then] there is a destruction of the fifth category [*anirvacanīya* (indescribability)].

13. Since there is neither a *viṣaya* [for *śāstra*] nor a *prayojana*, there is [also] no *adhikāri* (one eligible for studying the *śāstra*). In the light of these absences, there is also no *saṃbandha* [between the *viṣaya*, *prayojana*, and the *adhikāri*].

14. [Consider these passages from the *Bhagavad Gītā* (15.16–20):] "There are two entities in the world, perishable and imperishable. All beings are perishable. The one occupying the highest place [i.e., *Brahman*] is called the imperishable. And the highest entity [that] is different [from the perishable entities] is called the Supreme Self, who, pervading the three worlds, supports them [i.e., the three worlds]. Since I transcend the perishable and am higher than the imperishable, I am in the world and in the Veda and am known as the Highest Among Beings! Oh Descendant of Bharta [i.e., Arjuna], he who knows Me as the Highest Among Beings [and is] without delusion, he knows all and worships Me with his entire being. Thus, this preeminently secret *śāstra* is professed by Me. Oh Descendant of Bharta, having awakened to this [secret], one should be enlightened, fulfilling all duties."

15. [And this passage from the *Kaṭha Upaniṣad* (3.10–11):] "Higher than the *indriyas* (senses) are their objects. Higher than sense objects is the *manas* (mind). Higher than the *manas* is the *buddhi* (intellect). Higher than the *buddhi* is the Highest Being. Higher than the Highest Being is the unmanifest. Higher than the unmanifest is the *puruṣa* (Person). Higher than the *puruṣa* there is nothing at all. That is the goal, that is the highest state."

16. [*Brahma Sūtra* 3.3.59 indicates this:] "Importance [is given to meditation] on the Supreme Being as is the [centrality of] sacrifice. This is shown [by the *śāstra*]."

17. The superiority of Visṇu is declared by all of the *śruti* and by the Lord and [that] alone is the purpose of the *śāstra*.

18. There is a destruction of the darkness of the entire *māyā* position by the all-knowing sage [i.e., Madhvācārya] by means of [his] *tattvavāda* (position of reality). [And this is] to dispel the doubts of good men.

19. There is nothing equal to Nārāyaṇa [that is Viṣṇu/*Brahman*], nor was there, nor will be there. With these true statements, I conclude [my refutation of the *māyā* position].

MADHVĀCĀRYA'S *UPĀDHIKHAṆḌANA*

1. May [Lord] Nārāyaṇa [Viṣṇu], whose form alone is permanent [and filled with] countless qualities, who is free from all faults, [and] who is

the abode of Kamalā [i.e., an epithet of Lakṣmī, consort of Viṣṇu], be pleased. [Attributing] ignorance to the One Who Knows All is absolutely not proper.

2. If [you] hold that [this ignorance is] possible because of the difference [caused by] the limiting adjunct, then either it is [part] of the self-nature [of *Brahman*] or it is [caused by] ignorance. If it is intrinsic [to *Brahman*], then dualism is [established as] true.

3. When the cause [of the limiting adjunct] is [held to be] ignorance, then [there is the fallacy of] infinite regress or reciprocal dependence. Or [there is the] calamity of circularity. And, [moreover,] how can difference [be caused by] the limiting adjunct?

4. In all cases previously seen, [the limiting adjunct] is the indicator of a difference [that already] exists. [It does not] create new [differences]. When it[, the limiting adjunct, differentiates] portions from other portions it indicates a difference [that already] exists. [The limiting adjunct] is for the consideration of those who are stupid!

5. If not, then is there a relation of the limiting adjunct with one part [of the space] or with the whole? [If it were the first], with one part, then there would be infinite regress. [If it were the second], with the whole, then there is no difference [that is created].

6. And if one [self] is identical [with another, then] there would be no difference [between their individual] experience of pleasure and pain. Despite the difference [caused by] the limiting adjunct such as the hands, feet, etc.[, they are not experienced as different from the one who experiences them].

7. There is also the case of the *yogi* who investigates the experiences of different bodies. If [the bodies were] not [different from one another], then how can the *yogi*'s desire to investigate experiences [of different bodies be understood]?

8. [It may be argued that] possessing various bodies [is possible] without the plan [to investigate]. [If so, then] how is the *yogi* [able to choose] particular [bodies]?

9. If it were argued that [the difference in limiting adjuncts] is due to the difference in *karma*, then there would also be a difference in limiting adjuncts. And, if [this were the case], then there would be [the fallacy of] reciprocal dependence.

10. [There is] no fallacy [if there is] an intrinsic difference [between each individual] *ātman*. And [the position that they are all identical] is entirely inconsistent with perception and other [valid means of knowledge]. And this position [that there is identity] is incontrovertibly false.

11. By [observing] the characteristic behavior of other bodies, one concludes that [they each possess] an *ātman*. From this, [one concludes that] the individual *ātman* are different [from one's own *ātman*]. Everyone perceives this.

12. [The qualities of the individual *ātman*, such as] ignorance, insignificant power, suffering, and insignificant agency, are opposed to the qualities [of *Brahman*] such as omniscience and the like. [Everyone] perceives [this].

13. Viṣṇu's qualities such as omniscience, etc., are established in *śruti* [like *Ṛg Veda* 8.3.4: "He, with his might enhanced by *ṛṣis* thousandfold, has spread out like an ocean.] His greatness is [praised as] true [at solemn rites and his powers where holy singers rule"] and others.[4] From [such] statements [the aforementioned qualities ascribed to *Brahman*] cannot be false.

14. There is no reliable authority [which holds that] there is a fallacy in Vedic utterances. And even [if there were such an authority] it is not authoritative.

15. [If the identity theory were true] then the phrase "ignorance" is not [possible]. And [if this were the case, then] there is no subject to be explained [by the Vedas] nor the immediately adjoining [topic of purpose]. From there being no emergence of ignorance, who [would get the] fruit [of Vedic study]? The connection [between the subject to be explained, the purpose, and the eligibility of the student would be like the self-contradiction] of the hare's horn.

16. [If] the difficulty [in explaining the location of ignorance and the limiting adjunct] is [to be considered intellectual] ornamentation then the *ātman* [i.e., *Brahman*] would be ignorant! Complete darkness [i.e., ignorance] would be [His] ornamentation, [and] eternal suffering [His] crest-jewel!

17. Therefore, [the position that *Brahman* and *ātman* are different] is illustrated in *śruti* passages [such as *Ṛg Veda* 7.99.1: "They are not able to reach your majesty when you expanded beyond all limits"]. [And *Brahman*] is seen as different from the *ātman* by *śruti* passages [such as *Muṇḍaka Upaniṣad* 3.1.2: "Stuck on the very same tree, one person grieves, deluded by her who is not the Lord. But when he sees] the other, contented Lord [and his majesty, his grief disappears"]. [And, in] *śruti* passage [*Muṇḍaka Upaniṣad* 3.1.3]: "When [the seer sees that *puruṣa* (Person), the gold-colored, the creator, the Lord, as the womb of *Brahman*. Then shaking off the good and the bad, the wise man becomes spotless and attains the highest identity]" the [mere] similarity [of the

individual *ātman*] to the *ātman* [i.e., *Brahman*] always [indicates] difference.

18. In order to eternally please the Lord of Śrī [i.e., Lakṣmī], discerning reality [as it is], the sun of omniscience illuminated the world, which is pervaded by the darkness of the position of illusion.

19. I bow to that Lord of Indirā [i.e., Lakṣmī], whose form is a lovely and who is [characterized by] abundant bliss and innate intelligence and who grants the experience of eternal bliss [to his devotees].

FROM MADHVĀCĀRYA'S *VIṢṆUTATTVA(VI)NIRṆAYA*

1. *Ekajīvavāda* (the view that there is only one *jīva* [namely *Brahman*]), is incoherent.

2. When the imagination is [produced] from only one [*jīva*'s] *ajñāna* (ignorance) then [that *jīva*,] knowing "everything is [merely] imagination" cannot endeavor to enlighten [imaginary] students.

3. [Why?] Recognizing "this is [all] in a dream," one does not labor to [give away one's] monetary inheritance to the dream-son. [Similarly, why would one bother to teach one's students when they are merely products of one's own imagination?]

4. But, unaware of being in a dream, he may labor [in this way] in the dream itself.

5. Given that many [people] are seen [and they all might be dreaming], it is not possible to have firm conviction as to whose dream it is.

6. But in dream[s,] it is certain [that] after awaking, [only] one [person, namely the dreamer,] remains.

7. Here, [in this case,] it is not possible [to be certain about who is the dreamer and who is being dreamed].

8. It is also impossible that reality is to be conceived as of imaginary by each [individual *jīva*]. These alternatives cannot arise [as possibilities]. [One can only conclude that] there would be no imagination in reality.

9. Moreover, there is no *pramāṇa* (means for valid knowledge) [showing] that it [i.e., reality] is to be conceived [of as imagination by each and every *jīva*].

10. [If] the imagination [derives from] the ignorance of the student, then when [the student] becomes a teacher, he himself [becomes the product of] imagination! Learning properly [from] the books [i.e., sacred texts] would be disastrous!

11. No one would be able to attain *mokṣa*. When one learns the texts,

then one [becomes a teacher and] suffers [becoming the product] of the student's imagination!

12. If one *jīva* was a *bhedavādin* (one who follows the view [that there is a] difference [between the *jīva* and *brahman*]), then there is a confirmation of it [i.e., difference]. There is never an elimination of difference and[, therefore,] no one would attain *mokṣa*.

13. By this [reasoning], whatever is imagined [by this one *jīva*], that is [reality]. When those following *ekajīvavāda* (the view that there is only one [*jīva*]) are imagined to be in eternal Hell, then this would be so!

14. [From these arguments, it follows that] there is no proof whatsoever that everything is a [product] of the imagination of one *jīva*.

NOTES

1. For further information about the establishment of Madhvācārya's dates see B. N. K. Sharma, *History of the Dvaita School of Vedānta and Its Literature* (Delhi: Motilal Banarsidass, 1981), 77–79.
2. *evaṃvidhāni sūtraṇi kṛtvā vyāso mahāyaśāḥ | brahmarūdrādideveṣu manuṣyapitṛpakṣiṣu | jnānaṃ saṃsthāpya bhagavānkriḍante puruṣottamaḥ,* "Having produced the *sūtras,* the great Vyāsa, who is the Supreme Person, the Lord, established knowledge in Brahma, Rūdra, and other Gods, in men, forefathers, and birds" (Madhvācārya, *Brahma Sūtra-bhāṣya* 0).
3. *vāyuṃ hareḥ sutaṃ,* "Vāyu is the son of Hari (Viṣṇu)" (Madhvācārya, *Chāndogyopaniṣadbhāṣyam* 3.15.1).
4. Translation of the *Ṛg Veda* is from R. T. H. Griffith, *The Hymns of the Rgveda.*

FURTHER READING

Sarma, Deepak. *Epistemology and the Limitations of Philosophical Inquiry: Doctrine in Mādhva Vedānta.* Oxford: RoutledgeCurzon, 2005.

——. *An Introduction to Mādhva Vedānta.* Aldershot: Ashgate, 2003.

Sharma, B. N. K. *History of the Dvaita School of Vedānta and Its Literature.* Delhi: Motilal Banarsidass, 1981.

——. *Philosophy of Sri Madhvācārya.* Delhi: Motilal Banarsidass, 1986.

GENERAL BIBLIOGRAPHY

Anacker, Stefan. *Seven Works of Vasubandhu: The Buddhist Psychological Doctor.* Delhi: Motilal Banarsidass, 1984.

Arnold, Dan. *Buddhists, Brahmins, and Belief: Epistemology in South Asian Philosophy of Religion.* New York: Columbia University Press, 2005.

———. "Of Intrinsic Validity: A Study of the Relevance of Pūrva Mīmāṃsā." *Philosophy East and West* 51.1 (2001): 26–53.

Bartley, C. J. *The Theology of Rāmānuja.* London: RoutledgeCurzon, 2002.

Bhatt, Govardhan P. *Epistemology of the Bhāṭṭa School of Pūrva Mīmānsā.* Chowkhamba Sanskrit Studies 17. Varanasi: Vidya Vilas Press, 1962. (Republished as *The Basic Ways of Knowing: An In-Depth Study of Kumārila's Contribution to Indian Epistemology.* Delhi: Motilal Banarsidass, 1989.)

Bhattacharya, Kamaleswar. *The Dialectical Method of Nāgārjuna.* Delhi: Motilal Banarsidass, 2005.

Bilimoria, Puroshottama. *Śabdapramāṇa: Word and Knowledge.* Dordrecht: Kluwer Academic, 1988.

Burley, Mikel. *Classical Sāṃkhya and Yoga: An Indian Metaphysics of Experience.* London: Routledge, 2007.

Burton, David F. *Emptiness Appraised: A Critical Study of Nāgārjuna's Philosophy.* London: Curzon, 1999.

Carman, John B. *The Theology of Rāmānuja.* New Haven: Yale University Press, 1974.

Chakrabarti, Kisor Kumar. *Classical Indian Philosophy of Mind: The Nyāya Dualist Tradition.* Albany: State University of New York Press, 1999.

Chakravarti, V. R. Srisaila. *The Philosophy of Sri Rāmānuja.* Chennai: V. R. S. Chakravarti, 1974.

Chatterjee, Ashok Kumar. *The Yogācāra Idealism.* Delhi: Motilal Banarsidass, 1962.

Chatterjee, Satischandra, and Dhirendramohan Datta. *An Introduction to Indian Philosophy.* Calcutta: University of Calcutta, 1939.

Clooney, Francis X. *Theology After Vedānta: An Experiment in Comparative Theology.* Albany: State University of New York Press, 1993.

———. *Thinking Ritually: Rediscovering the Pūrva Mīmāṃsā of Jaimini.* De Nobili Research Library 17. Vienna: Brill, 1990.

D'Amato, Mario. "Three Natures, Three Stages: An Interpretation of the Yogācāra *Trisvabhāva*-Theory." *Journal of Indian Philosophy* 33 (2005): 185–207.

Dasgupta, Surendranath. *A History of Indian Philosophy*, vol. 1. Cambridge: Cambridge University Press, 1922.

Deutsch, Eliot. *Advaita Vedānta: A Philosophical Reconstruction*. Honolulu: East–West Center Press, 1969.

D'Sa, Francis X., S.J. *Śabdaprāmāṇyam in Śabara and Kumārila: Towards a Study of the Mīmāṃsā Experience of Language*. De Nobili Research Library 7. Vienna: Brill, 1980.

Dundas, Paul. *The Jains*. 2nd ed. London: Routledge, 2002.

Faddegon, B. *The Vaiceṣika-System, Described with the Help of the Oldest Texts*. Wiesbaden: Dr. Martin Sandig, 1969.

Fort, Andrew O. *Jīvanmukti in Transformation: Embodied Liberation in Advaita and Neo-Vedānta*. Albany: State University of New York Press, 1998.

Franco, Eli. *Perception, Knowledge, and Disbelief: A Study of Jayarāśi's Scepticism*. Delhi: Motilal Banarsidass, 1994.

Ganeri, Jonardon. *Indian Logic: A Reader*. Richmond, Surrey, UK: Curzon Press, 2001.

Griffiths, Paul J. *On Being Mindless: Buddhist Meditation and the Mind–Body Problem*. La Salle, Ill.: Open Court, 1986.

Halbfass, Wilhelm. *India and Europe: An Essay in Understanding*. Albany: State University of New York Press, 1988.

——. *On Being and What There Is: Classical Vaiśeṣika and the History of Indian Ontology*. Albany: State University of New York Press, 1992.

Harvey, Peter. *An Introduction to Buddhism: Teachings, History, and Practices*. Cambridge: Cambridge University Press, 1990.

Hiriyanna, M. *Outlines of Indian Philosophy*. Great Britain: George Allen and Unwin Ltd., 1932.

Hirst, J. G. Suthren. *Śaṃkara's Advaita Vedānta: A Way of Teaching*. London: Routledge-Curzon, 2005.

Ingalls, Daniel H. H. *Materials for the Study of Navya-Nyāya Logic*. Delhi: Motilal Banarsidass, 1988.

——. "Saṃkara on the Question: Whose Avidya?" *Philosophy East and West* 3.1 (1953): 69–72.

Jaini, Padmanabh S. *The Jaina Path of Purification*. Berkeley: University of California Press, 1979.

Jha, Ganganatha. *Pūrva-Mīmāṃsā in Its Sources*. Benares: Benares Hindu University, 1942.

King, Richard. *Early Advaita Vedānta and Buddhism: The Māhāyana Context of the Gauḍapādīya-kārikā*. Albany: State University of New York Press, 1995.

——. *Indian Philosophy*. Edinburgh: Edinburgh University Press, 1999.

Koller, John M. "Skepticism in Indian Thought." *Philosophy East and West* 27.2 (1977): 155–164.

Larson, Gerald James. *Classical Sāṃkhya: An Interpretation of Its History and Meaning*. Delhi: Motilal Banarsidass, 1979.

Larson, Gerald James, and Ram Shankar Bhattacharya. *Sāṃkhya: A Dualist Tradition in Indian Philosophy*. Princeton: Princeton University Press, 1987.

———. *Yoga: India's Philosophy of Meditation*. Delhi: Motilal Banarsidass, 2008.

Lipner, Julius. *The Face of Truth*. Albany: State University of New York Press, 1986.

Mahadevan, T. M. P. *The Philosophy of Advaita*. New Delhi: Arnold-Henemann, 1976.

Malkovsky, Bradley. *The Role of Divine Grace in the Soteriology of Śaṃkarācārya*. Leiden: Brill, 2001.

Malvania, Dalsukh, and Jayendra Soni. *Jain Philosophy, Part 1*. Delhi: Motilal Banarsidass, 2007.

Matilal, Bimal K. *The Central Philosophy of Jainism (Anekānta-Vāda)*. Ahmedabad: L. D. Institute of Indology, 1981.

———. "The Jaina Contribution to Logic." In *The Character of Logic in India*, ed. Jonardon Ganeri and Heeramann Tiwari, 127–139. Albany: State University of New York Press, 1998.

———. *Nyāya-Vaiśeṣika*. Wiesbaden: Harrassowitz, 1977.

Nakamura, Hajme. *A History of Early Vedanta Philosophy, Part One*. Delhi: Motilal Banarsidass, 1983.

———. *A History of Early Vedanta Philosophy, Part Two*. Delhi: Motilal Banarsidass, 2004.

Padmarajiah, Y. J. *A Comparative Study of the Jain Theories of Reality and Knowledge*. Delhi: Motilal Banarsidass, 1963.

Phillips, Stephen H. *Classical Indian Metaphysics: Refutations of Realism and the Emergence of "New Logic."* Delhi: Motilal Banarsidass, 1997.

Potter, Karl, ed. *Advaita Vedānta up to Śaṃkara and His Pupils*. Delhi: Motilal Banarsidass, 1981.

———. *Indian Metaphysics and Epistemology: The Tradition of Nyāya-Vaiśeṣika up to Gaṅgeśa*. Princeton: Princeton University Press, 1977.

———. *Presuppositions of India's Philosophies*. Delhi: Motilal Banarsidass, 1991.

Rahula, Walpola. *What the Buddha Taught*. New York: Grove Press, 1959.

Ram-Prasad, Chakravarthi. *Advaita Epistemology and Metaphysics: An Outline of Indian Non-Realism*. London: RoutledgeCurzon, 2002.

Riepe, Dale. *The Naturalistic Tradition in Indian Thought*. Seattle: University of Washington Press, 1961.

Robinson, Richard H., Willard L. Johnson, and Thinisasaro Bikku. *Buddhist Religions: A Historical Introduction*. Belmont, Calif.: Thomson, 2005.

Sarma, Deepak. *An Introduction to Mādhva Vedānta*. Aldershot: Ashgate, 2003.

———. *Epistemology and the Limitations of Philosophical Inquiry: Doctrine in Mādhva Vedānta*. Oxford: RoutledgeCurzon, 2005.

Sen Gupta, Anima. *Classical Sāṃkhya: A Critical Study*. Delhi: Munshiram Manoharlal, 1981.

Shah, Nagin J. *Jaina Theory of Multiple Facets of Reality and Truth*. Delhi: Motilal Banarsidass, 2000.

Sharma, B. N. K. *History of the Dvaita School of Vedānta and Its Literature*. Delhi: Motilal Banarsidass, 1981.

———. *Philosophy of Sri Madhvācārya*. Delhi: Motilal Banarsidass, 1986.

Sharma, Chandradhar. *A Critical Survey of Indian Philosophy*. London: Rider, 1960.

Siderits, Mark. *Buddhism as Philosophy*. Aldershot: Ashgate, 2007.

Srinivasachari, P. N. *The Philosophy of Viśiṣṭādvaita*. Chennai: Adyar Library and Research Centre, 1978.

Stcherbatsky, F. Th. *Buddhist Logic*, vol. 1. New York: Dover Publications, 1962.

Van Buitenen, J. A. B. *Rāmānuja's Vedārthasaṃgraha*. Poona: Deccan College Postgraduate and Research Institute, 1956.

Vidyabhusana, Satis Chandra. *A History of Indian Logic: Ancient, Mediaeval, and Modern Schools*. Delhi: Motilal Banarsidass, 1988.

Waldron, William S. *The Buddhist Unconscious: The Ālaya-Vijñana in the Context of Indian Buddhist thought*. London: RoutledgeCurzon, 2003.

Westerhoff, Jan. *Nāgārjuna's Madhyamaka: A Philosophical Introduction*. Oxford: Oxford University Press, 2009.

Whicher, Ian. *The Integrity of the Yoga Darśana: A Reconsideration of Classical Yoga*. Albany: State University of New York Press, 1998.

Williams, Paul. *Mahāyāna Buddhism: The Doctrinal Foundations*. New York: Routledge, 1989.

Williams, Paul, and Anthony Tribe. *Buddhist Thought: A Complete Introduction to the Indian Tradition*. New York: Routledge, 2000.

INDEX